Emig, Emich, Amick, Emmick

Emig, Emich, Amick, Emmick
A Family in the New World

By David Emmick

The flying A

Flying A Books
Issaquah, Washington

Emig, Emich, Amick, Emmick
Copyright © 2007 by David J. Emmick

Emig, Emich, Amick, Emmick
2nd Edition
Copyright © 2014 by David J. Emmick

Flying A books may be ordered through lulu.com

Flying A Books
Issaquah, Washington

ISBN: 978-0-6151-7428-0 (pbk)
ISBN 2nd Edition: 978-1-312-45462-0

ISBN 2nd Edition Paperback: 978-0-615-17428-0

available exclusively at www.lulu.com

Printed in the United States of America

In memory of those who came before us.

Montani Semper Liberi

Mountaineers Forever Free

Contents

Acknowledgments

I thank Barbara Nichols who was instrumental in getting me started in genealogy. I thank Louise E. Reithel for her knowledge of Nicholas Emmick and the Kentucky line. I also thank Director Beth Lander and Donna Humphrey in the Research Department at Spruance Library for their help in locating material. Thanks also go to the Springfield Township Historical Society, Nancy Gonshor and the staff at the Pendleton County Clerk's office in Franklin as well as the staff at the Pendleton County Historical Society who also helped in locating key documents. There were many others too numerous to name here who helped with identifying family and contributed stories. Thank you all.

Second Edition: Thanks to Jeff Munn for corrections to the map of the Pendleton County farm as well as pictures and description of the Amick door.

Foreword

I remember my father telling me about his ancestors. The oral tradition of our family heritage passed down from his father and his father before him. He told me we had come over during the revolutionary war as Hessian troops paid by the English; a father and two sons or three brothers. The father's name was "Christopher" and the son's name "Nicholas." Another son was born in America. When the British lost the war, the father and son deserted and took off into the forest as the English would not pay passage back to Germany. I've also heard that there might have been an Indian bride.

Well, some of the story is correct and some is melded with other history. Based on research, we came over before the revolutionary war and might have come from Hessen – thus making us "Hessians." A father and mother with two sons did come over. They had a son in America but I am descended from the first born: Heinrich. Several of the family members did fight in the revolutionary war, but they fought as patriots. After the war, several members of the family moved west into the forests of Virginia. The son Heinrich married Catharina Nicola (Nicholas) and this might be the origin of the names in the above family story. Henry fought with his cousin Christopher Nicholas. There is also a Nicholas Emmick later in the family that moves to Kentucky. Christopher may also be a reference to the ship – the Christian - they came over on. I did find an Indian princess on my grandmother's line but not on this one; but I have found an Indian princess mentioned on unproven Amick family branches.

Family oral history can be right on and some completely wrong, almost fabricated. Looking at the above story you can see how things get translated moving from one generation to another and another until the tale is almost unrecognizable. Genealogy is a science. It deals with facts. You can document genealogy by working from the present back as well as back and down to today. Make genealogy family group sheets for each one of your parents with their parents and their children and so on. Make these group sheets up for as far back as you can go and then start with your parents and get their birth, marriage and death certificates as each one has valuable information. Then do that for each of your brothers, sisters and spouses. You will not be able to get all of them and they get harder and harder to obtain until you will only find death notices as most states did not require these records until into the 1900's. Also obituaries in newspapers are a good source but only as good as the person who submitted the information so watch it there. This is one of the best ways to start. Then add all the family history and stories to each individual and the information on members of the family you did not know about you get from the family bible, records and oral history. Include deeds and warrants if available. Then, one goes to the census. With names, birth dates and locations the census data is an additional source, but without knowledge beforehand can easily confuse family lines with the same names. It's the family oral history, tales and stories that add spice to the family heritage. But you need to start with the facts and keep a clear and rational outlook.

One of the things I've learned is that it's important to visit the places and meet the people in our family's history– to personally go to the places and talk with people still there. This is referred to as "boots on the ground" by the army. Anyone can memorize facts and figures, the real way to learn anything is to get out and experience it and let your curiosity lead you. I've always found more pieces to the puzzle that way and it's so much more fun!

There are two main family lines of Amicks covered in this work: Henry Amick who fought in the Revolutionary War and Nicholas Emmick, Henry Amick's cousin, who also fought in the Revolutionary War. I'm descended from Henry. I've also included related families: the Kellers, Nichols, Propsts, Pitsenbarger and Steinbach. Although the family name has various spellings early on the families in West Virginia spelled it Amick while the Kentucky families spelled it Emmick. With so many Johns, Henrys and Jacobs it's hard to keep them all straight. I'll try to give each one enough context to follow the right line.

My ancestry is: My dad: Robert Emmick, his father: Edward Emmick, his Father: Jacob Emmick [who married Emma Sampson daughter of Naoma Propst], his father Henry Emmick [who married Jane Nichols], his father: Jacob Amick, his father: Henry Amick, his father: Henry Emig, and his father Georg Emig.

This book is for the children; may they keep the stories alive.

I'll leave you with this little poem:

The Elusive Ancestor
By Merrell Kenworthy[1]

I went searching for an ancestor. I cannot find him still.
He moved around from place to place and did not leave a will.
He married where a courthouse burned. He mended all his fences.
He avoided any man who came to take the U.S. Census.

He always kept his luggage packed, this man who had no fame.
And every 20 years or so, this rascal changed his name.
His parents came from Europe. They should be upon some list of
passengers to U.S.A., but somehow they got missed.

And no one else in this world is searching for this man.
So, I play geneasolitaire to find him if I can.
I'm told he's buried in a plot, with tombstone he was blessed;
but the weather took engraving, and some vandals took the rest.

He died before the county clerks decided to keep records.
No Family Bible has emerged, in spite of all my efforts.
To top it off this ancestor, who caused me many groans,
Just to give me one more pain, betrothed a girl named JONES.

Second Edition: *Additional War of 1812 documents were found. Jacob Amick's wife needed to apply for widow's benefits and having two Jacob Amicks in Pendleton County in the war complicated the application. She had to submit many documents. This has been updated in the book Into the Wilderness as many of the documents are circa 1870 with references to the 1812 documents. The other Jacob Amick's documents have been added to the Supplement. Also updated are maps and details of the Pendleton Amick farm now owned by Jeff Munn. There are a few spelling and format changes. Note there are a lot of citations with misspellings. I have not labeled them as is typical with [sp?] as there are just too many of them.*

Settling the Wilderness

Johan Georg Emig, his wife and two young children, arrived in Philadelphia on September 13, 1749. Most of the passengers were from the Palatine region or Rhine Valley with some listed specifically from Wurttemberg, Alsace and Zwieback but it is not known what area Georg and family came from. The western part of the Rhine is alternately French or German through history – they still eat sauerkraut in Alsace.

Johan in German is a name prefix similar to Mr. and can be discarded. Georg is spelled without an "e" in German and translates with the "e" into English. The last name "Emig" is the suspected European spelling as it occurs in some of the Pennsylvania documents and later in the German language Virginia church documents. The English clerks and even Georg at times translated the name as Awe, Amick, Emich, Ering, Ihmig and later Emick. Prior to Daniel Webster, there was no agreed on method of spelling in America, not even an agreed upon alphabet. Clerks spelled things the way they wanted to spell them with the letters they liked. The name M-mick or M-ick in German can be spelled in various ways, but as the name is pronounced it is classic High German. The name is pronounced Em or Am with or without an umlaut for the beginning; and ich in High German, ick in Low German and English, or ig in French. The west side of the Rhine has been in alternating German or French control for hundreds of years.

The first generation family…

Family Tree First Generation

Johan Georg EMIG (1714 - 1773)
+Maria Elisabeth (1736/1738 - 1799)
      Johan Heinrich EMIG (1737/1739 - 1777)
      Johan Philip EMIG (1745 -   )
      Johan Georg EMIG (1751 – 1829)

+ indicates spouse

Arriving in the New World

The Amicks came over to the New World long before the Revolutionary War. The family came from Germany along the Rhine River probably from Hesse. At that time the name was spelled Emig, but various spellings have been used as the English clerks tried to translate from German.

Johan Georg Emig and his wife Maria and two sons took a ship from Rotterdam in 1749 to Philadelphia. Many of the passengers were from Wurttemberg, Alsace, & Zweibrach. These areas are in Germany along the Rhine. In *Pennsylvania-German Pioneers*, vol. 1, the ship's list is reproduced.

Johan Georg and Maria Elisabeth Emig with two children, Johan Heinrich (about 1737-1739) and Johan Philip (about 1741-1745) are listed on the ship's list in 1749 of the ship Christian with Thomas Brady, Master, from Rotterdam, but last from Cowes in England and arriving in Philadelphia on the 13 Sep 1749.[2]

Current Map of Rhine area

The map above includes Amsterdam in the north; note the area of the Rhineland-Palatinate, Alsace-Lorraine and Frankfort. Rotterdam is near The Hague marked on the map above.

George took the Oath of Allegiance on September 13, 1749. One hundred and 11 persons are listed from "Wurtonberg, Alsace, & Zweibrach" on the passenger list of the three hundred total persons on board. Emig is listed as ERIG on the ship's list. The facsimile signature on page 441 was written as George Erig (note misspelled last name and "e" at the end of Georg in the English style.[3]

It is likely, but not certain, that Georg came from Germany from the area along the Rhine River. Nearly all of the German emigrants at this time were from the Rhine Valley, the Palatinate. This would include Alsace and Hesse.

This agrees with Maude Emmick's family history written around 1950. She remembers Henry (son of Jacob AMICK, Henry AMICK, Johan Heinrich, and Johan Georg) who was born in 1817 telling her his remembrances from 1860 to 1870 that the family came from Frankfort Germany and settled in Germantown, Pennsylvania. She remembers: "I can't tell you when our ancestors came from Europe to America, but they settled in Germantown,

Philadelphia. The name at that time was Amick. Some of them called themselves Von Amick. Grand Dad (Henry) always referred to his ancestors as 'Low Dutch'".[4,5] Henry may have heard this from the Nicholas Emmick line when he settled in Indiana across from the Emmick plantation in Kentucky around the time of the Civil War.

Maude states:[6]

> There were relatives who had moved to Indiana before Grand Dad [Henry]. They spelled the name Emmick. They persuaded Grand Dad [Henry] that Emmick [does Maude mean Amick] was a Dutch corruption of the name, which had taken place during their sojourn in Germantown. They claimed that we were not Dutch but German from Frankfurt, Germany.
> I can't tell you when our ancestors came from Europe to America, but they settled in Germantown, Philadelphia. The name at that time was Amick. Some of them called themselves Van Amick. Whether they were German or Dutch I don't know. Grand Dad Emmick said, "German or Low Dutch, what's the difference?" Perhaps when they lived in Europe, Germany belonged to Holland or Holland belonged to Germany, -- I am a little vague about history concerning that period. Anyhow the Germans and the Dutch in Philadelphia had many of the same customs, the same religious beliefs, and the same superstitions, ate the same dishes, and intermarried, to the extent that they felt like one nationality. Grand Dad always referred to his ancestors as "Low Dutch," which to us would mean Holland Dutch. But more about that later.

This is also consistent with Geneva Amick Dyer's account in *Fourteen Children, The Family of John Amick of West Virginia*. Her reference to Henry, Jacob and John are to the brothers who came out from Virginia to Pennsylvania. There are actually three generations back farther then these brothers who landed first in America. There is no record of the sister dying at sea.[7] Geneva writes:

> The Amick family is of German descent. There are several traditions about the coming of the "Amick" family to America, but I am not able to give an authentic account. My father's cousin, David Amick, whom we always called "Uncle Dave," because he was near the same age of our uncles, told me there were three brothers, Henry, Jacob, and John, who came to America, and settled in Pennsylvania. He told me

also that a sister started with them, but died, and was buried at sea. I believe it was Henry, who is our great grandfather.

A teacher of the German language in one of our western colleges said the name Amick was originally spelled Emig. Uncle Dave said when our people first came to America; they spelled it Emick, and then changed it to Amick.

Some of our family in Kansas and California now spell their name Emick. When I was in Oregon, and Washington, many of my friends pronounced my name as if it did begin with "E," instead of "A," and often spelled it that way.[8]

This is also consistent with *The History of Nicholas County* where Henry, Jacob and John are mentioned.[9] It is assumed this is from the same source as Geneva's.

Amick, German. The Amick family probably came to America in the German Mennonite emigration from the Palatinate. The family tradition has it that three brothers: Henry, Jacob and John came together and settled in Pennsylvania. Later one of the brothers came to Pendleton County; and there in 1780 his son, John, was born.

Of note is a Bible that Georg willed to Trinity Church. The German bible was published in Basel, Switzerland in 1747 and is now at the Bucks County Historical Society. Basel is on the Rhine River.

Also do not confuse our line with the Amick family that emigrated about the same time on the *Pink John and William*. That family Amick is sometimes confused with ours on the Web and elsewhere. They came from the area of Alsace Lorraine. That family settled in parts of Pennsylvania and South Carolina. There is also an Emmick family that entered New York earlier and settled on the Hudson River. These families could only be more distantly related. Families descended from the Bucks County line are identified here.

The family is definitely of German decent and probably from along the Rhine. The way the name is pronounced, it is High German. The Emich/Emig name is a famous and frequently used name in the area of the Palatine.

Along the Rhine River is an ancient principality called the Palatinate. It contains the cities of Manheim, Worms, Spires and Heidelberg. The area was devastated by the Thirty Years War from 1618 to 1648 which finally ended with the Treaty of Westphalia in 1648. This treaty did not stop the warfare; invasions continued for many years that left the area in ruin.[10]

William Shirer presented a background of this period of German history in his book *The Rise and Fall of the Third Reich*. He described what led up to the thirty Years War and its consequences as follows:[11]

There is not space in this book to recount adequately the immense influence that Martin Luther, the Saxon peasant who became an Augustinian monk and launched the German Reformation, had on the Germans and their subsequent history. But it may be said, in passing, that this towering but erratic genius, this savage anti-Semite and hater of Rome, who combined in his tempestuous character so many of the best and the worst qualities of the German—the coarseness, the boisterousness, the fanaticism, the intolerance, the violence, but also the honesty, the simplicity, the self-scrutiny, the passion for learning and for music and for poetry and for righteousness in the eyes of God—left a mark on the life of the Germans, for both good and bad, more indelible, more fateful, than was wrought by any other single individual before or since. Through his sermons and his magnificent translations of the Bible, Luther created the modern German language, aroused in the people not only a new Protestant vision of Christianity but a fervent German nationalism and taught them, at least in religion, the supremacy of the individual conscience. But tragically for them, Luther's siding with the princes in the peasant risings, which he had largely inspired, and his passion for political autocracy ensured a mindless and provincial political absolutism which reduced the vast majority of the Garman people to poverty, to a horrible torpor and a demeaning subservience. Even worse perhaps, it helped to perpetuate and indeed sharpen the hopeless divisions not only between the classes but also between the various dynastic and political groupings of the German people. It doomed for centuries the possibility of the unification of Germany.

The Thirty Years' War and the Peace of Westphalia of 1648, which ended it, brought the final catastrophe to Germany, a blow so devastating that the country has never fully recovered from it. This was the last of Europe's great religious wars, but before it was over it had degenerated from a Protestant-Catholic conflict into a confused dynastic struggle between the Catholic Austrian Hapsburgs on the one side and the Catholic French Bourbons and the Swedish Protestant monarchy on the other. In the savage fighting, Germany itself was laid waste, the towns and countryside were devastated and ravished, the people decimated. It has been estimated that one third of the German people perished in this barbarous war.

The Peace of Westphalia was almost as disastrous to the future of Germany as the war had been. The German princes, who had sided with France and Sweden, were confirmed as absolute rulers of their little domains, some 350 of them, the Emperor remaining merely as a figurehead so far as the German lands were concerned. The surge of reform and enlightenment which had swept Germany at the end of the fifteenth and the beginning of the sixteenth centuries was smothered. In that period the great free cities had enjoyed virtual independence; feudalism was gone in them and the arts and commerce thrived. Even in the countryside the German peasant had secured liberties far greater than those enjoyed in England and France. Indeed, at the beginning of the sixteenth century Germany could be said to be one of the fountains of European civilization.

Now, after the Peace of Westphalia, it was reduced to the barbarism of Muscovy. Serfdom was reimposed, even introduced in areas where it had been unknown. The towns lost their self-government. The peasants, the laborers, even the middle-class burghers, were exploited to the limit by the princes, who held them down in a degrading state of servitude. The pursuit of learning and the arts all but ceased. The greedy rulers had no feeling for German nationalism and patriotism and stamped out any manifestations of them in their subjects. Civilization came to a standstill in Germany. The Reich, as one historian put it, "was artificially stabilized at a medieval level of confusion and weakness."

Refugees from the area crossed the Channel to England. These refugees then migrated to New York and New Jersey. This migration is referred to as the Palatine migration. Several histories of Palatines to the New World are available.

The Germans came mainly from the Rhineland. A pamphlet from William Penn promising religious freedom had been translated into German and circulated there. In 1683 a group of Mennonites founded Germantown north of Philadelphia. The Germans around Philadelphia were known as the Pennsylvania Dutch – a corruption of Deutsch.[12]

During the War of the Grand Alliance (1689-97), Louis XIV troops ravaged the Rhenish Palatinate. Many of the early German settlers of Pennsylvania were refugees from this region. During the French Revolutionary and Napoleonic Wars, the Palatinate's lands on the west bank of the Rhine were incorporated into France, while its eastern lands were divided largely between neighboring Baden and Hesse.

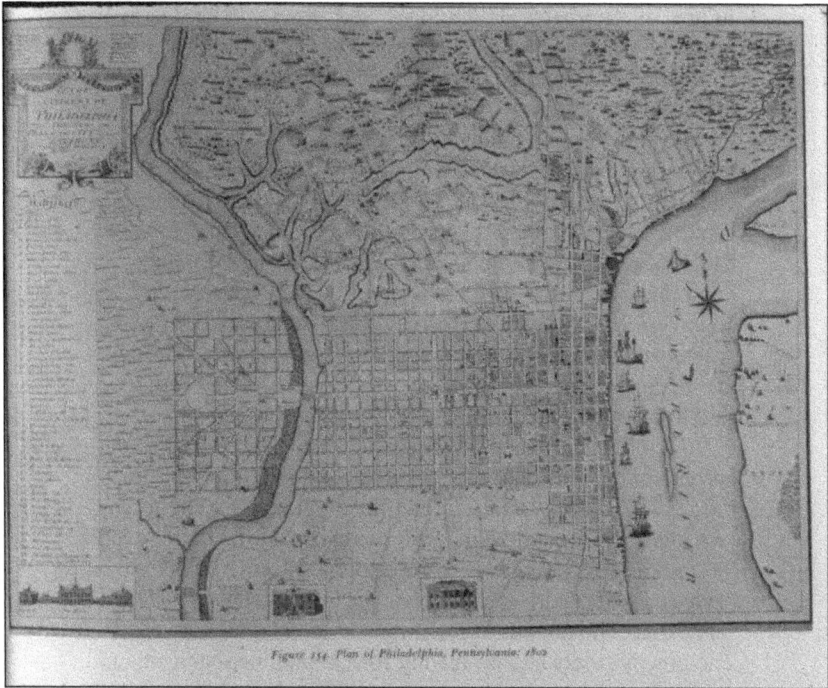

Plan of Philadelphia, Pennsylvania, 1802

Johan Georg Emig, the father, was born in Germany on July 13, 1715 and married his wife Maria in Germany about 1735. Georg and Maria and their two children Heinrich and Philip debarked from Rotterdam on the ship *Christian* in 1749 arriving in Philadelphia. The family when it arrived consisted of Father Georg, two sons and his wife. They came in at Philadelphia to settle Penn's Sylvania: Penn's woods. This land had been granted to William Penn and his heirs to be settled by Germans. After they arrived a son named George was born in the new world.

Ship at Penn's Landing
Penn's Landing was the site where the Englishman and Quaker, William Penn, stepped ashore
from the Delaware River in 1682. Picture taken 2007.

Drawing of the old Tun Tavern, Philadelphia, built 1685[13]

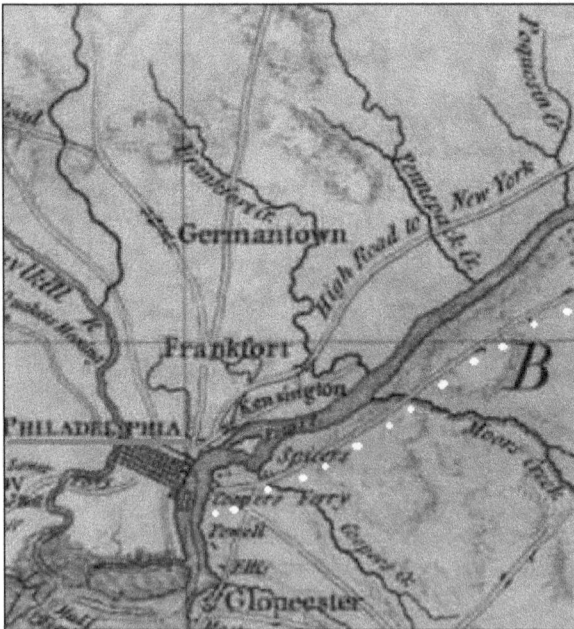

Germantown north of Philadelphia about 1777

Settling in America

Georg and his family settled first in Pennsylvania north of Philadelphia on the outskirts of Germantown. Philadelphia was the largest city in the colonies with some 30,000 people living in the city and surrounding countryside.[14] The family settled north of Philadelphia in Bucks County with some of the family later dispersing to Berks County to the west. Georg Emig built a grist and sawmill on Tohickon Creek.

Location of Bucks County Pennsylvania in relation to other counties

Haycock Mountain view from the north looking south from Highway 412 [Durham Road]
Taken 2007

Georg settled near Applebachsville close to Haycock Mountain in Bucks County. The area is described in *The History of Bucks County, Pennsylvania.*[15]

> Haycock contains two natural features of interest, the curiously-shaped mountain which bears its name, and Stony garden. Haycock mountain, situated in the eastern part of the township, was named by the early settlers from its resemblance to a cock of hay. Its height has never been ascertained, but the elevation is considerable, with a gradual slope to the top from which there is a prospect of unsurpassed beauty over a wide scope of country. About a mile to the northeast of the mountain there was a deer lick when the country was settled. Thomas McCarty found rattlesnakes on the mountain as late as 1819, and Jacob E. Buck says that he shot a large red-headed woodpecker on it in 1818, which bird disappeared from that section may years ago. Stony garden, on the road from Applebachsville to Stony point, two and a half miles from the former place, is a locality of curious interest. Leaving the road at a rude hamlet called Danielsville, and going through a wood a few hundred yards, over a surface

covered with the boulder drift, you come to a spot about an acre in extent covered with trap rock. The stones are of many and curious shapes and sizes, and must have been emptied down in the forest in the wildest confusion. Earth has never been found beneath the rocks, and they are entirely void of vegetation except a little moss and a few parasitic plants that have attached themselves to the hard stones.

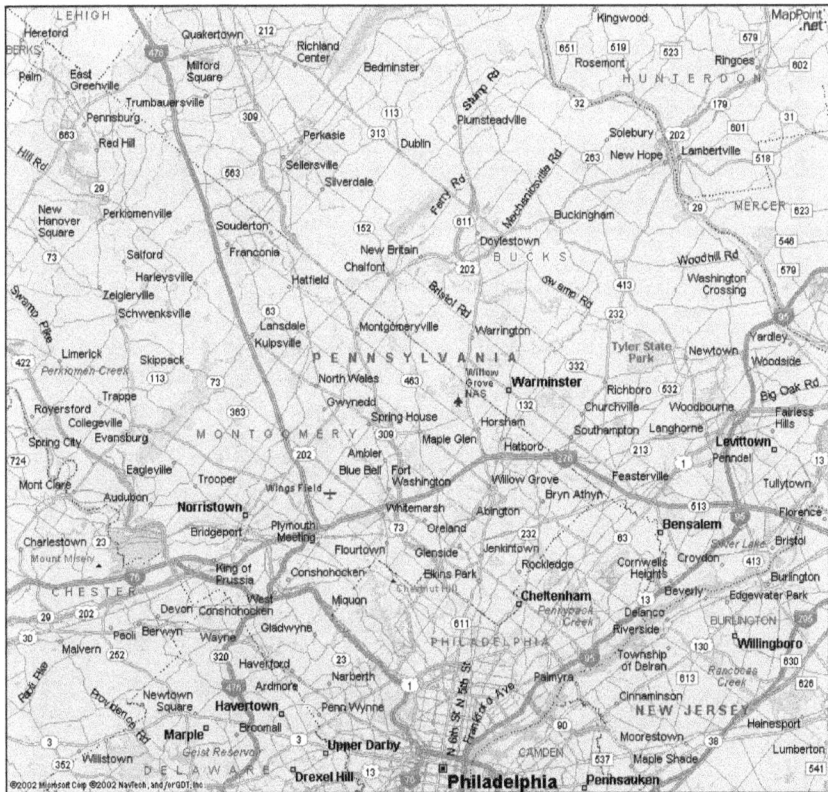

Current Map of area north of Philadelphia

Bedminster and Dublin are near the top of the map above. The Emig land is now under the reservoir at the top of the map. Germantown was north of Philadelphia, but has since been overtaken by the Philadelphia city limits. Bedminster is less then 20 miles outside Philadelphia or about two days travel by horse.

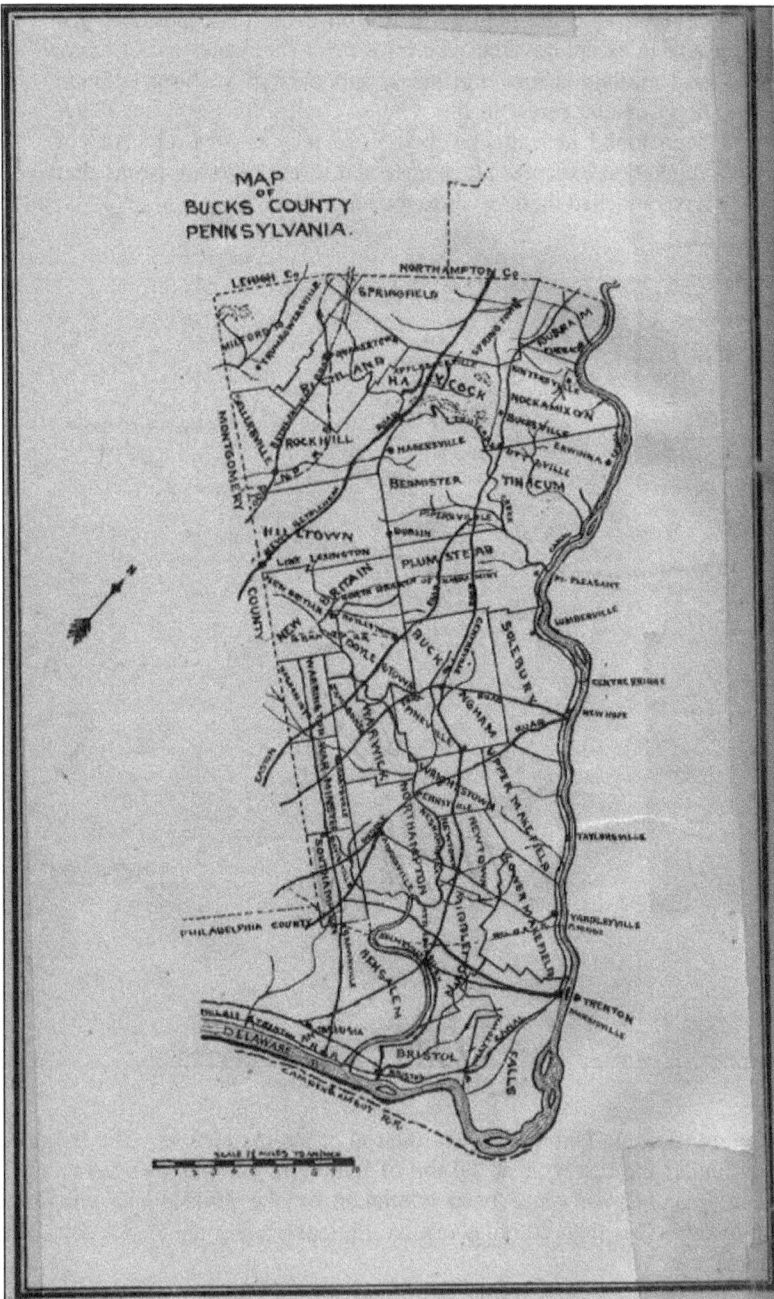

Early Map of Bucks County 1876 from *The History of Bucks County*

The area was originally owned by William Penn and the map above lays out the original township lines. Early documents about Georg mention Rockhill and Springfield. Haycock and Bedminster Townships were formed later and appear in later documents. This map is from *The History of Bucks County Pennsylvania* by W.W.H. Davis.[16]

In *The History of Bucks County, Pennsylvania*, Georg Emig is noted as one of the original settlers around Applebachsville with two hundred and thirty-one acres.[17] Note that Georg's property is next to Charles Dennis on the early map of Bucks County on the next page.

In *The History of Bucks County Pennsylvania* Davis states.[18]

> ...The Stokes tract, which was laid out for 300 acres and allowances, was found to contain 347 acres and 42 perches by the survey of Asher Woolman and Samuel Foulke, April 12, 1769. It lay at Applebachsville, and comprised the fine farms of the late General Paul Applebach. The old family mansion, more than a century old, is still standing.
>
> Joseph, the great-grandfather of Wilson Dennis, immigrated to America and settled near Egg Harbor, New Jersey, when he came to "the adjacent of Springfield," afterward Haycock, about 1746, and took up several tracts of land in this and Springfield township. He was a great hunter, and is said to have selected stony land because such soil yielded the most grass in the woods, and was sure to bring plenty of game. Wilson Dennis, the fourth generation, through Joseph, Charles, and Josiah, owns and lives on the tract that his ancestor received from the Proprietaries. March 1, 1756, 136 acres were surveyed to Valentine Rohr "in the lands adjacent to Springfield, upon a branch of Tohickon called Jo Toonum's run," by virtue of a warrant.
>
> This is an Indian name: Jo Toonum alias Neepaheilman, was one of the signers to the famous "Walking Purchase" deed, 1737, and probably a resident of Haycock. At one time Martins creek, Northampton county, was also called Tununis, or Toonums creek, no doubt after the same Indian.

Early Map of Bucks County 1681 listing the first owners

The original purchasers of land on the west side of the Bethlehem road, up to the Springfield line, were, in order, Allem, William Strawn, a Quaker, Valentine Rohr, Andrew Booz, Dutt, and Ludwig Nusbeckel [Nusbecker], whose land was on the east side of the road, opposite. Dutt Nusbickel (4) was born April 14, 1730, died January 10, 1818, and was buried in the Springfield graveyard. His wife died in 1795. They were both members of Springfield church, where his daughter, Elizabeth, was baptized August 10, 1760. Besides John Stokes, the original purchasers immediately around Applebachsville were William Strawn, **George Emig**, the original for Amey, who took up a tract of 231 acres, 89 perches, which was confirmed by Thomas and Richard Penn, July 13, 1768, who left the same to his son George, by will, in 1773. Emig, who was born July 13, 1715, died March 7, 1773, and was buried in the Springfield yard. In 1767 Stephen Acraman bought 138 acres of Lydia McCall, widow of George McCall, an early settler northwest of Applebachsville.

Davis continues:

The first constable returned was Henry Keller, at the September sessions, 1763. Haycock was, doubtless, named after the little mountain in it, which was so called because of its resemblance to a cock of hay, which name was given to it many years before the township was organized. Haycock is mentioned in a deed as early as 1737, and the creek which winds along the base of the mountain is called Haycock Run, in the boundary of Nockamixon, 1742. The mountain and run received their names from the earliest settlers in the township. Heinrich Keller, son of William and Gertraut Keller, was born in Weierbach, Baden, January 9, 1708, and married there, October 20, 1728, Julianna Kleindinst, born 1711, and with her and four of their children came to America in the ship "Glasgow," arriving in Philadelphia September 9, 1738. He was the ancestor of the family that gave the name to "Keller's" church. His son, John Keller, was a member of the state convention that formed the first constitution of Pennsylvania, 1776, and served in the assembly, 1776-1779, and was also a colonel of militia during the Revolution and saw active service.

Representative cabin of the period at Mercer Museum,
Doylestown, Bucks County, Pennsylvania, Taken 2007

Log House in Springfield Township near Haycock on Highway 212, Taken 2007

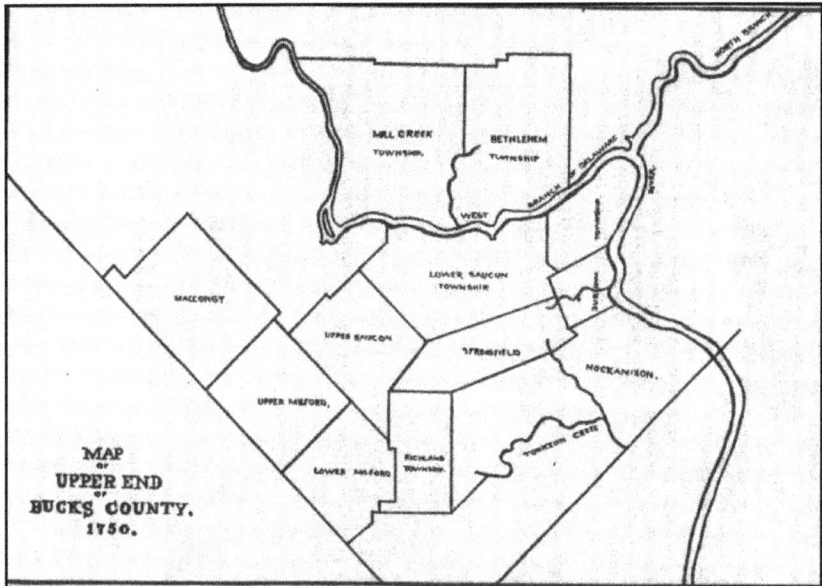

Map of Upper End of Bucks County, 1750

John Keller with Samuel Smith and Andrew Keckline were appointed in September 1778 to audit and examine the accounts of the administrators of the estate of Henry Amey. John Keller is an uncle of Henry's (Georg, Heinrich) wife Barbara Niemand.

Davis continues:[19]

> The accompanying map of the "Upper end of Bucks county" was copied from an old one drawn between 1742 and 1750. It gives the location of the townships formed in the upper section at that period after Springfield had been organized, but before its "adjacent" had been laid out and declared Haycock township. It shows several townships now in Northampton and Lehigh, namely: Bethlehem, Millcreek and Lower Saucon in the former, and Upper Saucon, Upper Milford and Macungie in the latter. That Williams township, organized 1750, is not given on it is evidence the original map was drawn prior to that year. Durham township was not organized until 1775.

Tohickon Church

Tohickon Union Church, organized 1752

One of the first records of the family is the baptism of Georg and Maria's son George at Tohickon Church. The family is listed in latter records of the Tohickon Church as well as Keller's Church founded a few years later. The Reformed Church is across the Tohickon Creek from Haycock Township where the family lived.

Johan Georg & Maria Elisabeth Emig's son Johan George was baptized at the Tohickon Reformed Church in Bedminster Township on April 21, 1751. The name in the record is spelled IHMIG. George Bergstresser, Jacob Riess and wife Catharine are listed as witnesses.[20] George MacReynolds in *Place Names in Bucks County, Penn.,* gives a later date for the organization of Tohickon Church. He states that in 1744, the German Lutherans founded Keller's Church which is still active today. In June 1745 the Tohickon

Reformed Church was organized in Bedminster Township with the Rev. John Conrad Wirtz, a native of Zurich, Switzerland, as the first pastor. The church is located on the old Bethlehem Road near Tohickon Creek.[21] The two churches are often confused. The churches were about 3 miles apart and never served by the same pastor.

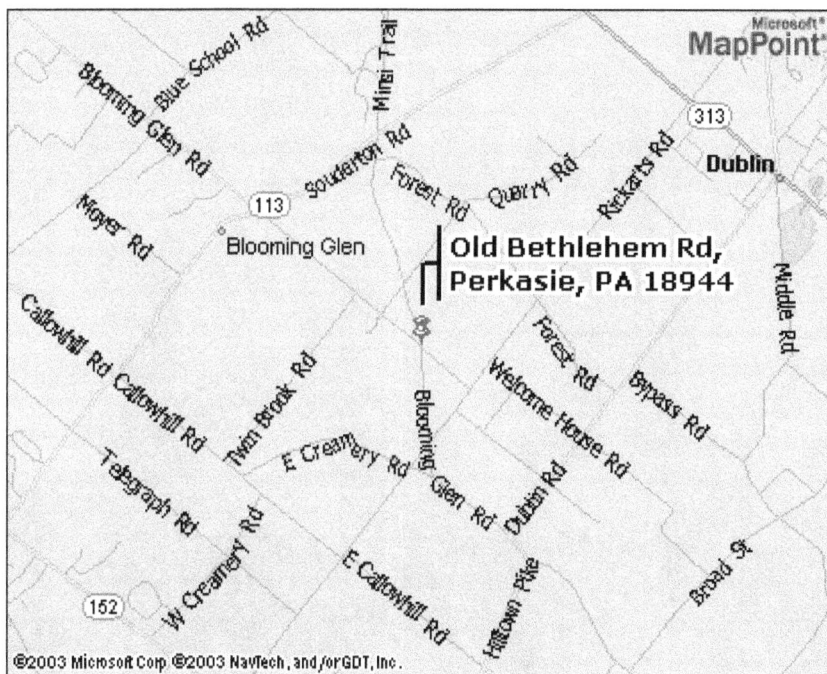

Directions to Tohickon Church
St. Peter's (Tohickon Union) Old Bethlehem Pike, Perkasie, Pennsylvania
Dublin to the right is a good reference point

Maria Elisabeth Emig was listed as a witness with Philip Geres at the baptism of a daughter of Philip and Anna Elisabeth Shaeffer at the Tohickon Reformed Church, Bedminster, Bucks, Penn. on December 12, 1757 (this is the first use of EMIG in America).[22]

Georg Emig took the sacrament to become naturalized on September 22, 1765 in Rockhill Township, next to Haycock. He is listed as Georg ERNIG. Son Johan Heinrich Emig took the sacrament to become a British citizen on July 7, 1765 with the same surname spelling. Johan Heinrich Emig took the sacrament in Haycock Township. His father-in-law Valentine Nicolas/Nicholaus and John Keller are listed as fellow worshippers.[23] This is the same misspelling as appears in the Buck County records. The original warrant is Emig but recorded by the clerk as Ernig.

Keller's Church

St. Mathew's Evangelical Lutheran Church known as Keller's Church[24]

Tohickon Church and Keller's Church are both documented in *The History of Bucks County, Pennsylvania.* The Tohickon Church was built first. Although Keller's Church was organized in 1744 and land granted in 1751, the building was not erected until after 1759. Johan Heinrich Emich (son of Georg) would later marry Catharina Nikla in the school house at Bedminster because Keller's Church had not yet been erected.[25]

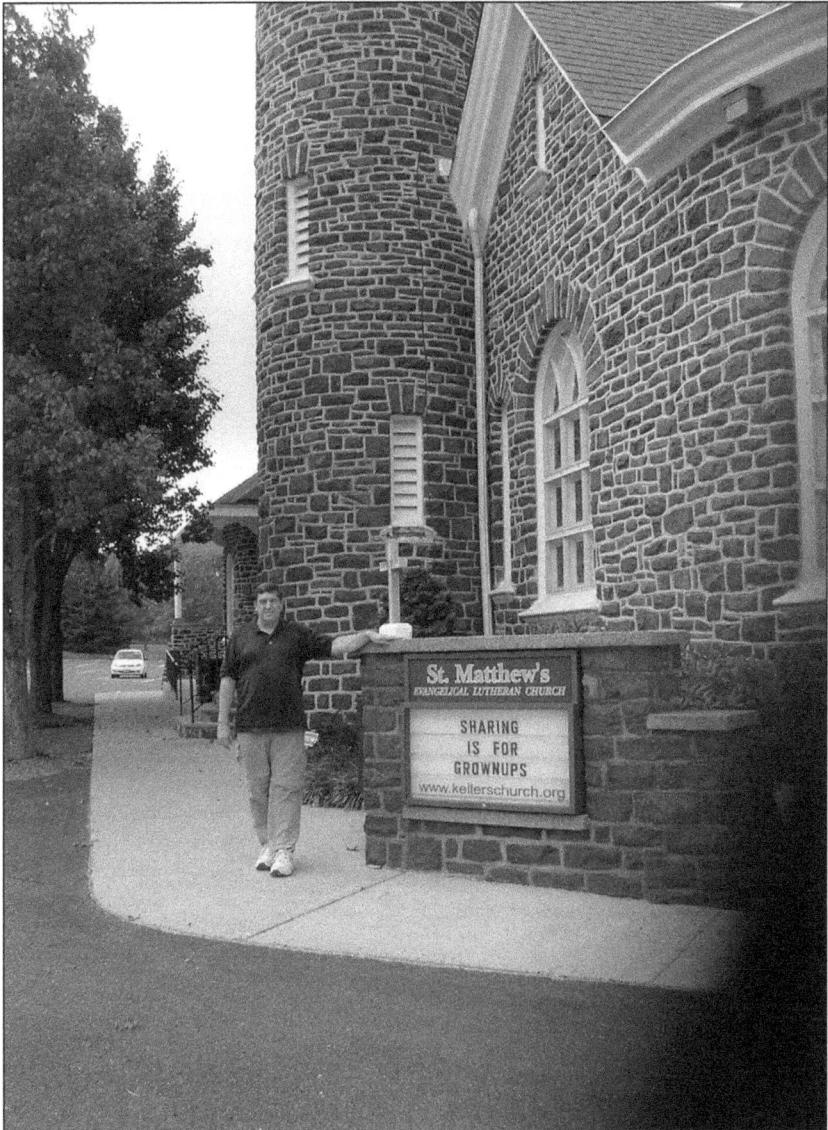

Author, David Emmick, at Keller's Church taken 2007

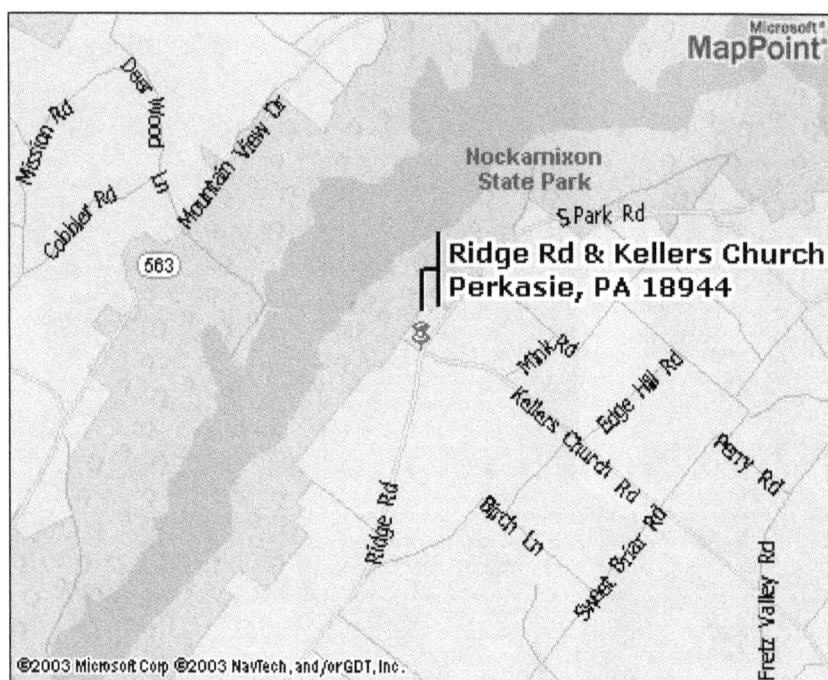

Directions to Keller's Church, also called St. Mathews, organized 1751
Ridge Road and Kellers Church Road, Perkasie, Pennsylvania

Location of Tohickon and Kellers Churches

PENN
Bucks Co
Henry [1]

Tohickon Creek

○Tohickon P.O.

Bedminster Township

⚤ Keller's Church

3 1/2 Miles

⚤ Tohickon Church

Church Hill P.O.

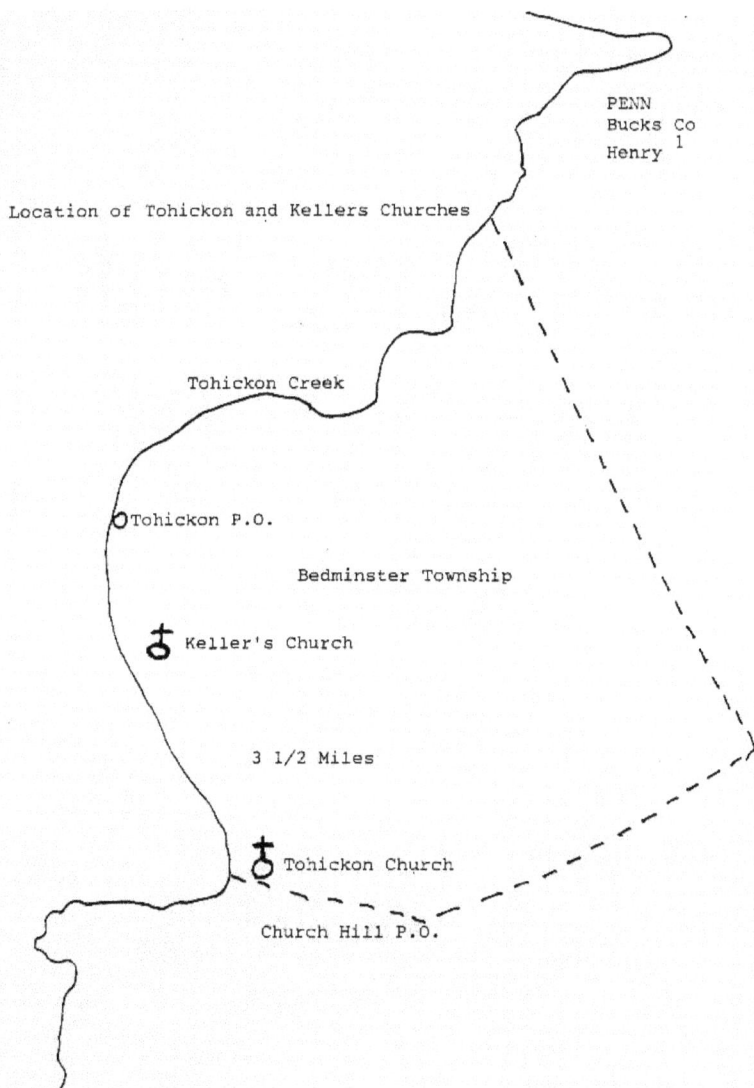

Sketch from Barbara Nichols[26]

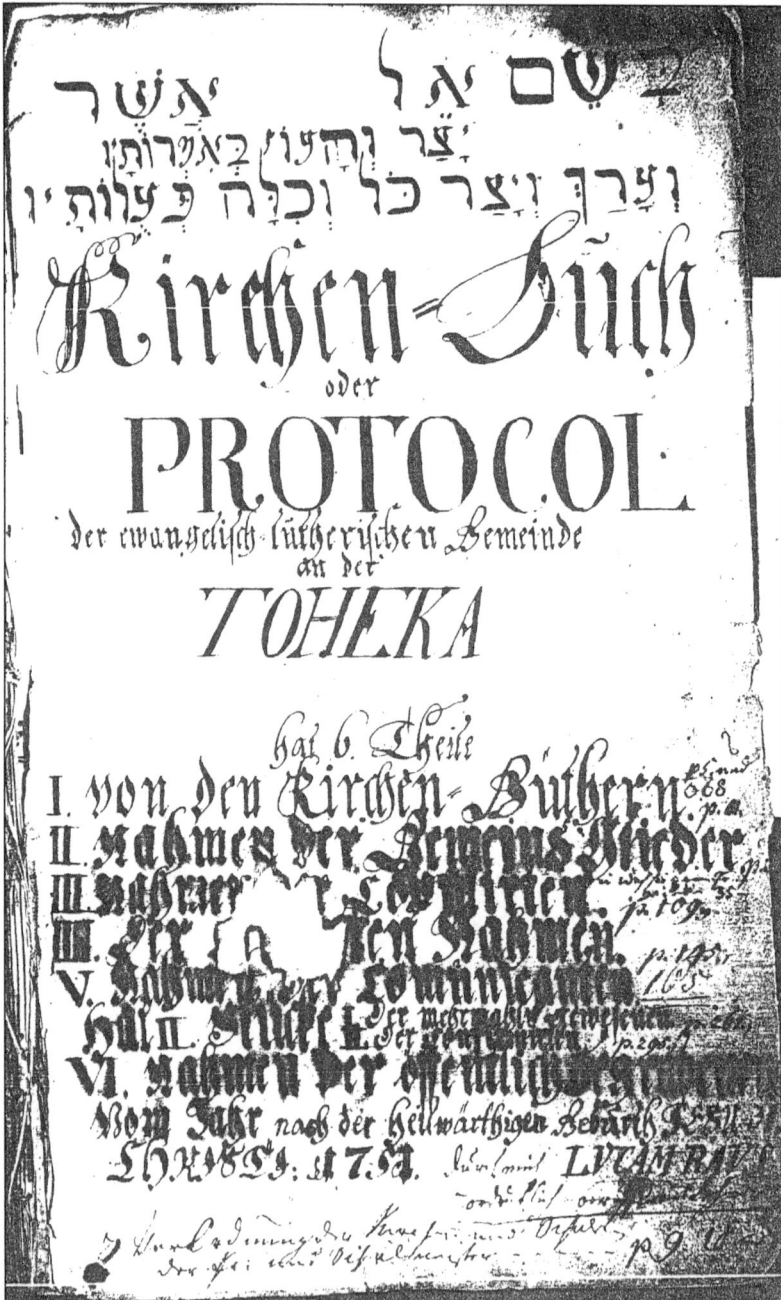

Kirchen Buch, Evangelich Lutheran Kirchen, at Toheka, 1759

Kirchen Buch, Evangelich Lutheran Kirchen, at Toheka, 1759

From *The History of Bucks County Pennsylvania* by W. W. H. Davis:[27]

> The oldest Reformed church in Bucks county is in Bedminster on the old Bethlehem road, near its crossing of Tohickon creek, and called the "Tohickon Church." It was organized, 1743, and subsequently became a union church, Reformed and Lutheran, and has remained so. The present Reformed pastor is Rev. James Kehm.
> Keller's church, Lutheran and Reformed, is situated on the Ridge road, leading from Bucksville to Sellersville, near Haycock mountain, and was organized early, the land it was built on was conveyed to Henry Acker, Henry Keller and Christian Stoneback for that purpose and an additional tract was subsequently purchased of John Ott. Henry Keller was one of the active leaders in the development of this church. In 1840, the Lutherans and Reformed became a union congregation, and joint owner of the real estate by deed dated January 1, 1858. The first union church was erected, 1841, at a cost $1,900, and a new building put up, 1894, at an expense of $12,000. It is modern in all its appointments with a seating capacity of 500; seats arranged in amphitheater form and a Sunday school annex. A movement to open a cemetery was made in 1874, incorporated the same year, and the first burial was 1876. It is not known when the first interment was made in the graveyard of Keller's church, but some of the grave stones are as old as 1782. The first organ was brought from Germany, the gift of the Rev. Mr. Hecht, the pastor, but the present one was built at Quakertown in recent years. The church records, of the period of which we write, speak of the congregation as the "Vacant Evangelical Lutheran Congregation of the Tohickon, township of Bedminster, county of Bucks."

Keller's Church land warrant, granted by Henry Ocker, Henry Keller and Christian Stoneback (Steinbach), was taken on August 14, 1751 and surveyed on February 6, 1752 for 20 acres. A school house was completed first and used by the congregation for services. Abraham Nicla, son of Valentine Nicla (Nicolas) and his wife Anna Elisabeth was baptized in the school house on March 30, 1752.[28] Of note in the Early History of Keller's Lutheran Church, Bedminster Township, Bucks County, Rev. William Hinke notes that on June 15, 1754, Rev. Henry M. Muhlenberg wrote to Dr. Francke at Halle the following: [citation same as above]

> At a river called Tohicon, about twenty-two miles from
> Providence [now Trappe, Muhlenberg's home] there is a
> fairly large congregation of High German Lutherans, who for
> ten years [1744-1754] have been visited as much as possible
> by our Ministerium, and was last served by Messrs. Rauss
> and Schult.

This is important in that it mentions the congregation was High German.
Lucas Rauss was the first pastor of Keller's Church in 1751.

Heinrich (now Henry), son of Georg and Catharina (now Catherine) were
communicants at Keller's Church from 1760 to 1777. Henry Keller's son John
Keller was an uncle of Henry's (Georg, Heinrich) wife Barbara Niemand.
John Keller would be appointed September 1778 to audit and examine the
accounts of the administrators of the estate of Henry Amey. Later, when
Henry's wife Barbara's father died in 1768 her mother Barbara Niemand
remarried Michael Steinbach, the son of Christian and Dorothy Steinbach.
Christian was one of the founders of Keller's Church.

The Original Family Homestead

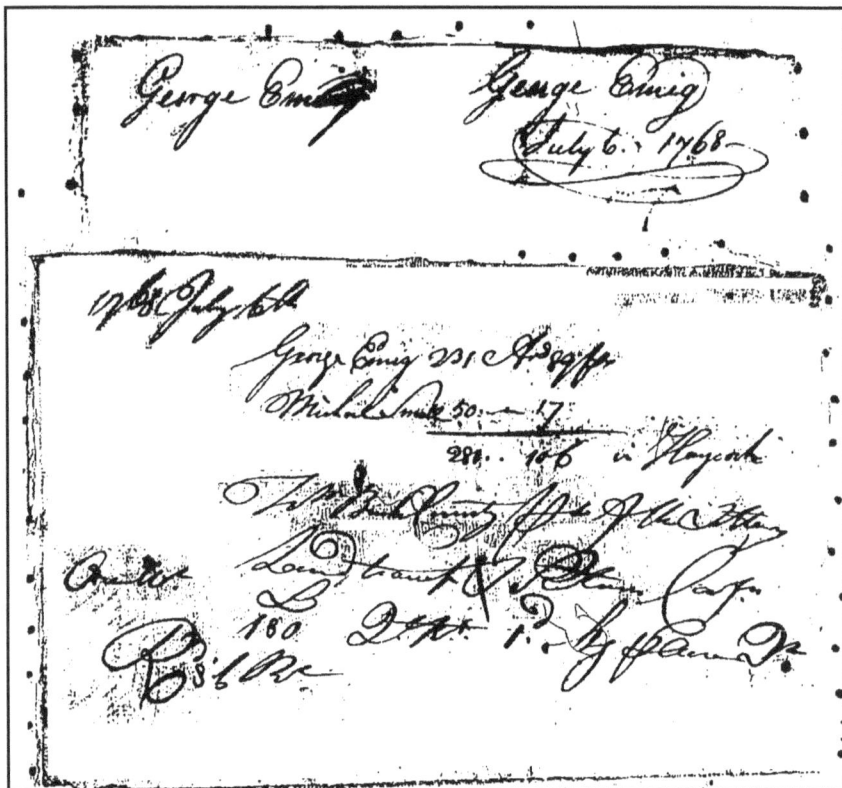

George Emig's application for a land warrant in Haycock, Bucks County, Pennsylvania, July 6, 1768. Land consisting of 281 acres and 106 perches

A land warrant was issued to Georg Emig in 1768. In the original warrant as found in Pennsylvania *Application for Warrants,* 1768, A-E, the spelling is EMIG[29] but the same warrant listed in *Pennsylvania Archives,* Series 3, Vol. 24, Bucks Co., p.125 has the spelling of ERNIG.[30, 31]

BUCKS.

No. of Warrant	Name of Warrantee	Descrip. tion of Warrant	Quantity	Date of Warrant	Date of Return	Acres Returned	Name of Patentee	Where Recorded			Where Survey is Copied	
								Vol.	Bk.	Page	Book.	Page.
42	Everard, Joseph	Accept	57.21	17 Feby. 1747	17 Feby. 1747	57.21	Joseph Everard	A	16	7	A49	65-86
40	" Frederick	Survey	20	30 Sept "	27 Jany.1768	28.120	Arnold Everhart	AA	6	153	A49	107
44	Everett, John	Accept	200	13 April 1748	13 April 1748	200	John Everett (Constel)	A	5	19	"	52
45	Ernhart, Philip	Survey	50	27 July "	23 " 1840	140.14	Michael Houseman	H	42	284	M.	519
69	" Jacob	"	25	5 Oct. "	12 March 1769	25.163	Jacob Ernhart	A	19	328	C50	111
46	Everd, Michael	"	50	4 Novr. "	16 Jany. 1822	4.60	Joseph Jones	H	20	602	C51	232
											C51	247
47	Erhbach, Lawrence	Accept	160	13 Jany. "	30 May 1785	170¾	Jacob Erbuch	P	3	593	B16	109
53	Eshbach, Christian	Survey	15	16 Feby. 1748	21 Jany. 1756	15	Philip Ginzinger	AA	1	21	C50	128
96	Eagner, Matthias etal	"	20	23 " "	22 " 1819	30.37	Trustees Lutheran Congn.	N	10	300	C51	180
51	"	"	25	27 " "	6 June 1703	35.80	Matthias Eagner	AA	2	105	C50	139
37	Effric, Johannes	"	10	2 March "	7 Augt. 1748	61.90	John Reinhold	H	1	310	C51	134
58	"	"	25	" " "	21 Nov. 1789	58¾	George Dutt	"	15	193	B2	42
					11 April 1810	13.11	Frederick Dotuns				C50	263
48	Eagner, Matthias	Accept	250	9 " "	9 March 1748	250	Matthias Eagner	AA		14	A49	51
49	Eble, John	Survey	100	23 " 1749	16 Novr. 1790	150¾	Conrad Reinkley	P	12	109	C14	255
50	Eastburn, John	"	"	7 June "	24 " 1752	282	Andrew Miller	A	17	322	K	2
53	"	"	"	50	7 " 1750	57.89	Jacob Stout	"	15	606	B.	187
54	Elster, Christopher	"	"	28 Sept "	5 March 1760	170	Daniel Heller	P	4	75	A26	15
55	Everard, Thomas	"	100	12 Oct "	1 " 1762	195	Thomas Everett	AA	5	484	A49	46
					6 Decr. 1759	56¾						
60	Eagner, Jacob	"	20	8 May 1750	6 June 1810	29.15	Jonathan Butz	H	4	124	C60	84
					13 Feby. 1808	18.117	Henry Drankle	"	25	187	C51	121
					28 Augt "	13.100	Charles Domckle	"	24	122	"	122
					8 Jany. 1840	9.70	John Lichtnawotter	"	27	332	"	257
59	Ehrhort, John	"	50	6 June "	2 June 1792	204.40	Daniel Heller	P	16	487	B.	203
61	Eryon, Matthias	"	"	20 Novr. "	14 July 1835	70.70	John S. Kestler	H	50	151	C53	134
62	Eggleston, James	"	25	10 April 1751	12 May 1810	10240	Valentine Albert	H	5	536	A51	134
63	"	"	"	" "	26 July 1813	58.100	Samuel Gulick	H	9	220	C60	179
											B.	215
64	"	Accept	110¾	8 June "	16 June 1781	110¾	James Eggleston	A	17	1	C50	101
65	Eberly, Rudolph	"	32	11 Oct "	28 " 1745	48.120	Rudolph Eberly	AA	6	307	A49	47
66	Everhart, Joseph	Accept	150	" Decr. "	23 Novr. 1782	149.160	Joseph Everhort	A	16	533	I.	457
67	Eberhart, Joseph	Survey	50	29 Jany. 1753	1 Feby.1762	67.96	Joseph Eberhart	"	"	371	R.	37
69	Esch, Peter	"	20	8 Oct. 1759		74.105					C52	246
70	Everrighter, Michael	"	25	12 Augt. 1765	24 July 1766	55.56	Michael Everrighter	AA	7	105	A49	55-85
71	Eannick, Jacob	"	"	14 Oct. 1766	8 Feby. 1778	137.137	John Walker	"	18	224	A3	193
72	Eden, Samuel	"	40	" Augt. 1766	23 Decr. 1768	54.104	Nicholas Paws	"	4	167	C50	202
73	"	"	100	13 April 1767		100	" "	"	"	"	C50	260
74	Emig, George etal	Accept	221.106	6 July 1768	12 July 1768	231.89	George Emig	AA	10	451	C50	163
					" " "	56¾	Michael Small	"	"	491	"	"
75	Edwards, William	Survey	70	14 Oct. 1786	27 Jany. 1789	75.86	William Edwards	P	14	403	C65	85
76	Erwin, Hugh	Inbound	10	13 Decr. 1811	16 " 1811	11.107	Hugh Erwin	H	5	229	C60	107
78	" William	"	3	" " "	19 "	7.(6)	John S. Stover	H	47	116	C65	113
					23 Feby. 1840	16.103					C60	113
77	"	"	2	" " "	19 Jany. 1811	2.306	William Erwin	H	5	229	C60	135
79	" "	"	5	10 " 1811	20 Feby.1812	14.16	" "	"	7	26	"	135
80	Ely, John Jr.	"	4.99	5 July 1814	21 Decr. 1816	5.155	John Ely Jr.	"	16	8	B.	246
81	Erwin, William	Accept	25.157	13 Feby. 1821	14 Feby. 1821	25.157	William Erwin	"	17	584	C51	315

Pennsylvania State Archives; RG-17; Records of the Land Office
WARRANT REGISTERS, 1733-1957. [Series #17.88];
BUCKS COUNTY WARRANT REGISTER PAGES,
Page 171, line 74 (near bottom), Application for Warrants, 1768, A-E, 6 July 1768

WARRANTEES OF LAND

IN THE

COUNTY OF BUCKS.

1733-1889.

(197)

COUNTY OF BUCKS—1733-1889.   125

	Acres.	Date of Survey.
Erbaegh, Lawrence, ...	160	Jan. 13, 1748-9.
Eshbach, Christ'n, ...	15	Feb. 16, 1749.
Eagner, Mathias, &c., ...	20	Feb. 23, 1749.
Eagner, Mathias, &c., ...	25	Feb. 27, 1749.
Elfrie, Johannes, ...	10	March 2, 1749.
Elfrie, Johannes, ...	25	March 2, 1749.
Eagner, Mathias, ...	250	March 9, 1748-9.
Ebble, John, ...	100	March 28, 1749.
Eastburn, John, ...	100	June 7, 1749.
Eastburn, John, ...	50	June 7, 1749.
Elder, Christopher, ...	50	Sept. 28, 1749.
Everrard, Thomas, ...	100	Oct. 18, 1749.
Eagner, Jacob, ...	20	March 8, 1750.
Ehrhart, John, ...	50	June 6, 1750.
Eergon, Mathias, ...	50	Nov. 20, 1750.
Eggleston, James, ...	25	April 10, 1751.
Eggleston, James, ...	25	April 10, 1751.
Eggleston, James, ...	110½	June 8, 1751.
Eberley, Rudolph, ...	25	Oct. 11, 1751.
Everhart, Joseph, ...	150	Dec. 11, 1751.
Eberholt, Joseph, ...	50	Jan. 29, 1752.
Esch, Peter, ...	20	Oct. 8, 1754.
Everrighter, Mich'l, ...	25	Aug. 12, 1755.
Eanwick, Jacob, ...	25	Oct. 14, 1756.
Eden, Samuel, ...	40	Aug. 14, 1758.
Ellicott, John, ...	100	April 13, 1767.
Ernig, George, & Als., ...	281, 106	July 6, 1768.
Edwards, William, ...	70	Oct. 14, 1786.
Erwin, Hugh, ...	10	Dec. 18, 1810.
Erwin, William, ...	3	Dec. 18, 1810.
Erwin, William, ...	2	Dec. 18, 1810.
Erwin, William, ...	5	Dec. 10, 1811.
Ely, John, Jr., ...	6, 39	July 5, 1814.
Erwin, William, ...	25, 157	Feb. 13, 1821.
Fisher, John, ...	50	Feb. 2, 1733.
Fealty, Michael, ...	100	March 20, 1733.
Foulke, Hugh, ...	200	March 22, 1733-4.
Freylick, Mich'l, ...	150	June 25, 1734.
Fraley, Mich'l, ...	50	Dec. 6, 1736.
Fry, William, ...	200	Dec. 30, 1736.
Foreman, Benj., ...	250	March 3, 1737.
Farguson, Hugh, ...	300	March 20, 1737.
Fry, Johannes, ...	150	April 2, 1737.
Feighly, Jacob, ...	150	Dec. 19, 1737.

Pennsylvania Archives, Series 3, Volume: XXIV, Chapter: Warrantees of Land in the County of Bucks. 1733-1889, p. 125

From *Application for Warrants,* 1768, A-E, the Original Warrant, note the correct spelling of Emig:[32]

1768 July 6th
George EMIG	231 Acres 89 Perches
Michael SMELL	50 17
Total	281 Acres 106 Perches

In Haycock, Bucks County per and of the Lottery Land tract and return - £180 2sh 1p.

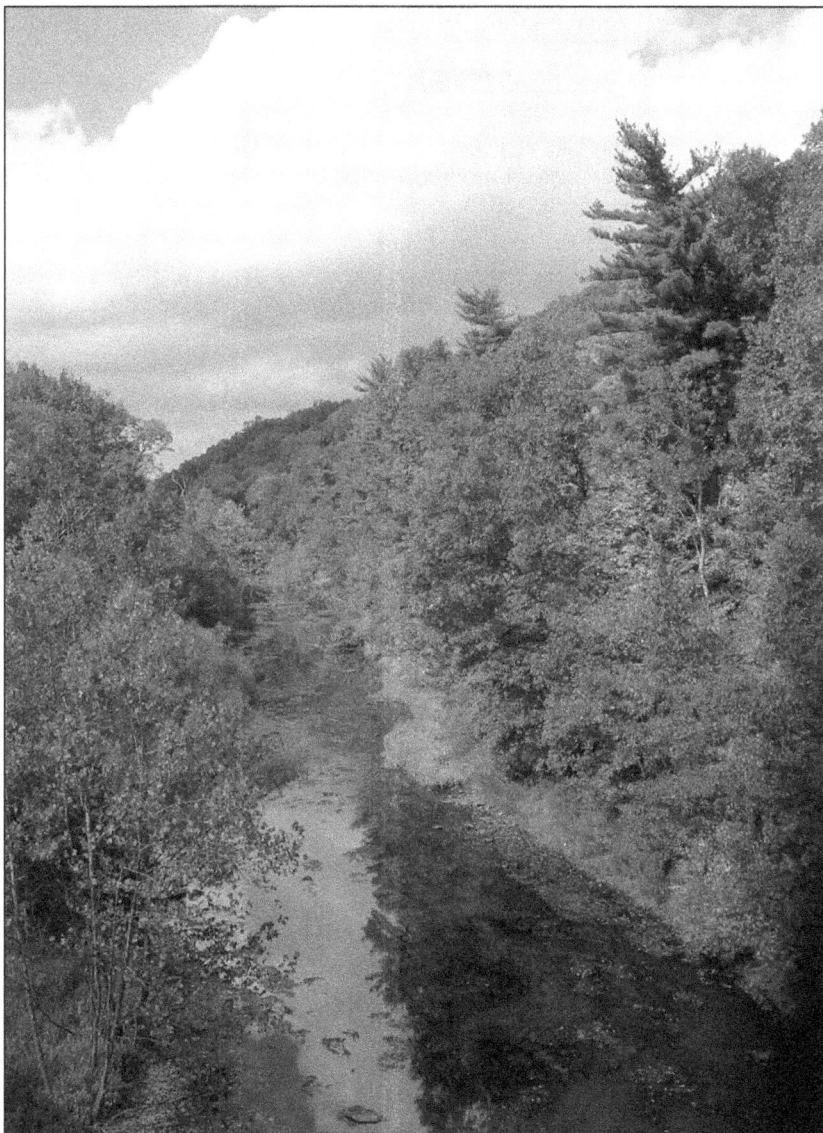

Tohickon Creek below the dam from the bridge on Ridge Road
Taken 2007

The land above is described in a deed and *Map of Lottery Land* that
follows. Georg EMIG obtained Lottery Land in the amount of 230 acres and
89 perches at Haycock Township on 13 Jul 1768 for a consideration of £249

with quit rent of 1 penny sterling per acre due per year. A survey of the land referred to as *Innovation* was made out to George Emig.

The original patent is found in the *Bucks County Pennsylvania Deeds*. The original is hard to read and states: "Beginning at a marked white oak thence by lands of Christian Gaynian & Peter Heft – thence by Charles Dennises land – thence by John Stokes land—to a corner of Michael Smelk land – containing 231 acres and 89 perches."[33]

The original homestead was flooded in the 1970's to form Lake Nockamixon. The website describes the history of the lake:[34]

> **History of Lake Nockamixon**
> The Tohickon watershed is 44.5 square miles in size. Tohickon Creek has historically been used as a source of power. At one time there were between 12 and 18 dams on the Tohickon furnished power to saw wood, grind grain, card wool, and lift water. Dams were used to make ponds where ice was cut during the winter and stored until needed in the summer months. The remains of two mills and four dams are located in Nockamixon State Park. One dam (in good condition) is located just behind the Weisel Youth Hostel on Richlandtown Road.
> …
> The land acquisition and construction of the park began in 1961. In the year 1965, the construction of Lake Nockamixon began. A total of 290 properties in Bedminster, East Rockhill, Nockamixon, Haycock, and Tinicum Townships were condemned to build the park. The construction of the dam began in October 1968. The dam was completed in June 1973 and the lake began filling at that time. It took about six months for the lake to fill completely. The relocation of Route 563 began in September of 1970 and was completed in 1972. Park electrical, water, and sewer system development took place between 1973 and 1975.
> …
> When Lake Nockamixon was created by a dam, its waters covered the sites of several homes and a few businesses.
> …
> The small town of Tohickon, formerly called Stovertown, was located along the creek just upstream of the present dam. Much of the rest of the lake site was farmland, including farmhouses, barns, and other associated farm buildings. All of the buildings in the area now covered by the lake were

demolished before the lake was filled. Many roads crossed the area now under the lake waters, and each road had a bridge where it crossed the Tohickon Creek. All of the bridges, except for the stone arch bridge at Tohickon village, were also demolished so they would not cause underwater hazards. The stone arch bridge is still there, under approximately 70 feet of water.

Nockamixon State Park looking south over the lake
The Emig homestead is under Lake Nockamixon.

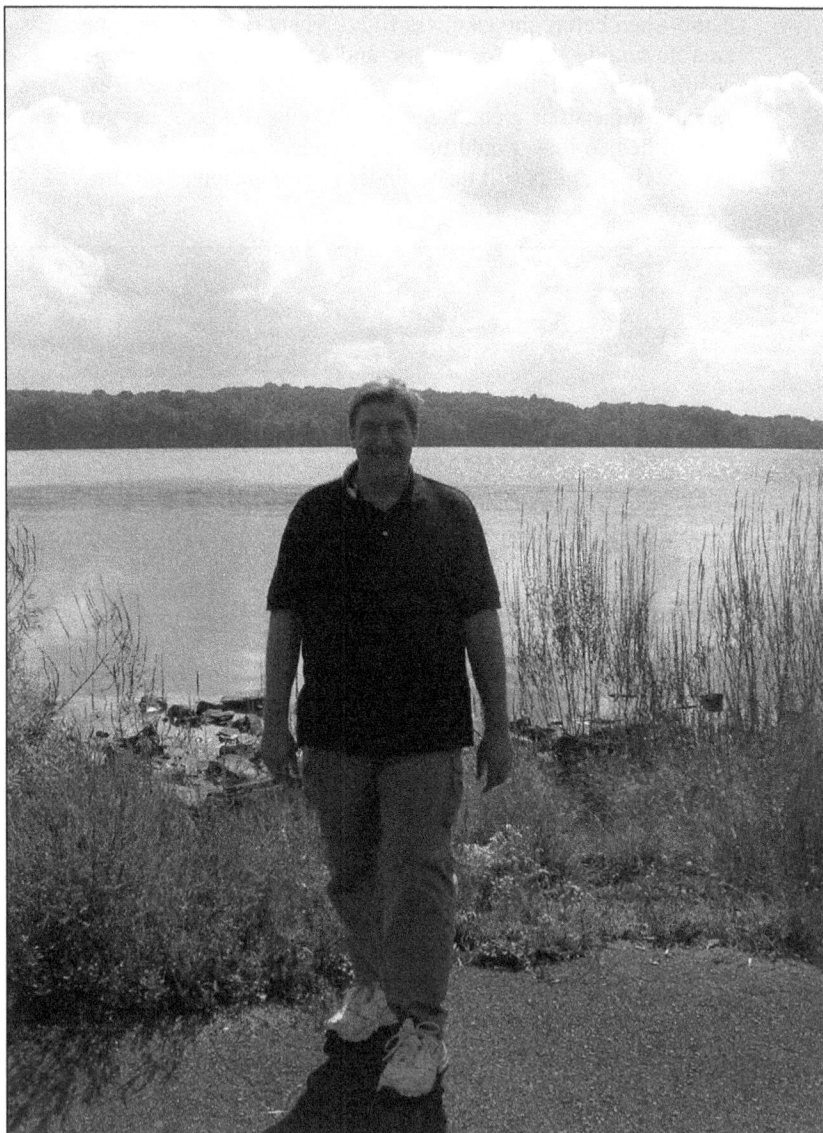

Author, David Emmick, overlooking Lake Nockamixon toward the family homestead
Taken 2007

Old Bethlehem Road heading east blocked by Lake Nockamixon near the family homestead
Taken 2007

Overlooking Lake Nockamixon toward the family homestead
Taken from Old Bethlehem Road looking northeast
Taken 2007

Home on Old Bethlehem Road near lake shows style of stone construction

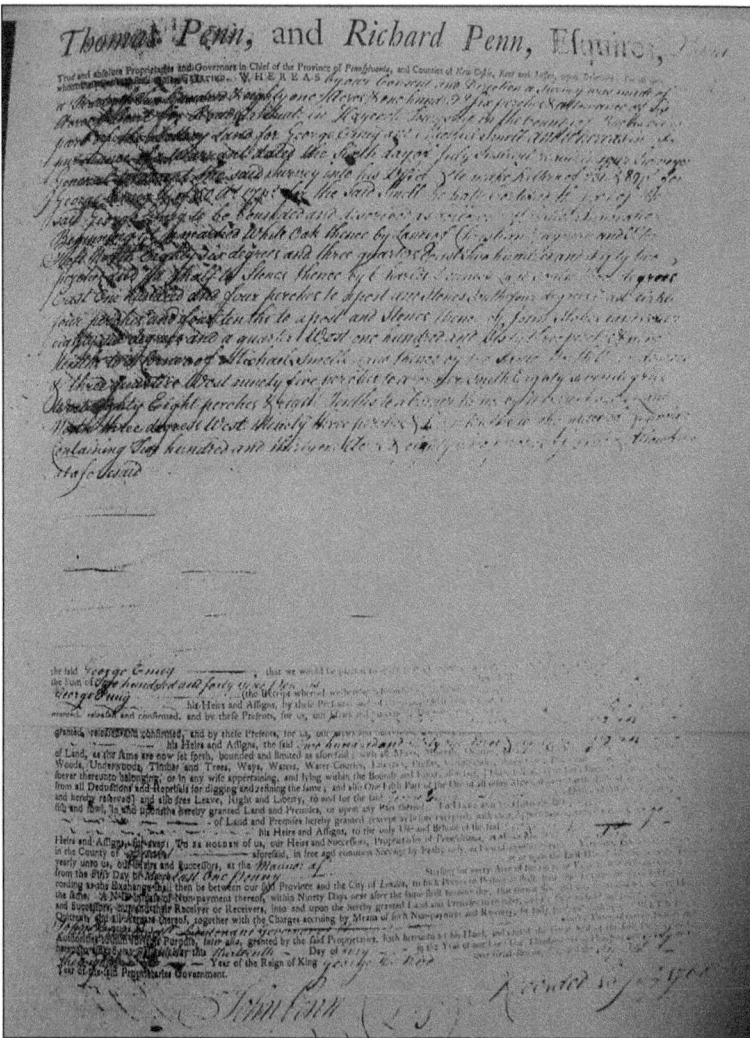

Bucks County, Penn. Deeds, Bk. AA #10. p. 433, George Emig on top of lower half
Very poor quality copy

In 1735, sons of William Penn, John and Thomas Penn, planned a lottery to liquidate holdings of absentee English landlords in Haycock and Springfield townships. The drawing for the lottery was not held but the purchasers of the tickets were allowed to take title to the land. The *Map of Lottery Land adjoining the Manor of Richland 1735* gives the owners names, amounts of land granted and dates. This corresponds to Georg's deed of 1768.[35]

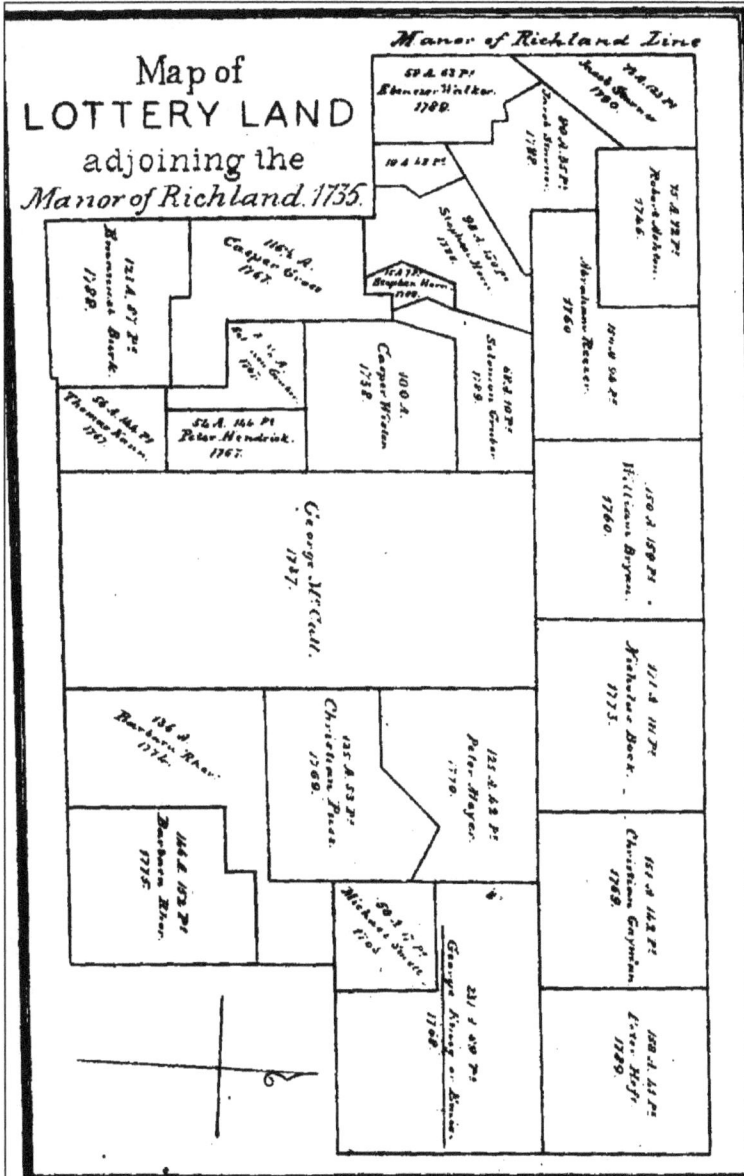

Map of Lottery Land adjoining Manor of Richland 1735
Copy or Original in Spruance Library, Doylestown, PA

The Map following is of Lower Haycock Township constructed from and compared with original drafts remaining on file in the Department of Interior Affairs of Pennsylvania, for the use and at the request of the Forestry Reserve Commission of Pennsylvania on December 8, 1924.[36]   Charles Dennis does not appear on the Lottery Map but does appear on this map on the far west edge.   The Dennis family is mentioned earlier as settlers of Applebachsville [also note Jacob Emick on the map].

The map bears the signature of James H. Craig, Dep. Sec. Internal Affairs. Heinrich Emig appears on this map as Henry Emigh, and the land located on Tohickon Creek.   Although Charles Dennis is not referenced on the *Map of Lottery Land adjoining the Manor of Richland 1735,* he is referenced on this map.

In 1766 Philip and Barbara Hahn Emig had a son, John Nicholas born September 15, 1766 and baptized October 12, 1766 at the Tohickon Reformed church at Bedminster with witnesses Michael Coppelbeger and wife.[37]

Map of Lower Haycock Township
Showing Warrant of Christopher Moyer dated 13 December 1709
Surveyed 21 October 1756 to Henry Emigh, see lower right for Henry Emigh
Copy of map at Bucks Co. Historical Society, Spruance Library

Copy of map at Bucks Co. Historical Society, Spruance Library
Detail showing Henry Emigh center

JOHN FRY

Chas. Denner etal.
A-48-211

JOHN DENNIS
50A. 84
Wt May 9, 1747
Sd May 15, 1764
A-45-226
Pat. Aug. 18, 1764
To Charles Dennis
A-A-518

Jno Fry

GEORGE EMIG
231 A. 89 P.
Lottery Land
Sd. Apr. 20, 1748
Called "Preble"
C-50-143
Pat. July 13, 1745
To George Emig
A-A-10-433

Christian Gayman & Peter Hess

John Stokes

MICHAEL SMELL
50A. 17 P.

Henry Moyer

Christian Puss

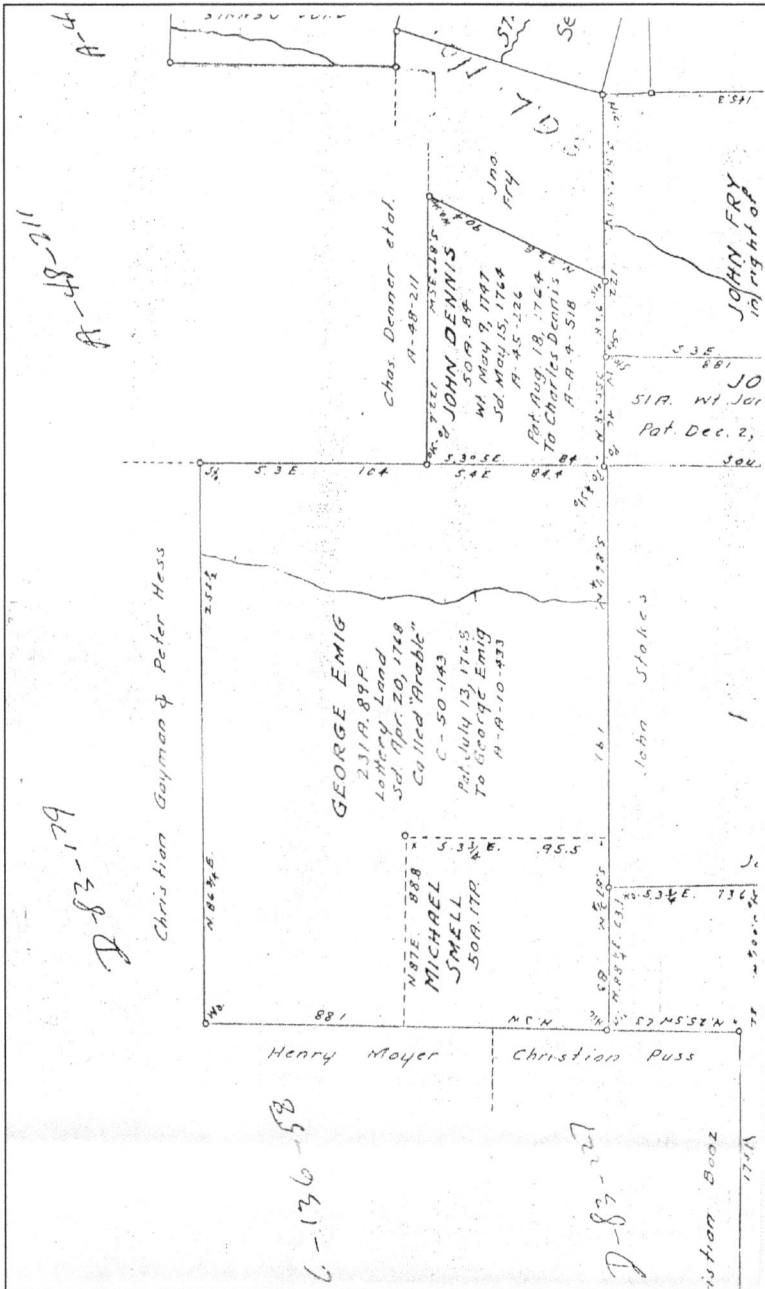

Copy of map at Bucks County Historical Society, Spruance Library
Detail, same map set, different map

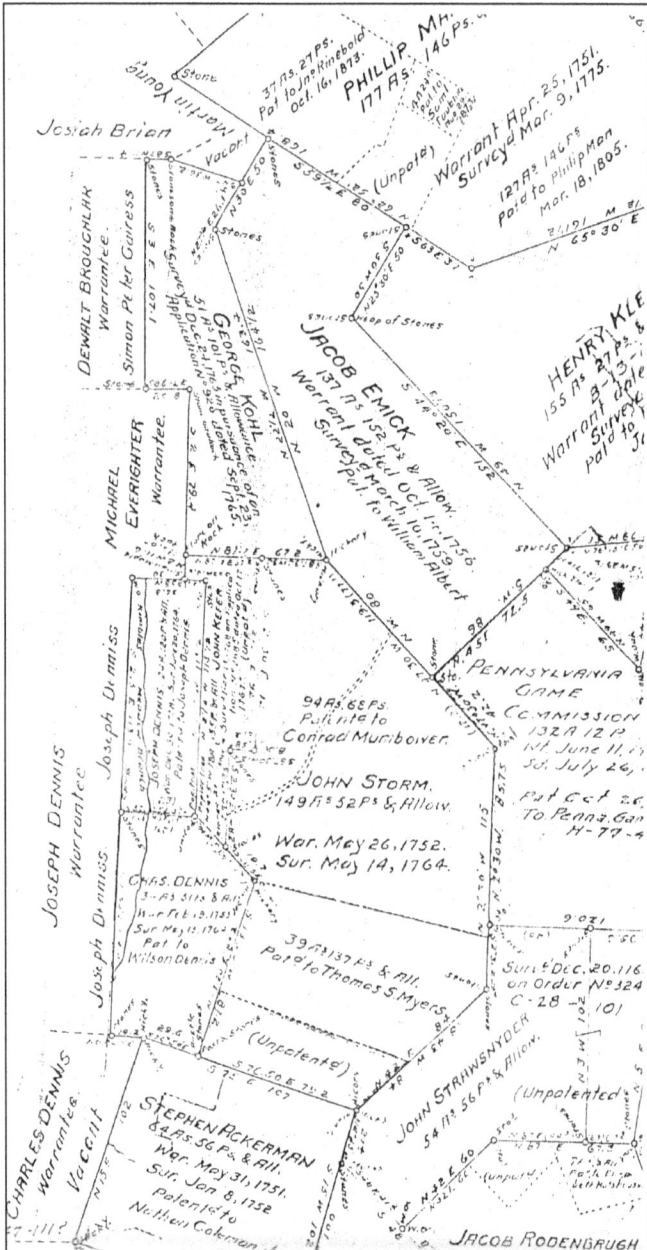

Copy of map at Bucks Co. Historical Society, Spruance Library
Detail, showing Jacob Emick (unknown relation) center

The Death of Johan Georg Emig

The old section of the graveyard behind Trinity Lutheran Church, Springfield Township,
taken 2007

Johan Georg Emig died at Springfield Township, Bucks County, Pennsylvania, March 5, 1773, and was buried at Trinity Union Church Cemetery, Springfield Township in the old cemetery. The marker lists born July 7, 1715, died March 5, 1773 aged 57 years, 7 months and 26 days but the inscription has since worn and is no longer easily found. The information about his grave was copied from a 1921 list prepared by B. F. Fackentha Jr. and the grave was not found or legible in 1981 when Linda Klosek prepared another list of graves in the cemetery.[38,39]

The old section of the graveyard at side of Trinity Lutheran Church, Springfield Township,
Taken 2007

His wife, Maria Elisabeth, as "Widow Emich" was buried on October 12, 1799 in Springfield in the Old Cemetery of Trinity Union Church along with husband George although no tombstone marks her grave. She is listed as Mary in the will of Georg but Maria in earlier records.[40]

Georg's will is listed in Wills of Bucks County, Pennsylvania[41] and states:

> Last Will & Testament: Georg Emig
> Drawn: 2 March 1773; Proved: 15 March 1773
> My wife Mary, she shall live upon my plantation during her life – My beloved son George Emig, all my real and personal estate
> Witness: Peter Seen, Michael Small & Peter Hest [Heist]

Georg Emig's Will,
Wills of Bucks County, Pennsylvania, Bk. B. 1773, pp. 315-316

Georg Emig's will
Wills of Bucks County, Pennsylvania, Bk. B. 1773, pp. 315-316

George Emig's estate inventory was valued at £908.[42]

Bucks County, Pennsylvania, Orphans' Court Records, File #563, 13 Sep 1774, Bk. A-2, p. 363

Georg Emig bequeathed his bible to the Dutch Reformed Church in Springfield. The Bucks County Historical Society Bible Records states: "The Bible, according to the last will and testament of Johann Georg Emig of Haycock twp, Bucks County, has been bequeathed to the High German Reformed Congregation in Springfield Twp, Bucks County for use in the public church service and has been surrendered by his estate, this taking place in the year of our lord 1780." [43]

If I only knew High German!
Author, David Emmick, at Spruance Library, Mercer Museum, Bucks County, Pennsylvania,
reading Georg Emig's family bible. Taken 2007.

Georg Emig's bible at Spruance Library, Mercer Museum, Bucks County, Pennsylvania.
Taken 2007

The family Bible of Georg Emig was published in 1747 at Basel, Switzerland by Emanuel Thurneyen. It was donated to the church and is still available. [44]

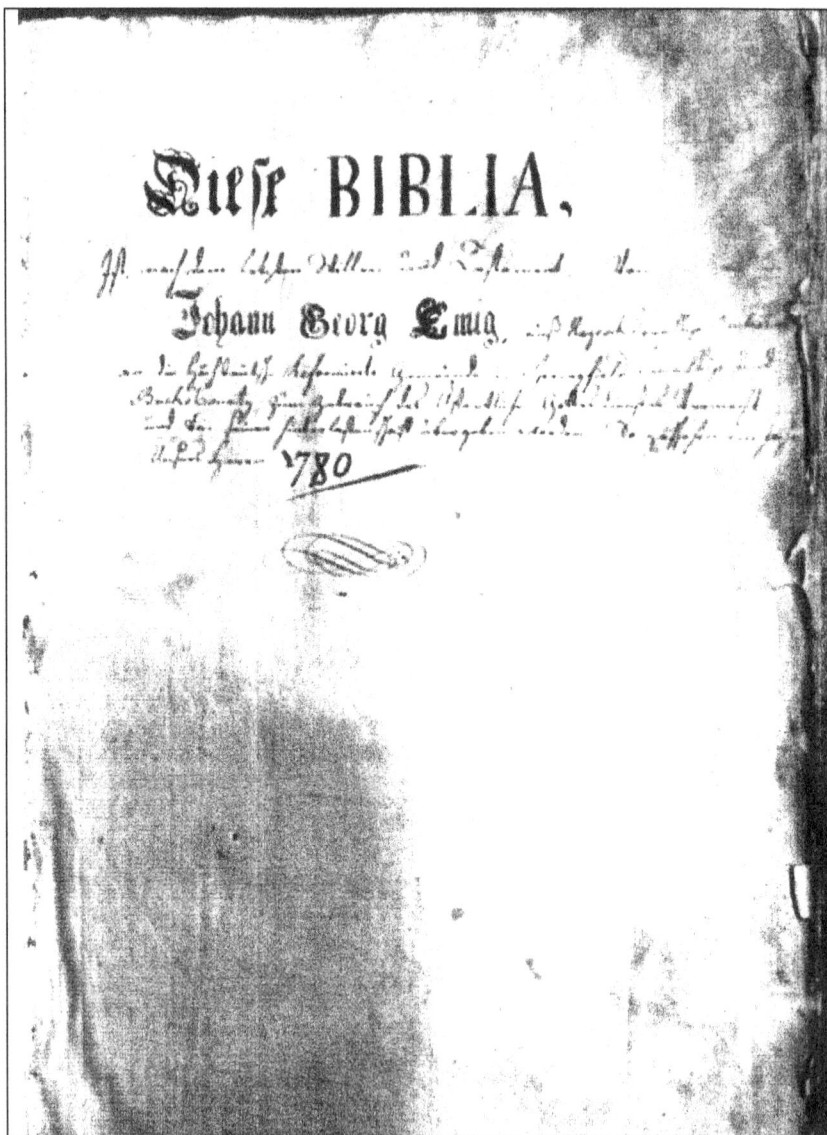

First page of Georg Emig's bible with inscription of donation dated1780.

BIBLIA,

Das ist:

Die Gantze

Heilige Schrifft,

Alten und Neuen Testaments,

Verteutschet durch

Doct. Martin Luth

Anietzo
Uber die alten Summarien, Concordantzer
Historien- und Namen-Register

Mit

Nützlichen, einem jeden Verſ. beygefü
accurat- und vollkommenen Summ
Neuen und lehrreichen Vorreden über viele B
Vorstellung der vornehmsten Materien oben a
Vermehrung der Parallel-Stellen, Einri
und Unterscheidung der Haupt- und M
durch eine besondere Schrift

GOTT zu Ehren

und allen Heils-begierigen Seelen zum Unterrich
verfasset und herausgegeben durch

M. Friedrich Gattler und M. Theodor Bernler,

Weiland Diener am Heil. Evangelio in der Kirche zu Basel.

Mit Ihro Röm. Käyſ. Majeſt. allergnädigſtem Privilegio, wie auch mit gnädigem Pr... C&M. Evangel
Orten der Eydgnosschafft, und Approbation E. E. Theologischen Facultät in der Hohen Schul zu Basel.

Neue Auflage,

Mit noch mehrern Auslegungen, ſammt einer verbeſſerte
Zeit-Rechnung und unterschiedlichen darzu dienlichen
neuen Figuren versehen.

BASEL,

Bey und in Verlag Emanuel Thurneysen, MDCC

Title page of Georg Emig's bible with publisher and dates, slightly torn.

Trinity Union Church

Trinity Lutheran Church, Springfield Township,
On the Old Bethlehem Road

Johan Georg Emig was buried at the Trinity Union Church Cemetery in Springfield Township in the old cemetery March 5, 1773. It is located on what was the Old Bethlehem Road west of Applebachsville north of Richardstown in Pleasant Valley [now 212]. The marker is no longer legible and the grave not immediately recognizable.

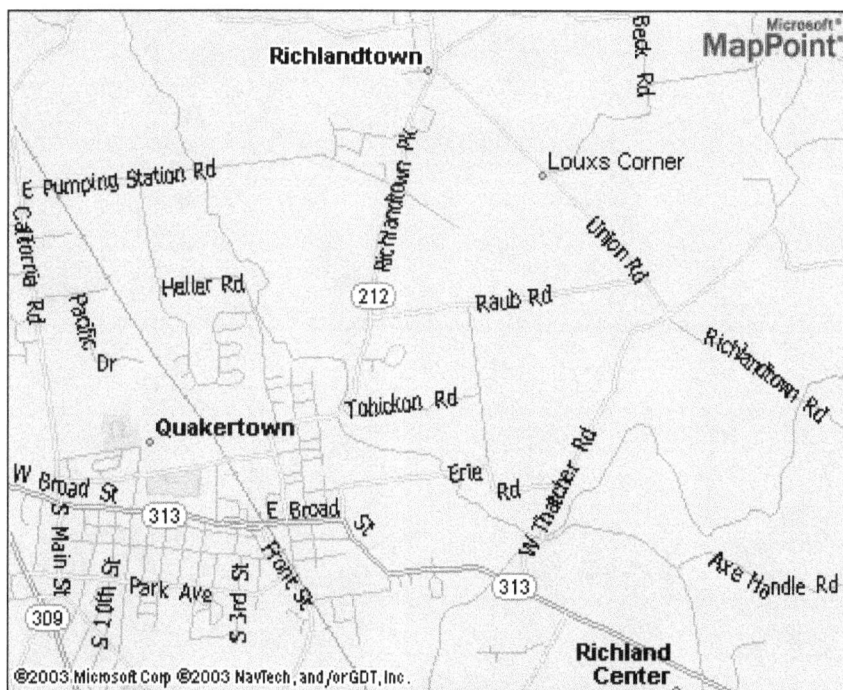

Trinity Church, Reformed and Lutheran, Main Street, Old Bethlehem Road,
Springfield, Pennsylvania, organized 1745
On Route 212 near Richlandtown in Pleasant Valley

The First Generation

The first generation family with grandparents repeated ...

Family Tree First Generation

Johan Georg EMIG (1714 – 1773)
+Maria Elisabeth (1736/1738 – 1799)
    Johan Heinrich EMIG (1737/1739 – 1777)
    +Anna Catharina NICOLAS (1739/1740 – 1832)
        Maria Elizabeth EMICH (1760 – 1761)
        Child EMIG (1761 – 1761)
        Henry AMICK (1762 – 1830)
        Julianna EMICH (1765 – 1841)
        Catherine Margaret EMICH (1768 – 1842)
        John Philip EMICH (1769 – 1850)
        Mary Magdalene EMICH (1772 – 1841)
        John George EMICH (1774 – 1827)
    Johan Philip EMIG (1745 -   )
    +Barbara HAHN
        Nicholas EMMICK (1766 – 1836)
        Maria Magdalena EMIG (1768 -   )
        Henry EMIG (1770 -   )
        Catharine EMIG (1772 -   )
    Johan Georg EMIG (1751 – 1829)
    +Anna Margaretha LERCH (1754 – 1829)
        George EMIG (1774 -   )
        Anna Maria EMIG (1778 – 1805)
        Johannes EMIG (1779 – 1849)
        Samuel EMIG (1782 -   )
        Petrus EMIG (1784 -   )
        Anthony EMIG (1789 – 1842)
        Joseph EMIG (1793 – 1842)
        Catharine EMIG (1795 -   )
        David EMIG (1798 -   )
        Magdalena EMIG (1800 -   )

Henry and George Emig

Johan Heinrich Emig married Catharine Nicolas, daughter of Valentine & Anna Elisabeth (Shenk) Nicolas\Nicolaus, early settlers at Haycock, Bucks County on December 4, 1759.[45]   Johan Heinrich Emig [Emich in these records] married Catharina Nikla (Nicolas) in the school house; Keller's Church had not yet been erected.[46] The family is well documented in church records for baptism and attendance.

Maria Elisabeth Emig, first child and daughter of Henry and Catherine, was born on September 5, 1760, and baptized September 28 at Keller's Church. Grandparents Valentine Nicola and wife Elizabeth were witnesses. She was named for her grandmother.[47]

Henry and Catherine lost their second child at birth. In the church records it states: "Aug 12 1761, Henry Emig's second child died and was buried the next day". The child was not named and buried the day after birth.[48]

Henry and Catherine's oldest son was born June 7, 1762, and named Henry [Henry Amick]. The church records state: "Henry of Henry Emig and wife Catherine, nee Nicolay, bapt. July 4, Sponsors Peter Keller and wife Catherine."[49]

Henry Emig is also listed in the general church records. In the church records listing members contributing to the minister and schoolmaster from Easter 1762 to 1763; Henry Emig paid 5sh, Henry Keller – 10sh and Valentine Nicola-15sh.[50]

Julianna, the daughter of Henry and Catherine, was born April 29, 1765 at Haycock and was baptized on June 11, 1765 at Keller's Church, Bedminster Township.[51]

Henry's brother, Philip, is mentioned in baptismal records in 1766. John Nicholas, born September 15, 1766, to Philip & Barbara (Hahn) Emig was baptized October 12, 1766, at Tohickon Reformed Church at Bedminster. Witnesses were Michael Coppelberger and wife.[52]

It is recorded that in 1767 Henry Emich and his wife Catherine attended communion and confession at Keller's Church at Bedminster on the fifth Sunday after Trinity, "but June 7 being Pentecost, they were admitted to communion and confession the next day".[53]

Catherine Margaret, daughter of Henry and Catherine Emig was baptized April 3, 1768. Sponsors were Peter Kubler and his wife Catharine.[54]

Henry and Catharine are listed in the church records at communion in April and August 1768, October 1769 and January 1779. The records state: "John Philip of Henry Emig and wife Catherine was born." John Philip Emig was born on December 11, 1769 and baptized January 1, 1770. The sponsors were John Philip Stein and wife Elizabeth.[55]

Maria Magdalena, daughter of Henry and Catherine was born January 30, 1772 and baptized June 8, 1772 by Rev. Peter Frederick Niemyer. Jacob Ness and wife Maria were Sponsors.[56]

Many immigrants were indentured servants and Henry had such a servant in 1773. In October of that year, Henry took out an advertisement for his return, the servant having run away. The advertisement placed by Henry Emig reads:[57]

Five Pound Reward

Run away, on the 26th of September last, from the subscriber, living in Haycock, Bucks County, a Dutch servant man, named Matthias Borell, speaks some English, is about 26 years of age, a middling long lean fellow, and has a sore on one of his cheeks which constantly keeps running; had on, when he went away, a new fashioned French hat, a red striped jacket, without sleeves, a darkish-colored ditto, a brown parched coat, velvet breeches, tow trousers, black ribbed stockings, a pair of cotton ditto, and wide shoes. Whoever apprehends said servant, and brings him to his master or secures him so that he may have him again, shall receive the above reward, and reasonable charges, paid by Henry Emig.

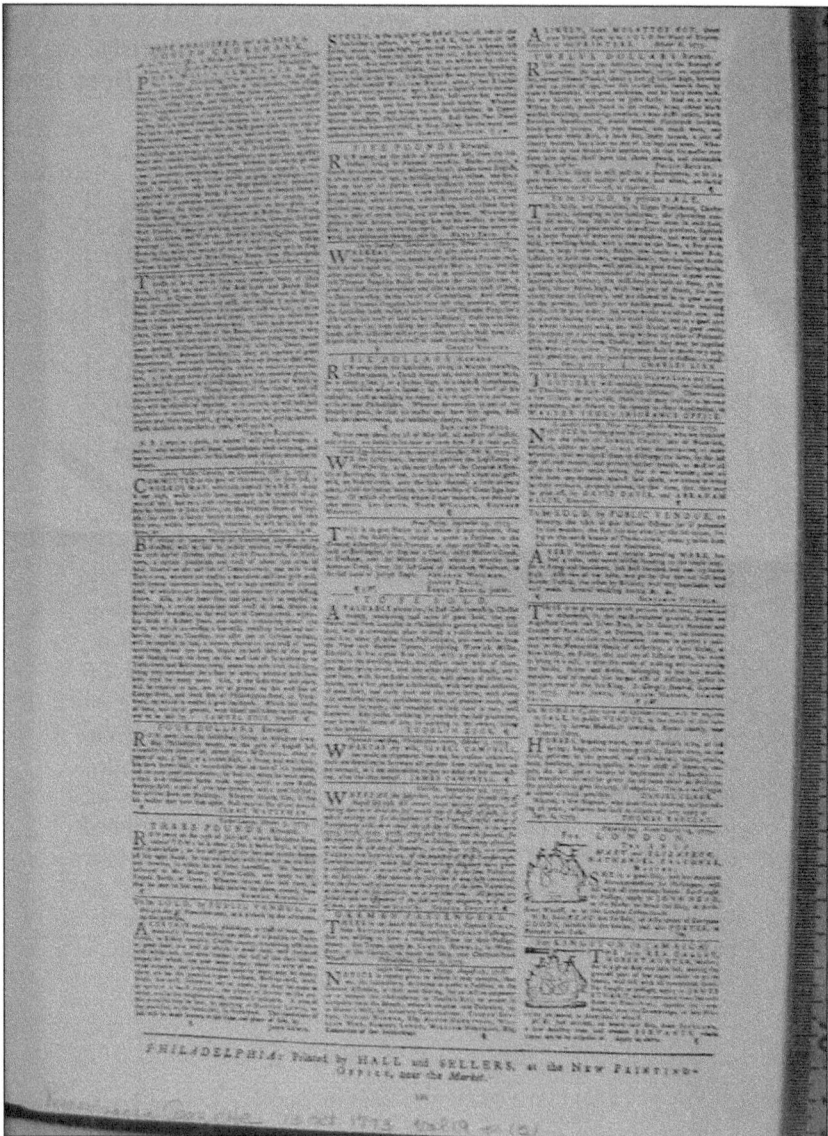

Pennsylvania Gazette of 13 Oct 1773, vol. 19, p. 131, Bucks County Historical Society

John George Emig, son of Henry and Catherine, was born April 6, 1774 and baptized August 20, 1774. John George Steinbach and wife were listed as sponsors.[58] Henry and Catherine Emig and Maria Elizabeth Emig (age 14 then) are listed as communicants of Keller's Church in 1774 and 1776.[59]

In the *History of Bucks County, Pennsylvania* Henry is mentioned several times having to do with roads. Also mentioned is John Keller. Henry and John Keller lived near Applebachsville named for General Applebach. The mills and locality are also described.

From *The History of Bucks County, Pennsylvania* by W. W. H. Davis:[60]

A bridge was built across the Tohickon in 1768, probably where the Bethlehem road crosses that stream, and the first in the township. We know next to nothing about the early township roads. The Bethlehem road runs across its western part, and early gave the inhabitants an outlet toward Philadelphia, and this main artery of travel was intersected by lateral roads as they were required to accommodate the wants of the inhabitants. In June 1765, Aaron Fretz, who owned a "water grist-mill" on the Tohickon, in Haycock, petitioned the court to open a road for him to get out from it. It was to run down through Bedminster, past Jacob Niece's smith shop, to meet a road from the Durham road to Perkasie. In 1774 Jacob Strawhen, Martin Sheive, William Bryan, John Keller, George Amey, and 18 others, remonstrated against a road that was to be opened in Haycock, and asked that it be reviewed, on the ground that it would be impossible for wagons to travel it, on account of its being so rough and rocky. This road must have passed across the region known as the "Rocks," the drift belt crossing the township from east to west, where, for the distance of a mile or more, the earth is covered thick with well-worn boulders from the size of a bushel basket to that of a small house. Considerable of this region cannot be cultivated.

John Fretz owned a mill in the township before 1764, and Henry Nicholas in 1790.

Haycock has but one village that deserves the name, Applebachsville, on the Old Bethlehem road, in the northwest part of the township. It contains about 30 dwellings, several of them brick, built on both sides of the road, with shade trees in front. Among the buildings other than dwellings, are a pubic schoolhouse, with a graded school, a union church, Lutheran, Reformed, and Mennonite, founded in 1855, built of brick, a brick hotel, and a store. [The Rev. J. F. Ohl was the Lutheran pastor from 1874 to 1889, G. C. Gardner, 1890-97, and Warren Nickel from 1897 to the present time. Keller's church belongs to the same parish.] Adjoining the village lived many years, and died, in 1872, General Paul Applebach, after whom it was named. He was its founder and did much to advance its prosperity. Down to within 28 years there was but one dwelling there, a centenarian, still standing by the roadside, the first new house being built in 1848, by General Applebach. It is the seat of a physician, who practices in the neighborhood. The country around the village is fertile and picturesque, but lying on the borders of the rock drift may loose boulders, that fell out of ranks, lie upon the surface and make cultivation somewhat difficult.

…

In Bedminster there is a labyrinth of roads, but we know little about those earliest laid out. It is a difficult thing to recognize local roads after the lapse of many years, and a change of the names of points that fixed them at their opening. The township is cut by three of the great arteries of travel that traverse the county: the Durham and Easton roads pass through the southeast corner of Bedminster, intersecting at Pipersville, the Old Bethlehem road forms the northwest boundary, while the Swamp road separates it from Hilltown on the west. The first township road, that we have a record of, was laid out in 1748, running from the road from "Colvin's ferry (on Delaware) to Philadelphia," to John Clymer's mill on Tohickon, and thence by the Presbyterian and Mennonite meeting-houses to the Old Bethlehem road. In 1755 a road was probably laid out from the Durham road to Jacob Stout's mill on the Tohickon and the Tohickon church, and thence toward the county line. A road was laid out in 1765 from Deep Run meeting-house to the Easton road, and the following year one was opened from the meeting-house to Tohickon church. About 1800 a bridge was built over Deep Run, near the meeting-house.

…

   John Clymer's mill, on the Tohickon, is thought to have been the first built in the township, and before 1749. The mills of Jacob Kraut, on Deep Run, and Joseph Tyson, on Cabin run, were erected next in order. We have authority for saying that the oldest mill in the township is supposed to have been built on the site of Angany's on a small stream that joins Deep Run, east of the Presbyterian church. These mills were followed by Jacob Stover's on the Tohickon, and Henry Black's oil-mill on Cabin run and Durham road, half a mile below Pipersville, since torn down. In 1753 the widow Sheaver owned a mill, but we do not know the location, and the same year a road was laid out from it to Deep Run meeting-house. One of the petitioners was Rev. Francis McHenry. Among early mills on the Tohickon were those of Ichabod Wilkinson, White's and Henry Lot's.

...

Bedminster has five villages, at least localities that bear the name, Pipersville, on the Easton road, in the southeast corner, Dublin, on the Swamp road, in the southwest corner, Hagersville and Keelersville on the Old Bethlehem road, in the northwest corner, and Bedminsterville, at the intersection of the roads that lead from the Mennonite meeting-house to Keller's shop and from the Durham to the Dublin road. Of these, Dublin is the most considerable. It is said to have taken its name from the old log tavern that first dispensed the good things of life to man and beast at this point. It was a double building and got the name of the "double-inn," and, in the course of time, the name was a little changed, and the hamlet that grew up around it was called Dublin.

...

Pipersville, Hagersville and Bedminsterville are post-villages, where offices were established 1845 and 1851. This township is well watered by Cabin, Deep, Wolf, Deer and Mink runs, branches of Tohickon and by the north branch of Perkiomen. The surface is rolling, with but few hills, the soil is generally fertile, and produces good crops under careful German tillage.

Another petition for a public road is recorded in *Bucks County Pennsylvania, Petitions for Roads.* From the General Quarter Session held at Newtown, June 1767, for a public road "Laid out from Henry Emig mills to Henry Keller and thence through the widow Bishops land to the Lutheran Meeting House to a Road leading across the county to the line of said county." The petitioned was signed by Valentine Nicklaus, William Diehl, John Keller, Henry Keller, John Doan, John Nicholas and others.[61]

Henry Emig mentioned here is our Henry Emig [Henry, Georg]; Valentine Nicklaus is Henry's grandfather, Anna Catharina Nicolas' father; and the Keller's are uncles of Henry Emig's wife Barbara Niemand.

Later, another petition for roads is made. Henry Nicholas petitioned the court of general quarter session in 1790 for a road from his grist and saw mill to a public road leading from Durham Road to Henry Trumbower's Tavern. The petition was signed Daniel Wiegner, Georg Emig, Georg Mast, Valentine Nicola, Peter Mills, Georg Nicola, Christian Nicola and others who were close relatives or neighbors of Heinrich Emig.[62]

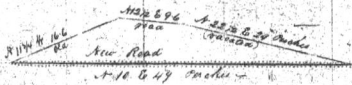

Petition for Roads, pp. 545-546

Record of Roads November Term...

fifteen perches to a post and South thirty five...
perches and seven tenths to a post; thence through...
Kressman and land belonging to Jacob Kressman...
degrees west twelve perches and eight tenths to a post thence...
Jacob Kressman deed South twenty seven degrees west twenty...
post South nineteen degrees and three quarters west fifty ten perches to a post...
South twenty five degrees and a quarter west twelve perches to a post and...
South fifteen degrees and a half west thirty three perches and five tenths...
to a post; thence through the said Jacob Kressman land and through land...
of Samuel Mann South thirty nine degrees west eighty three perches and...
three tenths to a post; thence through the said Samuel Mann land...
five degrees west thirty seven perches and five tenths thence through land...
of Jacob K. Mann South five degrees and three quarters west twenty...
perches to a post in a public road leading from the Durham road...
to the old Bethlehem road in land of Jacob K. Mann in the said...
Township of Springfield. A plot draft whereof is hereunto annexed...
... for town... and... this 16th day of October A.D. eighteen...
hundred and...

William S. Lena .... [Seal]

Anthony Frankie .... [Seal]

... the road ... approved and .... Jacob Van Buskirk .... [Seal]
... road ...
... ... J. W. Erdman .... [Seal]

Joseph Hange .... [Seal]

Jacob Stover .... [Seal]

... this page —

Petition for Roads, pp. 545-546

Henry Emig and his brother George Emig are listed in the tax records for 1775 as Amey. Henry Amey is listed as living in Haycock with his saw and grist mill on Tohickon Creek. His brother George Amey is also listed.[63]

George Amey 4 horse, 3 cattle, 8 sheep   200a Land 1-Servent
Henry Amey 1 Horse   3 cattle, 19 sheep   175a Land 1-Saw & Grist Mill

The family farm was left to George Emig, who was 24 years of age. The mill is part of disbursements made of the estate of Henry Emey "late of Haycock Township" on December 14, 1778, "Paid 1 pound 14 shillings, and 3 pence to repair the Mill."[64]

Henry Emig is also recorded as having four land patents with the spelling Emigh. John Penn, Esq., and John Penn, Jr., issued a patent to Henry Emigh, February 22, 1776.[65] Other patents of note:

> Seventy (70) acres, one hundred eleven (111) perches plus allowances, warranted 1749 to Christopher Browers called "Sower Crout".
>
> Eighty-five (85) acres, plus allowances, warranted, 1743, to Dennis Onam, called "Embeck".
>
> One Hundred twenty-two (122) acres, plus allowances, warranted 1744 to Dennis Onam called "Embden".
>
> Forty-seven acres (47) plus allowances, Warranted 1754 to Valentine Nicholas called "Kale".
>
> Three hundred twenty-four (324) acres, one hundred eleven perches (111) total.
>
> Valentine Nicholas, in his warrant application of 5 Nov 1754, received twenty (20) acres, more or less adjacent to Dennis Ent & Dennis Bourne on the "Tohiccon" Bucks County "pay 251".
>
> Signed by Richard Peters and addressed to Nicholas Sull, Surveyor, General.

Pennsylvania State Archives, Division of Land Records, Harrisburg PA. *Deed Book AA*, vol. 15, pp. 635-636

In Land Grants:[66]

- The First entry is called a *Petition* or Application
- Second, upon approval of the entry, a *Warrant* is issued.
- Third, *Survey* to measure the requirements of the entry and warrant. With a plat (map) showing the location in relation to land held by others with a written description using meters and bounds.
- Fourth, a *Patent* is issued and recorded. The title is secured through the patent.

Also of note is the Deed Recorded December 30, 1790 (when Henry moved to Virginia) in which Henry and Catherine Emich sold one hundred thirty acres and one hundred fifty-six perches of land to Catherine's brother, Jacob Nicholas of Haycock Township in consideration of three hundred and five pounds on April 24, 1776.[67]

Bucks County, Pennsylvania, Deeds, bk. 26, p. 49

Bucks County, Pennsylvania, Deeds, bk. 26, p. 50

Henry Emy died interstate before June 11, 1777. The inventory and appraisal of estate was filed by Thomas Armstrong and Jacob Bernt with Catherine and John Nicholas named as administrators. The estate was appraised at £447: 3sh: and 2p in personal goods and chattels with £45: 2sh: and 8p owed to the estate.[68]

Administration.

Nota Will

No. 1531

ESTATE OF

Henry Emy

REGISTER'S OFFICE

1777

Bucks County, Pennsylvania, Register of Wills, Doylestown, PA., Estate #1531

KNOW all Men by thefe Prefents, That

We *Catherine Emy John Nicholas Jacob Baun by Jacob Nicholas all of the Hay Cock Township in the County of Bucks* - - - - - -

- - - - - - are held and firmly bound unto *Joseph Hart* - - - - Regifter for the Probate of Wills and granting Letters of Adminiftration, in and for the County of *Bucks* - - in the Commonwealth of *Pennfylvania*, in the Sum of *One Thoufand* - - Pounds, to be paid to the faid *Joseph Hart or to* - - his certain Attorney, Executors, Administrators or Affigns. To the which Payment well and truly to be made, we bind ourfelves jointly and feverally for and in the Whole, our Heirs, Executors and Adminiftrators, firmly by thefe Prefents. Sealed with our Seals. Dated the *Twenty Seventh* Day of - - - in the Year of our LORD One Thoufand Seven Hundred and Seventy *Seven* -

THE Condition this Obligation is fuch,

That if the above bounden - - - *John* - *Nicholas Adminiftr* - - - - Adminiftrat *ors* of al: and fingular the Goods, Chattel - - - *Henry Emy* deceafed, do make, or caufe to be mad - - - ect Inventory of all and fingular the Goods, Chattels and Cre - - - id Deceafed, which have or. fhall come to the Hands, Poffeffion or Know - - of *them* the faid *Catherine Emy & John Nicholas* - - - or unto the Hands and Poffeffion of any other Perfon or Perfons for *them* and the fame fo made do exhibit, or caufe to be exhibited, into the Regifter's Office, in the County of *Bucks* - - at or before the *Twenty Seventh* Day of *July* - next enfuing, and the - - - Chattels and Credits, and all other the Goods, Chattels and Credits of the faid Deceafed, at the Time of his Death, which at any Time after fhall come to the Hands or Poffeffion of the faid *Catherine Emy or John Nicholas* - - or into the Hands and Poffeffion of any other Perfon or Perfons for *them* do well and truly adminifter according to Law. And - - do make, or caufe to be made, a true and juft Account of *them* faid Ad - - - on at or before the *27* - - Day of *June 1778* - And all the R - - - of the faid Goods, Chattels and Credits which fhall be found rema - - - Adminiftrators Account (the fame being firft examined and all - - - rt of the County of *Bucks* - -) fhall - - - - Perfon or Perfons refpectively as the faid Orphans C - - - Decree, or - - ence, purfuant to the true Intent and Meaning of the - - - Laws now in Force in this Commonwealth, fhall limit and appoint. A - - it fhall hereafter appear that any laft Will and Teftament was made by the - - Deceafed, and the Executor or Executors therein named do exhibit the fame into the faid Regifter's Office, making Requeft to have it allowed and approved accordingly: And if then the above bounden *Catherine Emy and John Ni* - - - being thereunto required, do render and deliver the faid Letters of Adminiftration (Approbation of fuch Teftament being firft had and made in the faid Regifter's Office) then this Obligation to be void and of none Effect, or elfe to remain in full Force and Virtue.

Sealed and Delivered
in the Prefence of

Tho Armftrong
Michel Smith

John Nicholas

Jacob Baunt

Jacob Nicola

Bucks County, Pennsylvania, Register of Wills, Doylestown, PA., Estate #1531

Bucks County, Pennsylvania, Register of Wills, Doylestown, PA., Estate #1531

To Wheat Suppos'd 50 Bushals @ 7/6 per Bushal | 18 | 10 | 0
To 4 Bushal Buckwheat @ 5/ per Bl | 5 | |
To a Brass Kettle - - - | 5 | 0 | 0
To 34 lb of Wool a 5/ per lb | 8 | 10 | 0
To 2 lb of Do a 1/6 per lb | 0 | 3 | 0
To a Cabbage Knife & go stole - | 0 | 4 | 0
To 2 Malt Barals & a Stake | 0 | 5 | 0
To a Bedstead & Bedding thereto belongin - | 4 | 5 | 0
To a Do - - Do - | 1 | 0 | 0
To 3 Little Wheels a 24/ & a long wheel | 1 | 10 | 0
To 6 Gums & a Beehive - - | 0 | 4 | 0
To a Side Saddle - - | 3 | 10 | 0
To a Box & a Beehive - - - | 0 | 1 | 6
To Ten yearn - - | 0 | 6 | 0
To a Waggon Cover - - | 1 | 10 | 0
To 2 Bags & 1/2 Bushal Flax | 0 | 12 | 9
To 10 Cow Chains a 3/ per Chane | 1 | 10 | 0
To Schreibers - - | 0 | 10 | 0
To 2 pear of Hall Hings & 2 Hings | 0 | 10 | 0
To a Bafket of Old Iron - | 0 | 5 | 0
To a Still & Drawing Knife - | 0 | 3 | 0
To 3 Hoaks & 3 Fleals | 0 | 1 | 6
To a Hay Fork a 2/ a Onuge a 1/ & a hilling Hoe a 3/ - | 0 | 11 | 0
To 2 old Shovels & a Turnipe Knife - | 0 | 2 | 6
To a Sythe & Cradle a 5/ & a Grass Sythe 7/6 | 0 | 12 | 6
To a Grubing Hoe & 2 Axes a 3/ & a | 0 | 11 | 0
To a Claves & Swingle Trees a 5/ in Ol | 0 | 5 | 0
To a Cros Cut Saw - | 2 | 10 | 0
To a Bafket & Beehive - | 0 | 2 | 0
To a Turning Bench - | 0 | 5 | 0
To a Chees Hage & Hopper - | 0 | 1 | 6
To Old Iron - - | 0 | 3 | 0
To a Froe & Hing - | 0 | 4 | 0
To a Sinning Chisel & Do - | 0 | 6 | 0
To 32 Molding Plean - | 0 | 17 | 0
To Plow Planes - - - | 0 | 6 | 0
To 6 Pleans - - | 0 | 10 | 0
To 2s Chifflig & Gages - - | 1 | 2 | 0
To 3 Files - - | 0 | 3 | 0
To 3 Augors - - | 0 | 3 | 0
To a 2 foot rule Compas & Sunreys - | 0 | 6 | 0
To 4 Augors - - - | 0 | 12 | 0
To Gages & Squars - - - | 0 | 1 | 0
| 36 | 10 | 9

Bucks County, Pennsylvania, Register of Wills, Doylestown, PA., Estate #1531

Soo frame Saw An Ades & Sundreys	1	5	0
To 2 Hane Saws	1	7	6
To 2 Hand Axes	0	10	0
To a Dog & Ruining Bench	0	6	0
To a Hitcher & Barral	1	1	0
To a Bed & Bedsteed	2	10	0
To a Do & Do	2	0	0
To a Small Chest	0	2	6
To a Bell & Small	0	3	0
To Earthen	2	0	0
To a Grine ... ple mill & Trough @ 15/ to Iron bolt	1	10	0
a 2/			
To Boards & Scantling	2	3	
To 450 ... Barrel	1	10	
To 300 ... Do	1	0	
To 300	0	16	
To 400	1	0	
To 380 ... Do	1	10	0
To Boords &	0	3	0
To 3 Slyds	8	3	0
To a Waggon	15	0	0
To Teuke Waggon	1	10	0
To a Stay	1	18	0
To Long Ladders	0	6	0
To a Cask a H... Buthal & a Sive	0	5	6
To a Windm	2	10	0
To a Straw	0	15	0
To a Saw	0	15	0
To 6 15 ... ed a 6 per Bu	1	19	0
To 4 B	0	13	0
To a C... Ci... y	0	7	
To a Cow & 2 Brine B... s & a pear of Hoples	5	3	
To 2 piess of Coylers ... Hems & Treases 6/ a Coller			
@ 18/ 2 Line Bridle	3	6	0
To a yea	15	0	0
To a Roan	25	0	0
To a Black ma & Colt	28	0	0
To a Brown Mare & Colt	34	0	0
To 9 yews & 9 Lambs	18	0	0
To 4 Sheep @ 25/ Each	5	0	0
To 4 Gees @ 6/ Each	0	12	0
To about 2 of Acre Flax in the ground	0	18	0
To Whate in the ground in the Orchard 2 a 5 a 0 per acre	15 & 15	0	
	187	15	6

Bucks County, Pennsylvania, Register of Wills, Doylestown, PA., Estate #1531

	£	s	d
To a Peice of Hemp in the ground	0	18	0
To About 4 Acres of Indian Corn @ 15/ the Acre	3	0	0
To a Cow	6	0	0
To a Wiffer	4	0	0
To a Bull	6	0	0
To a Cow	6	10	0
To a Cow	6	10	0
To a Haffer	4	0	0
To a Do	4	0	0
To a Do	4	0	0
To a Do	2	0	0
To a Cows	6	0	0
To a Do	8	0	0
To a Do	9	0	0
To a Do	7	0	0
To a Do	8	0	0
To a Do	7	0	0
To a Peice of Grass in the Oat[illegible]	1	0	0
To Flax in the ground & the Beech[illegible]	1	4	0
To Oates in the ground	0	15	0
To a Lot of Grass No 1	0	10	0
To a Lot of Do No 2	1	0	0
To a Lot of Do No 3	1	10	0
To a Lot of Do No 4	1	5	0
To a Lot of Do No 5	0	15	0
To a Lot of Do No 6	1	5	0
To a Lot of Do No 7	1	10	0
To a Lot of Do No 8	1	10	0
To about 5 Acres of Ray @ 25/ Per acre	6	5	0
To a Calfe	1	0	0
To 11 Popler Loges at the Sawmill	2	10	0
To 7 Oake saw Logs	1	0	0
To 300 Foot Popler Boards	1	0	0
To 200 Foot of Scantlin	0	10	0
To 3 pear of Slide [illegible]	0	6	0
To Garding Posts	0	5	0
To Scantling	0	7	0
To 700 Foot of Lathes	0	14	0
To 150 Foot of Popler Boros	0	9	0
To a ½ Bushal & a Bucket	0	3	3
To 34 Bushal of Flaxseed @ 6/ per Bushal	10	4	0
To 4 Hhds @ 4/ Each	0	16	0
To a Grindstone & a Tube	0	4	0
To 200 Foot Walnut Boards	0	15	0
To 90 Foot Popler Do	0	6	0
To 2 Sives	0	6	0
To a waggon Screw	1	0	0
	132	2	3

Bucks County, Pennsylvania, Register of Wills, Doylestown, PA., Estate #1531

Bucks County, Pennsylvania, Register of Wills, Doylestown, PA., Estate #1531

Since Henry died young leaving orphans, the family is well documented. Petition of September 14, 1778, presented by John Nicholas, administrator of Henry's estate and Catherine Amey, widow of Henry Amey deceased, requested the court to appoint guardians for minor children of the deceased, named as: Julianna, Catherine, Philip, Magdalene and George. The court appointed John Mill guardian of the minor children.

Petition of September 14, 1778, presented by Henry Amey and Elisabeth Amey, "children of said deceased, now of proper age," asked to choose a guardian for themselves. They chose John Mill who was then appointed their guardian.[69]

John Keller, Samuel Smith and Andrew Keckline were appointed in September 1778 to audit and examine the accounts of the administrators of the estate of Henry Amey late of Haycock twp., dec'd, by Catherine Amey and John Nicolas, administrators. Inventory contained £492: 5sh: 10p and further credited with £253: 6sh: 10p goods sold for above appraised value for a total estate value of £750: 12sh: and 8p and signed by John Keller, Samuel Smith and Andrew Keckline dated 8 March 1779.[70]

The land is now under present day Lake Nockamixon in Bucks County. Anna Catharina (Nicolas) Emig remarried at Keller's Church, Bedminster in 1779 to Frederich Bremauser\Premaour, son of Gottfried and Anna Catherine Breamauser. Her will was probated 10 September 1832 at Doylestown, Bucks county seat leaving three children Catherine, Gertrude and John.

The Keller's are neighbors and later relatives. John Keller is a member of the assembly and later a Colonel in the militia. Additional research into the Keller family may help with tracking the Amick family back into Europe. From Keller's History:

> Henry of Heinrich Keller arrived in Philadelphia on the good ship "Glasgow" September 9th, 1738. From the records of Keller's Church, we have the following: "Heinrich Keller was born January 9th, 1708 and died October 18, 1782, his father's name was Wilhelm Keller and his Mother's name was Gertraut, in Weierbach, out of Naumburch, Braden and came to America September 9th, 1738. On the 20th of October, 1728, he married Juliana, born in 1711: her Father's name was Peter Kleindinst and Mother's name Anna Maria, also out of Weierbach, Naumburch. Her Father held an Office there." Their eldest child Peter died within a week of their landing and seven others were born to them in Pennsylvania. After Henry (Heinrich)'s arrival, the first record of him as a landholder was in 1750, when he purchased of Thomas and Richard Penn 150 acres in Bedminster township, on the northwest side of the Ridge road. This tract he conveyed to

Michael Yost in 1752. His residence at that date as shown by the deed was Bedminster. In the year 1734, a tract of 300 acres on the north side of the Tohickon, in Haycock township, was sold to Henry (Heinrich) Keller on May 10, 1757.

On November 05, 1754, Henry (Heinrich) Keller obtained a warrant for the survey of 21 acres and 136 perches at the northwest corner of the above tract and the draft of survey, on file at Harrisburg, shows that the Davis tract was then in the tenure of Henry (Heinrich) Keller. It is therefore probable that Henry (Heinrich) Keller took possession of the tract soon after his sale of his Bedminster land in 1752, under an agreement to purchase that was not completed until the date of the over the Tohickon into Bedminster township at two or three points, caused by curves of the creek. Of this tract of 300 acres purchased of Davis, Henry (Heinrich) Keller and Juliana, his wife, 1772, conveyed about 225 acres in three practically equal tracts to their sons Henry, Peter and Christopher. His son John had purchased a large tract adjoining his father in 1772 of David Graham. Henry (Heinrich) Keller was a man of prominence in his community. He was the first constable of Haycock township, and was frequently named by the Court or selected by the parties to assist in the settlement of estates.

And continues…

Henry (Heinrich) was the chief founders of Kellers' Church in 1746. He purchased a large tract of land extending across the Tohickon Creek into Haycock Township and lived there until his death. He was one of the trustees who, on July 28, 1751, secured title to the twenty-acre tract upon which the first church, known as "Kellers," was erected; and he was one of the elders and trustees of that church until he died.

Estate of
Henry Amey
629
+ for Auditors

The Petition of Catharine Amey + John Nicolas Execut[rs] of the Estate of Henry Amey of Haycock Township dec[d] Humbly sheweth that your petitioners have fully administered the Estate of the said dec[d] to the best of their knowledge and now pray the Court will appoint suitable persons to examine the accounts of their administration in order that if they be just & true, they may receive your worships judgment & confirmation or such duties as the law in that case can direct &c.   Catharine Amey — John Nicolas

The Court taking into consideration the Petition of Catharine Amey and John Nicolas, do appoint John Keller, Samuel Smith [...] the [...] the accounts of their administration [...] auditors so appointed do make a report of their proceedings [...] the next Orphans Court to be held at [...] the [...] day [...]

Pet for Guardians

The Petition of John Nicolas of Haycock Township [...] ty of Bucks administrator [...] the Estate of Henry Amey of the s[d] Township dec[d] Humbly sheweth that your Petitioner with Catharine Amey widow of the said dec[d] having duly administered on the Estate of the said dec[d] beg[s] the Honorable Court will be pleased to appoint Guardians for the five following children of the said dec[d] — Juliana, Catharine, Philip, Magdalene, George and your petitioners as in duty bound shall ever pray &c.   John Nicolas
Catharine Amey

The Court taking into consideration the Petition of John Nicolas & Catharine Amey, administrators to the Estate of Henry Amey do appoint John Hull for the Guardian of the said Children

Petition of [...] Henry [...] for Guardian

The Petition of Elizabeth Amey & Henry Amey the children of Henry Amey of the Township of Haycock dec[d] Humbly sheweth that your Petitioners are now of proper age to chuse a Guardian for themselves, that they pray the Honorable Court to appoint John [...] who is their choice to represent them in the management of the Estate of their dec[d] Father & your Petitioners as in duty bound shall ever pray.   Elizabeth Amey — Henry Amey.

[...] taking into consideration the Petition of Elizabeth Amey & Henry [...]

Bucks County, Penn. Orphans' Court Records, File #629, Book B

Bucks County, Penn. Orphans' Court Records, File #629, Book B

Bucks County, Penn. Orphans' Court Records, File #629, Book B

Graveyard of Keller's Church, location of Henry Emig's grave is not known.
This is the old area behind the church.

I lost my keys out of my pocket when I took my camera out. It was to the left of the picture behind the garden. Could this be Henry telling me where his grave was?
Graveyard of Keller's Church, location of Henry Emig's grave is not known. This is the old area behind the church looking at the new addition and the grave fronts.
Grave of Catherine Nicholas center with many Keller graves of the period behind.

Philip Emich and Nicholas Emmick

```
┌─────────────────────────────────────────────────────────────┐
│                  Family Tree Second Generation                │
│                                                               │
│  Johan Philip EMIG (1745 -   )                                │
│  +Barbara HAHN                                                │
│          Nicholas EMMICK (1766 – 1836)                        │
│          Maria Magdalena EMIG (1768 -   )                     │
│          Henry EMIG (1770 -   )                               │
│          Catharine EMIG (1772 -   )                           │
│                                                               │
└─────────────────────────────────────────────────────────────┘
```

Johan Philip Emig was born between 1741 and 1745. He arrived in the new world with his parents and brother on September 13, 1749.

In 1766 Philip and Barbara Hahn Emig had a son, John Nicholas born September 15, 1766 and baptized October 12, 1766 at the Tohickon Reformed Church at Bedminster with witnesses Michael Coppelbeger and wife.[71] Philip Emig, the son of Johan Georg Emig dropped from Bucks County records after 1773, the year after his father died.[72]

There is much confusion in the records as at least two lines of Emig/Emich families live near Philadelphia. The association to the Bucks County line of the family instead of the York County line of Amicks is strongly influenced by Nicholas Emmick and Henry Amick (Bucks County line) moving together as cousins to Pendleton County before Nicholas moved to Kentucky. Also note there is no "Henry" listed in the York line and Nicholas later fights in the Revolutionary War in the same company as Henry Emig assumed to be his brother.[73]   To add to the confusion, the York line is referenced in Berks County documents as well.[74]

Berks County is also the home of Daniel Boone before he led settlers over to Kentucky; he was in the First Pennsylvania Battalion from Berks County in the revolutionary war. This was a line Battalion and not a militia company as Nicholas and his brother Henry were in. Nicholas would migrate out to Kentucky at about the same time as Boone.

The Family in the Revolutionary War

Henry Amick is documented as a patriot in the Revolutionary War on muster rolls dated 1781. His father, Henry Emig, died in early June of 1777 before the battle of Brandywine. The Bucks County Militia had been called out in defense but no records of Colonel Keller's muster rolls are available before 1781. Henry Emig's cause of death is not recorded but he likely served in the militia as all able bodied men where called out. He may have died of a communicable disease as many soldiers contacted diseases while serving. The family is generally documented in companies of Colonel John Keller with many family members serving. Nicholas Emmick and his brother Henry are documented in the Berks County Militia.

The Revolutionary War

Henry Emig was born in 1762 making him 18 in 1780. Being of age 18 in 1780, he would have been eligible for the militia. He is listed on the muster roll in 1781. His father Heinrich Emig would have served as well, since all able bodied men in Bucks County were required to serve.[75] No documents listing Heinrich have survived. Heinrich Emig died in July of 1777 at age 40. This is before the Battle of Brandywine and the retreat of General Washington across the Delaware to Valley Forge. The Bucks County Militia would have been called out to protect Philadelphia while Washington moved to attack the British. The major battles that the Bucks County militia fought were in 1776 and 1777. The young Henry Emig would not likely have fought in these battles being just 15, but his father, cousins and Colonel John Keller, his future uncle, may have. Henry married John Keller's niece, Barbara Niemand, after the war in 1784. Colonel Keller was the commander of the Third Battalion of the Bucks County Militia and is listed in a letter from George Washington.

Bucks County in the Revolutionary War

The French and Indian War had cost the British Crown dearly in treasure. With the English people already heavily burdened with taxes, the British Parliament instituted taxes on the colonies. After all it was the colonies that were the major beneficiaries of the war. However, the severity and randomness of the taxes riled the colonists. It was the lack of representation in how the taxes would be applied that was the biggest issue. "Taxation without representation" became a rallying cry that united the various colonies. The various governments of the colonies met to petition the king but were rebuked. The country moved toward war with the Boston Tea Party in 1773. By September 5, 1774, the First Continental Congress assembled in Philadelphia as the shot heard round the world was fired at Lexington. The war began in 1775 and the Second Continental Congress named George Washington commander-in-chief. The first major battle of the War took place at Bunker Hill on June 17, 1775. On July 4, 1776 the Congress adopted Thomas Jefferson's Declaration of Independence.

On Christmas night 1776, George Washington slipped across the Delaware with some 2,400 men. Near dawn at Trenton, the Americans surprised a garrison of 1,500 Hessians.

During the War the Bucks County militia was commanded by Brigadier General James Potter until 1778.[76] At that time General Potter went on leave and John Lacey Jr. was promoted to Brigadier General. John Lacey Jr. was a miller from Bucks County[77] and had joined the Bucks County Militia as a captain in 1775.[78,79] He served as a captain in the 4th Pennsylvania Continental Regiment with General "Mad" Anthony Wayne, at Fort Ticonderoga. General Wayne had him arrested on charges but Captain Lacey was exonerated by a court-martial. [80]   He resigned his Continental commission and returned to Pennsylvania.[81]   In May 1777, he was given a commission as lieutenant colonel in the militia[82] and in January of 1778 he was promoted to brigadier general, and given the command of Brigadier General James Potter. At age twenty-five, Lacey was the youngest general in the American forces.[83]

From Keller's History[84] Colonel John Keller was a member of the Pennsylvania Provincial Assembly for the colony representing Bucks County.

State House of the Province of Pennsylvania
"Independence Hall," Philadelphia

Constructed between 1732 and 1756 as the State House of the Province of Pennsylvania it is
nicknamed "Independence Hall"
Taken 2007

Interior of Independence Hall
Horace E. Scudder, *A History of the United States of America*
(New York: Sheldon and Company, 1897)

Interior of State House of the Province of Pennsylvania, Philadelphia. This is where John Keller
and the Bucks County representatives sat in session, although the furniture is arranged as it was for
the second meeting of the Continental Congress it would have been similarly configured for the
State Convention of 1776. Taken 2007

Interior of State House of the Province of Pennsylvania, Philadelphia
This is where John Keller and the Bucks County representatives sat in session
Picture of author, David Emmick, taken 2007

In 1775 Joseph Kirkbridge was listed as the Colonel of the First Battalion of Bucks County Militia and Doctor John Beatty as Colonel of the Second Battalion. On July 10, 1776, the Committee of Safety called up a militia force of four-hundred troops to be led by Colonel Joseph Hart for the "Flying Camp" under the command of Brigadier General Hugh Mercer of Virginia. The Flying Camp never realized its potential and was disbanded by November. Joseph Hart is also a member of the Supreme Council and his signature is on many later documents commanding the forces. [85]

The commanders in 1776 were:

First Battalion	Col. Joseph Kirkbridge	
Second Battalion	Col. Arthur Erwin	
Third Battalion	Col. John Keller	
	with	Lt. Col. Joseph Sevets
	and	Col. Andrew Kechlien
Flying Camp	Col. Joseph Hart	

John Keller was a representative for Bucks County to the Pennsylvania State Convention on July 15. With John Keller representing Bucks County were Joseph Hart, John Wilkinson, Samuel Smith, William Vanhorn, John Grier, Abraham Van Middleswarts and Joseph Kirkbride. Dr. Benjamin Franklin was elected the convention president.[86]

PROVINCIAL COMMISSIONS.   757

For the county of Westmoreland.

James Barr,	John Carmichael,
Edward Cook,	James Perry,
James Smith,	John M'Clellan,
John Moore,	Christopher Lavingair.

TUESDAY, July 16, 1776.

Dr. Benjamin Franklin was unanimously chosen President.
Col. George Ross was unanimously chosen Vice-President.
John Morris, Esq. was chosen Secretary.

Mr. Jacob Garrigues was chosen assistant clerk to the Secretary.

Mr. Morris not being in the city at present, Col. Matlack is requested to perform the duty of Secretary till Mr. Morris may return.

The qualification and profession of faith recommended by the conference of committees, held at Philadelphia on the 25th of June last, were read, taken and subscribed by all the members now present, viz:

Benjamin Franklin,	Robert Smith,
Timothy Matlack,	Samuel Cunningham,
Frederick Kuhl,	John Mackey,
Owen Biddle,	George Ross,
James Cannon,	Bartram Galbreath,
George Clymer,	Joseph Sherrer,
George Schlosser,	John Hubley,
David Rittenhouse,	Henry Slaymaker,
Frederick Antis,	Alexander Lowrey,
Henry Hill,	John Hay,
Robert Loller,	James Edgar,
Joseph Blewer,	Francis Crazart,
John Bull,	James Smith,
Edward Bartholomew,	Robert M'Pherson,
Joseph Hart,	Joseph Donaldson,
John Wilkinson,	John Harris,
Samuel Smith,	Jonathan Hoge,
John Keller,	William Clarke,
William Vanhorn,	William Duffield,
John Grier,	James Brown,
Joseph Kirkbride,	James M'Clean,
John Hart,	Jacob Morgan,
Thomas Strawbridge,	Gabriel Hiester,

On December 19, 1776, General George Washington sent orders to Colonel Joseph Kirkbridge First Battalion; Colonel Arthur Erwin, Second Battalion; Lt. Colonel Joseph Sevets for Col. John Keller Third Battalion; Colonel Andrew Kechlien and Colonel Joseph Hart of the Flying Camp (just dispended) to march to Philadelphia.[87]   Of note: John Keller and Andrew Keckline with Samuel Smith were the appointed auditors of Henry Amey (Emig)'s estate; Henry's father in September 1778. Washington's orders were:

> To Col. KIRKBRIDE
> of Bucks County Pennsylvania Militia
>
> Sir,
> The Honorable Council of Safety of the State of Pennsylvania having, by a Resolve passed the 17th. day of this inst December, Authorized me to call forth the Militia of the County of Bucks, to the Assistance of the Continental Army under my Command, I hereby require you, immediately to issue Orders to the Captains of your Regiment, to summon the Officers and Privates of their Companies to meet on the 28th. day of this instant, at the usual place for their joining in Battalion, with their Arms and Accoutrements in good Order, and when so met, march immediately to the City of Philadelphia and there put yourself under the Command of Major Gen. PUTNAM·. And you are further required to make me an exact return of the names and places of abode of such Officers and privates, as refuse to appear with their Arms and Accoutrements, at the time and place appointed, that they may be dealt with as the resolve, above referred [sic] to, directs.
> Given under my Hand at Head Quarters this 19th day of December· 1776.
>   G. WASHINGTON

Note: the same letter was also addressed to Colonels Joseph HART, Andrew KECHLEIN, Arthur ERWIN (EWING), and Joseph SABITTS [sic – SEVETS; Lt. Col. under Col. Keller], of the Pennsylvania Militia.

Christmas night 1776, George Washington slipped across the Delaware with some 2,400 men to attack the Hessian troops at Trenton.

General Washington ordered Bucks County militia to march to Morristown, New Jersey. Colonel Smith was from Cumberland.[88]

> To Col. KIRKBRIDE
> Bucks County Pennsylvania
> Head Quarters Morris Town,   14th Jan 1777
> Sir,
> Colo. SMITH being ordered to march up to this place with the Jersey Militia and form a Brigade under General DICKINSON, you are hereby directed to collect as many of the Militia of your County as will mount the necessary guards at the Ferries, where Colo. SMITH was posted. You will take particular Care to keep all the Boats, except such as are necessary for the Ferry, drawn up and well guarded, under the care of a good Officer.
>   I am Sir Yours &
>   G. WASHINGTON

The election of officers in spring of 1777 placed Hugh Tomb as Colonel of the First Battalion with Lieutenant Colonel James McMasters and Major as John Folwell. John Folwell had served as a captain in Joseph Hart's flying camp. The Second Battalion had Arthur Erwine elected as Colonel, Robert Robinson as Lieutenant Colonel and William Hart as Major.[89]

John Keller was listed as elected to Colonel of the Third Battalion of Bucks County Militia on May 6, 1777, with Lieutenant Colonel Joseph Sevets, Major Thomas Long and Captains: First Company – Phillip Steeves, 2nd – Jacob Shoop, 3rd – David Mellenger, 4th – Jacob Buck, 5th – George Wilkert, 6th Josiah Bryan, 7th – George Heilein and 8th – George Harlocker.[90]

The Forth Battalion was commanded by William Roberts who had served as a captain with Joseph Hart's Flying Camp and Fifth Battalion commanded by Joseph McIlvaine who had been a major under Joseph Kirkbridge, First Battalion.

The unit strength in 1777 was listed as

First Battalion	Hugh Tomb	490
Second Battalion	Arthur Erwin	520
Third Battalion	John Keller	551
Forth Battalion	William Roberts	600
Firth Battalion	Joseph McIlwain	630

For a total strength of 2,791
By order of Joseph Kirkbride, Lieut. B.C.
And signed Samuel Smith, S.L.B.[91]

Note the misspelling of names Erwine and McIlvaine.

Andrew Keckline (one of Henry Emig's auditors of his will) brother Peter raised a company of riflemen in Bucks County and was in command at the battle of Long Island 27th August, 1776 as part of Colonel Joseph Hart's "Flying Camp" where he was taken prisoner.[92] The Pennsylvania "Flying Camp" was attached to "Lord Stirling's" force. Lord Sterling wrote to Washington that the English General Grant was killed by some of Peter Keichline's riflemen and the company suffered heavy losses.[93] Christopher Keller was an ensign in the Fourth Battalion where he participated in the Battle of Long Island.[94]

George Emig's Enlistment

George Emig from Haycock Township, Bucks County was listed on a report of fines for 1777-1778.[95]

Pennsylvania State Archives; ARIAS; the Archives Records Information Access System located at: http://www.digitalarchives.state.pa.us/index.asp; Revolutionary War Military Abstract Card File, Emich, George

The Battle of Brandywine

In 1777 British General Howe moved to take Philadelphia.

Sketch from the *Pictorial Field Book of the Revolution* by Benson J. Lossing; 1850

In late July 1777 General Howe leading 17,000 British soldiers arrived at the head of Elk River in Maryland. Howe marched towards Philadelphia. General Washington moved his troops of the Continental Army between General Howe and the city. One of the fiercest battles of the war, the Battle of Brandywine, occurred on September 11, 1777, as Washington defended the British advance on Philadelphia. Washington was forced to withdraw. American casualties were estimated at about 1,200 and the British at about 1,900.

By midday of July 12 the American forces had reached the Schuylkill River and crossed the bridge over the Middle Ferry a couple miles north of Philadelphia. This protected the supply cities of Reading and Valley Forge as well as the munitions works at Coventry and Warwick. The British split their forces and Cornwallis headed for White Horse Tavern while Howe moved up the Wilmington Pike toward Boot Tavern. Cornwallis attacked to begin the Battle of the Clouds at about 1 pm. As rain poured down in torrents, Washington retreated across the Schuylkill still keeping his army between the British and the supply cities and he sent the bulk of the American forces to Reading Furnace. Howe occupied Philadelphia on the nineteenth.

Washington directing his troops at the Battle of Brandywine, Library of Congress

In late summer of 1777, Bucks County militia were recorded stationed at Bristol under the command of Colonel Hugh Tomb, at Billingsport under Lieutenant Colonel James McMasters who had been a major of the First Battalion of Bucks County militia in 1776 served under Colonel Beatty and Lieutenant Colonel John Folwell who had been captain of the 5th company in the same First Battalion in 1776.[96]

192   ASSOCIATED BATTALIONS

STATION OF BUCKS COUNTY COMPANIES.

At Bristol, July 31, 1777, under Command of Col. Hugh Tomb:

Captain William McConkey,	50
Captain John Thompson,	47
Captain William Pugh,	56
Captain Jacob Shrup,	30
Captain Nicholas Patterson,	36
Total Rank and File,	219

At Billingsport, August 13, 1777, under Command of Lieutenant Colonel James McMasters:

Captain Robert Ramsey,	31
Captain John Thomas,	43
Captain John Wood,	49
Captain David Mellenger,	109
Total Rank and File,	232

At Billingsport, August 26, 1777, under Command of Major John Folwell:

Captain Abraham DuBois,	31
Lieutenant John Keith,	25
Captain Robert Thorn,	
Captain John Harrison,	27
Captain Jacob Bourch,	30
Total Rank and File,	192

At Billingsport, November 12, 1777:

Captain Zephaniah Lott,	15
Captain Henry Lott,	19
Captain Abraham Britton,	8
Captain Elijah ——,	10
Total Rank and File,	52

On September 11, 1777, the Supreme Executive Council in Philadelphia ordered the mobilization of all able bodied men in Bucks County to support General Washington.

From excerpts of the Minutes of the Supreme Executive Council of Pennsylvania September 11, 1777 [see Supplement for complete listing]:[97]

> ...As the Enemy is near at hand & this minute engaging our Army under the Command of his Excell'y Gen'l WASHINGTON,
> Ordered, That every able bodied man in the County of Bucks, turn out with his Arms, accoutrements & blankets, & that those who cannot furnish themselves with Arms to take with them Axes, spades, & every other kind of entrenching Tools, & that Colonel ROBERTS, ERWIN & KILLER [sic], rendezvous at Sweed's Ford, and that Colo's TOOMB & McELWAINE rendezvous at this City.
> ...Ordered, That the Officers commanding the Militia of the County of Bucks, now at the Barracks, do immediately send a guard of Four Men to Robin Hood Ford, over the Schuylkill, four Men to upper Ferry, Four Men to the Bridge, & four Men to Gray's Ferry, to take care of the Artillery placed at those places.

The British moved to Valley Forge forcing Washington to protect Reading which opened Philadelphia to British attack. The citizens of Philadelphia removed the Liberty Bell to Allentown for safekeeping. On September 26, Howe entered Philadelphia with 3,000 men while Cornwallis held back in Germantown with 9,000 to establish a defensible position.

From the book American Military History:[98]

> When Howe finally began to stir in June 1777, Washington posted his army at Middlebrook, New Jersey, in a position either to bar Howe's overland route to Philadelphia or to move rapidly up the Hudson to oppose an advance northward. Washington confidently expected Howe to move northward to form a junction with Burgoyne, but decided he must stay in front of the main British Army wherever it went. Following the principle of economy of force, he disposed a small part of his army under General Putnam in fortifications guarding the approaches up the Hudson, and at a critical moment detached a small force to aid Schuyler against Burgoyne. The bulk of his army he kept in front of Howe in an effort to defend

Philadelphia. Forts were built along the Delaware River and other steps taken to block the approach to the Continental capital by sea.

In the effort to defend Philadelphia Washington again failed, but hardly so ignominiously as he had the year before in New York. After maneuvering in New Jersey for upward of two months, Howe in August put most of his army on board ship and sailed down the coast and up the Chesapeake Bay to Head of Elk (a small town at the head of the Elk River) in Maryland, putting himself even further away from Burgoyne. Though surprised by Howe's movement, Washington rapidly shifted his own force south and took up a position at Chad's Ford on Brandywine Creek, blocking the approach to Philadelphia. There on September 11, 1777, Howe executed a flanking movement not dissimilar to that employed on Long Island and again defeated Washington. The American commander had disposed his army in two main parts, one directly opposite Chad's Ford under his personal command and the other under General Sullivan guarding the right flank upstream. While Lt. Gen. Wilhelm van Knyphausen's Hessian troops demonstrated opposite the ford, a larger force under Lord Cornwallis marched upstream, crossed the Brandywine, and moved to take Sullivan from the rear. Washington lacked good cavalry reconnaissance, and did not get positive information on Cornwallis' movement until the eleventh hour. Sullivan was in the process of changing front when the British struck and his men retreated in confusion. Washington was able to salvage the situation by dispatching General Greene with two brigades to fight a valiant rear-guard action, but the move weakened his front opposite Kynphausen and his forces also had to fall back. Nevertheless, the trap was averted and the Continental Army retired in good order to Chester.

The Battle of Germantown

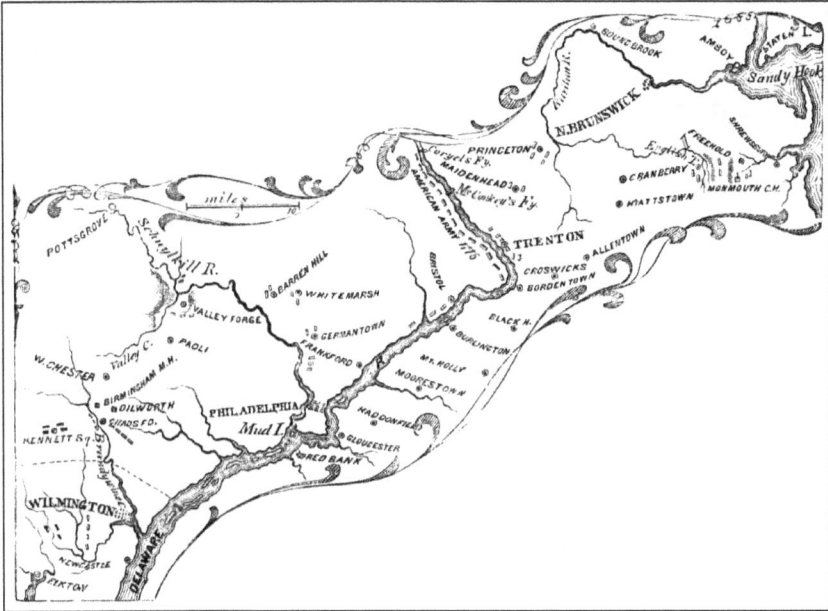

Sketch from the *Pictorial Field Book of the Revolution* by Benson J. Lossing; 1850

Washington attacked the British at Germantown on October 2, 1877 in a surprise move. The morning went well but fierce fighting at the Cliveden mansion slowed the American advance under Henry Knox. Washington was forced to retreat with the British in pursuit. The Americans lost 152, the British 537.

Battle of Germantown, Chew's house. Engraving by Rawdon, Wright, and Harch
from drawing by Koeltner. 148-GW-94; US National Archives

Cliveden, Judge Chew's House
Taken 2007

Battle of Germantown, Attack on Judge Chew's House, 1879
by Robert Hinshelwood Copy after Chappel; Smithsonian American Art Museum, 1978.152.91

From the book American Military History:[99]

Howe followed with a series of maneuvers comparable to those he had executed in New York, and was able to enter Philadelphia with a minimum of fighting on September 26. A combined attack of British Army and Navy forces shortly afterward reduced the forts on the Delaware and opened the river as a British supply line.

On entering Philadelphia, Howe dispersed his forces, stationing 9,000 men at Germantown north of the city, 3,000 in New Jersey, and the rest in Philadelphia. As Howe had repeated his performance in New York, Washington sought to repeat Trenton by a surprise attack on Germantown. The plan was much like that used at Trenton but involved far more complicated movements by much larger bodies of troops. Four columns—two of Continentals under Sullivan and Greene and two of militia—moving at night over different roads were to converge on Germantown simultaneously at dawn on October 4. The plan violated the principle of simplicity, for such a maneuver was difficult even for well-trained professionals to execute. The two columns of Continentals arrived at different times and fired on each other in an early morning fog. The two militia columns never arrived at all. British fire from a stone house, the Chew Mansion, held up the advance while American generals argued whether they could leave a fortress in their rear. The British, though surprised, had better discipline and cohesion and were able to re-form and send fresh troops into the fray. The Americans retreated about 8:00 a.m., leaving Howe's troops in command of the field.

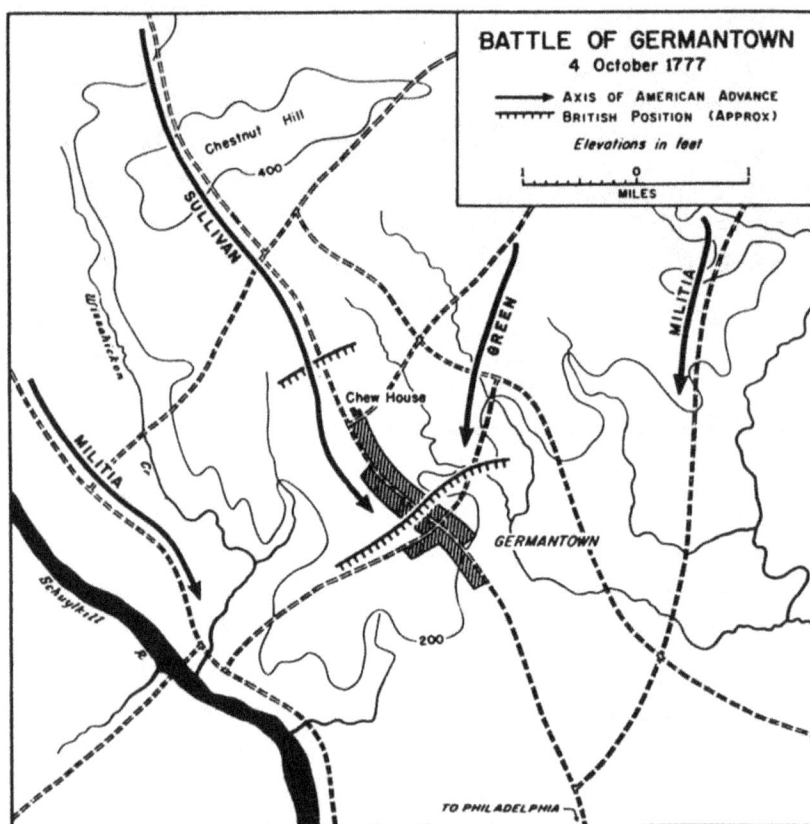

Battle of Germantown Map from *American Military History*, Page 75

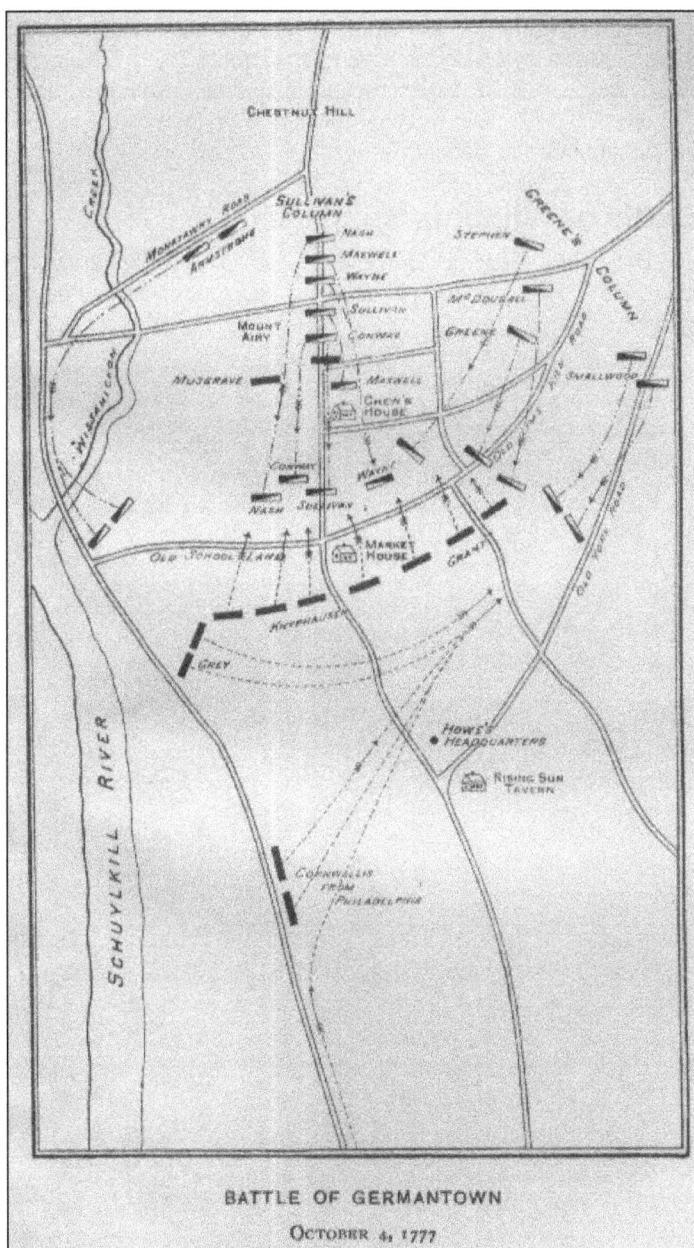

Map of the Battle of Germantown
The American Revolution by John Fiske, Vol. I;
Boston and New York, Houghton, Mifflin and Company, The Riverside Press, Cambridge.1891

The British controlled Philadelphia but the Americans controlled the surrounding area and the Delaware River. On October 19, 1877 General Howe withdrew several thousand British troops from Germantown into Philadelphia.

On October 23, 1777, the Supreme Executive Council called up the Bucks County Sixth and Seventh Battalions.[100]

The Battle of Whitemarsh

Early in December General Howe launched a surprise attack on the Continental Army encamped at Whitemarsh. The Americans had been alerted and were well prepared.

Washington at the George Emlen House, Whitemarsh, Pennsylvania
by Henry Ogden Alexander Collection of the New-York Historical Society

After several days of skirmishing the armies withdrew to winter camps: the British to Philadelphia and the Americans to Valley Forge on the Schuylkill River.

View from the British positions at the Battle of White Marsh.
Ink on paper, by cartographer Johann Martin Will.

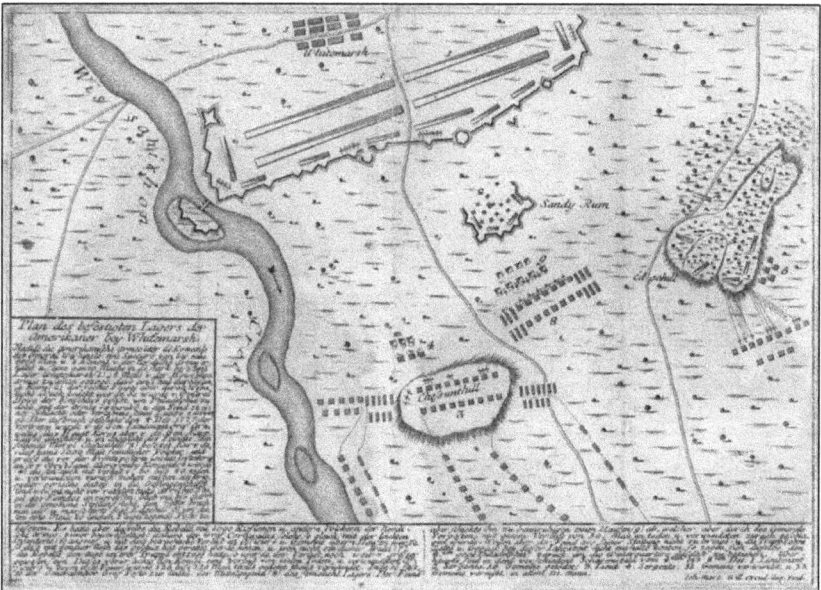

Map of the **Battle of White Marsh,**
Plan des befestigten Lagers der Amerikaner beÿ Whitemarsh by Johann Martin Will.
Map, Augsburg, Germany: 1777. Library of Congress, Geography and Map Division

From the book American Military History:[101]

> After Germantown Howe once again concentrated his army
> and moved to confront Washington at Whitemarsh, but finally
> withdrew to winter quarters in Philadelphia without giving
> battle. Washington chose the site for his own winter quarters
> at a place called Valley Forge, twenty miles northwest of the
> city. Howe had gained his objective but it proved of no lasting
> value to him. Congress fled west to York, Pennsylvania. No
> swarms of loyalists rallied to the British standards. And Howe
> had left Burgoyne to lose a whole British army in the north.
> It was the rising militia, rather than Washington, who were to
> provide the Northern Army with its main reinforcements.

Current map of Whitemarsh in lower left, just outside of Philadelphia
Bedminster (Richland Center) is about 20 miles to the north

Richland Center (Bedminster) and Plumsteadville are near the top of the
map of current Whitemarsh.   Whitemarsh is on the bottom center near
Interstate Highway 76; note Bucks County, Berks County and Philadelphia.
Whitemarsh is about 20 miles from the Emig Homestead.

The Forth Battalion was commanded by Lieutenant Colonel John Lacey on December 3, 1777. He was promoted to Brigadier General on January 9, 1778.[102]

Valley Forge

General Washington at Valley Forge

Washington retired to winter quarters at Valley Forge in the winter of 1777-1778.

From the book American Military History:[103]

Valley Forge

The name of Valley Forge has come to stand, and rightly so, as a patriotic symbol of suffering, courage, and perseverance. The hard core of 6,000 Continentals who stayed with Washington during that bitter winter of 1777-78 indeed suffered much. Some men had no shoes, no pants, no blankets. Weeks passed when there was no meat and men were reduced to boiling their shoes and eating them. The wintry winds penetrated the tattered tents that were at first the only shelter.

The symbolism of Valley Forge should not be allowed to obscure the fact that the suffering was largely unnecessary. While the soldiers shivered and went hungry, food rotted and clothing lay unused in depots throughout the country. True, access to Valley Forge was difficult, but little determined effort was made to get supplies into the area. The supply and transport system broke down. In mid-1777, both the Quartermaster and Commissary Generals resigned along with numerous subordinate officials in both departments, mostly merchants who found private trade more lucrative. Congress, in refuge at York, Pennsylvania, and split into factions, found it difficult to find replacements. If there was not, as most historians now believe, an organized cabal seeking to replace Washington with Gates, there were many, both in and out of the Army, who were dissatisfied with the Commander in Chief, and much intrigue went on. Gates was made president of the new Board of War set up in 1777, and at least two of its members were enemies of Washington. In the administrative chaos at the height of the Valley Forge crisis, there was no functioning Quartermaster General at all.

Washington weathered the storm and the Continental Army was to emerge from Valley Forge a more effective force than before. With his advice, Congress instituted reforms in the Quartermaster and Commissary Departments that temporarily restored the effectiveness of both agencies. Washington's ablest subordinate, General Greene, reluctantly accepted the post of Quartermaster General. The Continental Army itself gained a new professional competence from the training given by the Prussian, Friedrich Wilhelm von Steuben.

Steuben appeared at Valley Forge in February 1778 arrayed in such martial splendor that one private thought he had seen Mars, the god of war, himself. He represented himself as a baron, a title he had acquired in the service of a small German state, and as a former lieutenant general on the staff of Frederick the Great though in reality he had been only a captain. The fraud was harmless, for Steuben had a broad knowledge of military affairs and his remarkable sense of the dramatic he combined with the common touch a true Prussian baron might well have lacked.

Washington had long sensed the need for uniform training and organization, and after a short trial he secured the appointment of Steuben as Inspector General in charge of a

Valley Forge, Library of Congress

training program. Steuben carried out the program during the late winter and early spring of 1778, teaching the Continental Army a simplified but effective version of the drill formations and movements of European armies, proper care of equipment, and the use of the bayonet, a weapon in which British superiority had previously been marked. He attempted to consolidate the understrength regiments and companies and organized light infantry companies as the elite force of the Army. He constantly sought to impress upon the officers their responsibility for taking care of the men. Steuben never lost sight of the difference between the American citizen soldier and the European professional. He early noted that American soldiers had to be told why they did things before they would do them well, and he applied this philosophy in his training program. His trenchant good humor and vigorous profanity, almost the only English he knew, delighted the Continental soldiers and made the rigorous drill more palatable. After Valley Forge, Continentals would fight on equal terms with British Regulars in the open field.

George Washington and a Committee of Congress at Valley Forge. Engraving, 1866, from
painting by W.H. Powell. 148-GW-184; US National Archives

Fighting together in the American Revolution, Washington and Lafayette at Valley Forge, Dunsmore, John Ward, artist. "Washington and Lafayette at Valley Forge." Reproduction of a 1907 painting. St. Paul, Brown & Bigelow, copyright 1907. Prints and Photographs Division, Library of Congress

The family has not been documented as state line troops but little documentation of the state line muster rolls survive.

Valley Forge location of Pennsylvania line troops commanded by General Wayne, taken 2007

Washington's headquarters at Valley Forge, taken 2007

The Prayer at Valley Forge

The Prayer at Valley Forge painted by H. Brueckner. c1866[104]
Prayer at Valley Forge. Engraving by John McRae from painting by Henry Brueckner.
148-GW-201.

From eyewitness testimony of Isaac Potts:[105]

> I was riding with Mr. Potts near to the Valley Forge where the army lay during the war of ye Revolution, when Mr. Potts said, 'Do you see that woods & that plain? There laid the army of Washington. It was a most distressing time of ye war, and all were for giving up the Ship but that great and good man. In that woods (pointing to a close in view) I heard a plaintive sound as of a man at prayer. I tied my horse to a sapling & went quietly into the woods. To my astonishment I saw the great George Washington on his knees alone, with his sword on one side and his cocked hat on the other. He was at Prayer to the God of the Armies, beseeching to interpose with his Divine aid, as it was ye Crisis & the cause of the country, of humanity & of the world. Such a prayer I never heard from the lips of man. I left him alone praying. I went home & told my wife. We never thought a man could be a soldier & a Christian, but if there is one in the world, it is Washington. We thought it was the cause of God & America could prevail.

The Battle of Crooked Billet Tavern

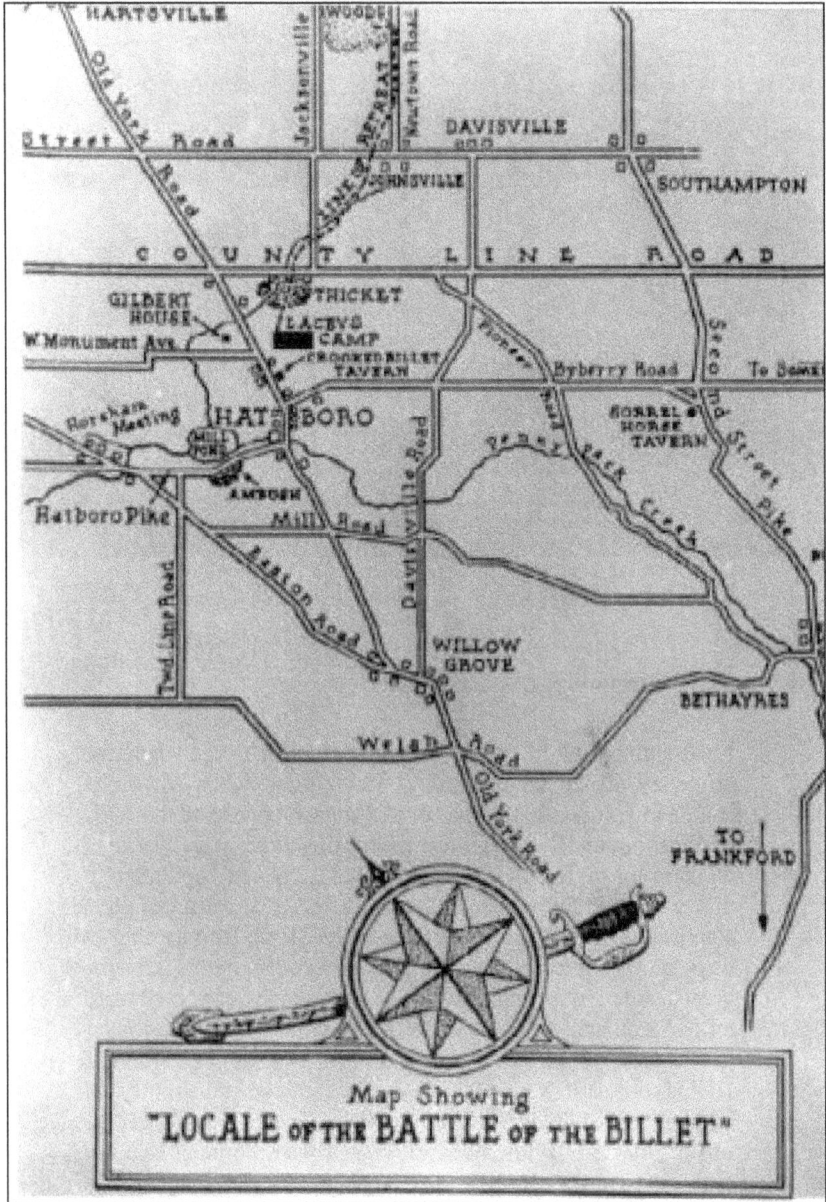

From the: *Royal Pennsylvania Gazette,* Philadelphia, May 5, 1778

Brigadier General John Lacey, Jr. was charged with patrolling the area north of Philadelphia in order to warn the troops at Valley Forge of attack from the British located in Philadelphia. On the morning of May 1, 1778, General Lacey's command was attacked near the Crooked Billet Tavern. He was able to withdraw his troops to a nearby wood and continued to withdraw further until the British broke off and withdrew back to Philadelphia leaving twenty-six killed and eight wounded.

Crooked Billet is about 20 miles south of Bedminster and about 10 miles south of Doylestown; just north of Philadelphia.

Road sign for Crooked Billet, taken 2007

From *The History of Bucks County, Pennsylvania:*[106]

> General Lacey frequently had his headquarters at Doylestown and this was his depot of stores. We find him here March 19, 1778, and copy the following from his order book: "Parole, Salem; countersign, Wilmington; officer of the day tomorrow, Major Mitchel; detail, three captains, three sergeants, four corporals and 48 privates. Officers of all grades are cautioned not to quarter out of camp." Lacey and his men

Road sign for Crooked Billet, taken 2007

did not want for the good things of life while soldiering in Bucks county. The receipts of the purchasing commissary cover payments for veal, beef, flour, mutton, whiskey, not a rifled article, turkeys and fowls. His troops, while encamped at the Crooked Billet, now Hatboro, were surprised by the British at daylight May 1, 1778, and it was only by boldness and good management that he was able to prevent the capture of his entire force. Spies, well acquainted with the situation, had given General Howe full information, who sent out strong detachments of cavalry and infantry. They took possession of all the roads, closing in upon Lacey, his camp was almost surrounded before their presence was known. Extricating his command he retreated across Warminster toward the Neshaminy. When it became evident that the enemy intended to evacuate Philadelphia, Washington requested the militia of Bucks county to hang upon his flanks in his march through New Jersey, and General Lacey (9) ordered the battalions of Colonels Keller, Roberts, Toms, and McIlvain to turn out for this service. [Colonel Joseph McIlvain died February 17, 1787, and was buried in St. James's yard, Bristol.]

Area to the side of the school at Crooked Billet, taken 2007

After the battle there were reports of British atrocities, including the British Rangers led by Major John G. Simcoe, burning captured militia soldiers alive.[107]

Testimony of British Atrocities at Crooked Billet, May 1, 1778

Deposition of Colonel Frederick WATTS & Saml. HENRY
14 May 1778
Bucks, ss.

> Personally appeared before me, one of the Justices of the Peace for the County of Bucks, Coll. Frederick Watts and Saml. Henry, and being qualified as the law directs, deposeth & sayeth, that on the first day of May Instant, a part of Genl Laceys Brigade was attacked by a number of the British Army, both Horse & Foot; the dispute was sharp, but their numbers being greatly superior obliged us to retreat. Upon our return the same day to the place of action, we found the bodies of the dead usid in a most inhuman & barbarous manner, the field in which some of the men fell there was

Buck Wheat Straw, which appeared to us they had taken &
set fire to, and threw the men into, whether quite dead or not
we cannot tell, but when found burnt to that degree that some
of them could not be known. We viewed the Corps of most
of the dead, & saw only two, as we remember, that had
escaped the most cruel Barbarity that had ever been
exercised by any civilised Nation; nay, Savage barbarity in
its utmost exertion of cruelty could but equal it.

Fr'k Watts,
Sam'l Henry. Sworn before me, this 14th day of May, 1778.
And'w Long.

Deposition of Wm. STAYNER
14 May 1778
Bucks, ss.

personally appeared before me, one of the Justices of the
Peace for the County of Bucks, Wm. Stayner, of the City of
Philada, and being quallified as the law directs, deposeth, &
sayeth, that several of the British Light Infantry informed
him, this Deponant, that in the Engagement with Genl Lacey
on the first of May inst., they Bayoneted some of Genl
Laceys men, after they had surrendered Themselves
Prisoners, others they threw into heaps of Buckwheat Straw,
while alive, and burnt them to death.

Wm. Stayner. Sworn before me, this 14th day of May, 1778.
Andrew Long.

Deposition of Thomas CRAVEN
15 May 1778
Bucks, ss.

Personally appeared before me, the subscriber, one of the
Justices of the Peace for the County of Bucks, in the State of
Pennsyla, Thomas Craven, Inhabitant of the township of
Warminster, Bucks County, deposeth & sayeth, that on the
first day May, after the Skirmish between the British and
Genl Laceys People, near the Billet, he was called on by one
of the British Light horse to carry some milch, &c., to one of
their Wounded Officers; when he came into the Field, he was

asked by a Trooper if he did not see some fires round the field, to which he said he did; the Trooper said they were men, & that their own Amunition set them on fire; after the British left the Ground he went again into the field, where he saw four or five men burnt to a shocking degree.

Thos. Craven. Sworn before me, this 15th day of May, 1778 And'w Long.

Deposition of Saml. ERWIN
15 May 1778
Bucks Co'y, ss.

The Examination of Saml. Erwin, upon Oath before me, Andrew Long, Esqr., one of the Justices of said Co'y, That the said Deponant sayeth, that on the first day of May, 1778, after the battle between the Militia, under command of Genl Lacey, and the English, he the Deponant saw a smoak in one of his Fields, and after the enemy had retreated went out to see what was the ocassion thereof; was much surprised to find one of the Militia men lying dead, his Clothes burning & near consumed, which had burnt the Body black; he thinks the man was set on fire before he was dead, from this circumstance that his arms were standing nearly erect; he further sayeth, he saw three other Bodies in Thos. Cravens Field burnt in an inhuman manner, & further said not.

Sam'l Erwin. Sworn before me, May 15th, 1778
And'w Long

Shortly after the battle General Washington relieved General Lacey of his command.[108]

Barren Hill

St. Peter's Church, Lafayette Hill, Pennsylvania[109]

On May 19, shortly after the Battle of Crooked Billet Tavern General Lafayette, just 20 years old, moved 2,000 troops on a reconnaissance as his first independent command to the heights of Barren Hill [now called Lafayette Hill]. The American line was deployed facing east toward Philadelphia parrallel to the Church Road.

Road Sign on Ridge Road, taken 2007

On May 20, he met the British forces commanded by General Howe and General Clinton advancing up the Ridge Road and Gray marching up the Germantown Road. General Lafayette gave orders for battle from the steeple of St. Peter's Church and troops used the graveyard wall for protection. As the battle progressed Grant with a column of 5,000 British Soldiers moved to cut off Lafayette's retreat by marching down the Ridge Road in his rear. He found himself surrounded on three sides by the enemy and the forth side blocked by the Schuylkill River. He was driven off by Howe's overwhelming forces and retreated down the Barren Hill Road to Matson Ford on the river. On Howe's departure Lafayette re-occupied the hill until recalled to Valley Forge on May 23, 1778.[110]

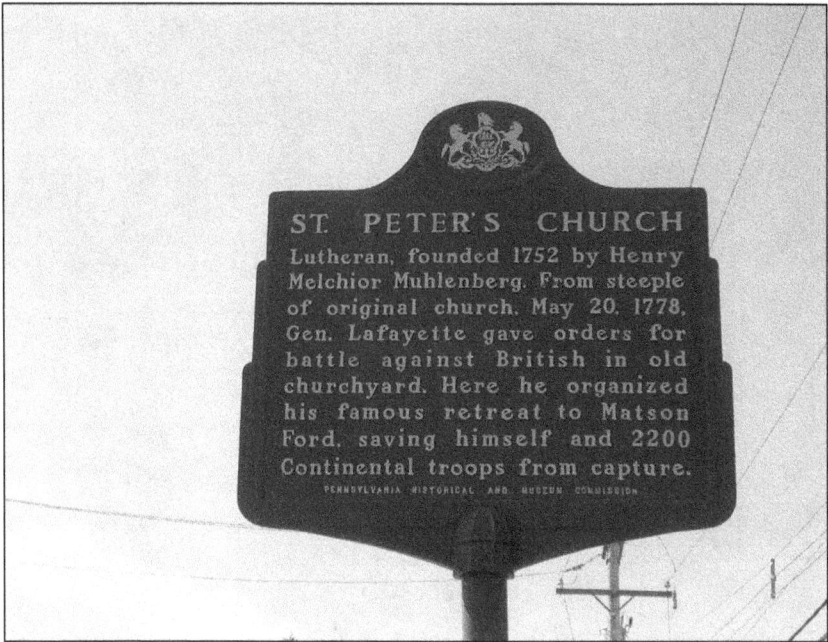

Road Sign for St. Peter's Church, taken 2007

Troops deployed in the graveyard of St. Peter's Church; taken 2007

The Retaking of Philadelphia

From the book American Military History:[111]

First Fruits of the French Alliance

While the Continental Army was undergoing its ordeal and transformation at Valley Forge, Howe dallied in Philadelphia, forfeiting whatever remaining chance he had to win a decisive victory before the effects of the French alliance were felt. He had had his fill of the American war and the king accepted his resignation from command, appointing General Clinton as his successor. As Washington prepared to sally forth from Valley Forge, the British Army and the Philadelphia Tories said goodbye to their old commander in one of the most lavish celebrations ever held in America, the Mechanize, a veritable Belshazzar's feast. The handwriting on the wall appeared in the form of orders, already in Clinton's hands, to evacuate the American capital. With the French in the war, England had to look to the safety of the long ocean supply line to America and to the protection of its possessions in other parts of the world. Clinton's orders were to detach 5,000 men to the West Indies and 3,000 to Florida, and to return the rest of his army to New York by sea.

As Clinton prepared to depart Philadelphia, Washington had high hopes that the war might be won in 1778 by a co-operative effort between his army and the French Fleet. The Comte d'Estaing with a French naval squadron of eleven ships of the line and transports carrying 4,000 troops left France in May to sail for the American coast. D'Estaing's fleet was considerably more powerful than any Admiral Howe could immediately concentrate in American waters. For a brief period in 1778 the strategic initiative passed from British hands, and Washington hoped to make full use of it.

Clinton had already decided, before he learned of the threat from d'Estaing, to move his army overland to New York prior to making any detachments, largely because he could find no place for 3,000 horses on the transports. On June 18, 1778, he set out with about 10,000 men. Washington, who by that time had gathered about 12,000, immediately occupied Philadelphia and then took up the pursuit of Clinton, undecided as to whether he should risk an attack on the British column while it was on the march. His Council of War was divided, though none of his generals advised a "general action." The boldest, Brig. Gen. Anthony Wayne, and the young major general, the Marquis de Lafayette, urged a "partial attack" to strike at a portion of the British Army while it was strung out on the road; the most cautious, General Lee, who had been exchanged and had rejoined the army at Valley Forge, advised only guerrilla action to harass the British columns. On June 26 Washington decided to take a bold approach, though he issued no orders indicating an intention to bring on a "general action." He sent forward an advance guard composed of almost half his army to strike at the British rear when Clinton moved out of Monmouth Court House on the morning of June 27. Lee, the cautious, claimed the command from Lafayette, the bold, when he learned the detachment would be so large.

In the early morning, Lee advanced over rough ground that had not been reconnoitered and made contact with the British rear, but Clinton reacted quickly and maneuvered to envelop the American right flank. Lee, feeling that his force was in an untenable position, began a retreat that became quite confused. Washington rode up amidst the confusion and, exceedingly irate to find the advance guard in retreat, exchanged harsh words with Lee. He then assumed direction of what had to be a defense against a British counterattack. The battle that followed, involving the bulk of both armies, lasted until nightfall on a hot, sultry day with both sides holding their own. For the first time the Americans fought well with the bayonet as well as with the musket and rifle, and their battlefield behavior generally reflected the Valley Forge training. Nevertheless, Washington failed to strike a telling blow at the British Army, for Clinton slipped away in the night and in a few days completed the retreat to New York. Lee demanded and got a court-martial at which he was judged, perhaps unjustly, guilty of disobedience of orders, poor conduct of the retreat, and disrespect for the Commander in Chief. As a consequence he retired from the Army, though the controversy over his actions at Monmouth was to go on for years.

Washington, meanwhile, sought his victory in co-operation with the French Fleet. D'Estaing arrived off the coast on July 8 and the two commanders at first agreed on a combined land and sea attack on New York, but d'Estaing feared he would be unable to get his deep-draft ships across the bar that extended from Staten Island to Sandy Hook, in order to get at Howe's inferior fleet. They then decided to transfer the attack to the other and weaker British stronghold at Newport, Rhode Island—a city standing on an island with difficult approaches. A plan was agreed on whereby the French Fleet would force the passage on the west side of the island and an American force under General Sullivan would cross over and mount an assault from the east. The whole scheme soon went awry. The French Fleet arrived off Newport on July 29 and successfully forced the passage; Sullivan began crossing on the east on August 8 and d'Estaing began to disembark his troops. Unfortunately at this juncture Admiral Howe appeared with a reinforced British Fleet, forcing d'Estaing to re-embark his troops and put out to sea to meet Howe. As the two fleets maneuvered for advantage, a great gale scattered both on August 12. The British returned to New York to refit, and the French Fleet to Boston, whence d'Estaing decided he must move on to tasks he considered more pressing in the West Indies. Sullivan was left to extricate his forces from an untenable position as best he could, and the first experiment in Franco-American co-operation came to a disappointing end with recriminations on both sides.

The fiasco at Newport ended any hopes for an early victory over the British as a result of the French alliance. By the next year, as the French were forced to devote their major attention to the West Indies, the British regained the initiative on the mainland, and the war entered a new phase.

From *The History of Bucks County, Pennsylvania* by W. W. H. Davis, Andrew Keckline was promoted to a majority on the field of Monmouth.[112] Andrew was a neighbor of Henry Emig and with John Keller and Samuel Smith were appointed on September, 1778 to audit and examine the accounts of the administrators of the estate of Henry Emig.

The Army Moves North

From *The History of Bucks County, Pennsylvania* the army moved north...[113]

Washington put the Continental army in march from Valley Forge, after a six months' residence upon its bleak hills, the 18th of June, to pursue the enemy in his retreat toward New York. General Lee, with six brigades, led the advance, via Doylestown to New Hope, where he crossed the night of the

20th, and Washington encamped at Doylestown the same evening with the main body. The weather was very stormy, and the army remained here until the next afternoon, occupying three encampments: on the south side of State street, west of Main, on the ridge east of the Presbyterian church, and along the New Hope pike east of the borough mill. Washington pitched his tent near the dwelling of Jonathan Fell, (10) now John G. Mann's farmhouse, and General Lafayette quartered at the house of Thomas Jones, New Britain, whose best bed was a little too short for the tall young Frenchman. The army was accompanied by some warriors of the Seneca nation, seeking the release of a captured chief, and attended by some friendly Oneidas and Tuscaroras. The army resumed its march for the Delaware the afternoon of the 21st, and crossed at New Hope the next day. While passing Paxson's corner a soldier shot the button from the top of a young pine, and the wound can still be seen [until the tree blew down a few years ago.]

And continues...[114]

From this time forward the stirring and active scenes of the war were removed to distant parts of the country. General Lacey was still in command in this county, keeping a watchful eye on the disaffected, now and then making an important arrest. In the summer of 1780 Bucks county sent her quota of militia to the camp at Trenton, in view of an attack upon New York, and the following year, when Philadelphia was again threatened, there was a concentration of troops at Newtown, under General James Irvine. In September 1781 the French and American armies, in march to meet Cornwallis in Virginia, passed through the lower end of the county. They crossed the Delaware at Trenton and the neighboring ferried on the morning of the 1st, and the same afternoon passed the Neshaminy at the rope ferry, encamping at the Red Lion in Bensalem that evening, and the next day marched through Philadelphia.

New Hope is just 20 miles east of Bedminster. Doylestown is about 10 miles south of Bedminster.

On November 26, 1778, the Supreme Executive Council acting on General Washington's request ordered 400 men of the first class of militia to guard

British prisoners through the state.[115] On December 4, 1778 additional orders for third and forth class militia were called up as well.[116]

Cornwallis sued for peace on October 17, 1781 ending the war. On February 27, 1782, the House of Commons voted against continuing the war. The Articles of Confederation became effective in March 1781.

Colonel John Keller in the War and Enlistments

John Keller's Battalion is listed in documents in 1781 at the end of the war.

AND MILITIA OF THE REVOLUTION.   209

Peter Roberts.
William Bennet.
John Shannon.
James Leddon.
Robert Mernes.
Jacob Kentner.
John Armstrong.
William McConky.

John Torlbert.
John McCammon.
Aaron Hagerman.
Jesse Brittain.
Benjamin Yeoman.
Robert Craige.
Thomas Wilson.

I do Certify that the foregoing is a true State of the Calvery for the County of Bucks, June 18th, 1781.

JACOB BENNET, *Capt.*

COL. JOHN KELLER'S BATTALION.

This battalion was in service in the fall of 1781. From several provision returns we learn that the number of the field and staff officers was ten, and eight companies, a total of 677 men. We have the rolls of only three companies, which follow.

Lieutenant Colonel.

John Keller.

Captains.

Gawin Adams.
Manus Yost.
Elias Roder.
Richard Stillwell.

John Thomas.
Daniel Hogland.
William Erwin.
Robert Patterson.

CAPTAIN ROBERT PATTERSON'S COMPANY.

Muster Roll of Captain Robert Patterson's Company, of the Second Regiment of Foot, in the service of the United States, commanded by Lieutenant Colonel John Kellar, of the Second Class of Militia, of the State of Pennsylvania.

Captain.

Robert Patterson.

Lieutenant.

Philip Slack.

Ensign.

Amos Shaw.

14—VOL. XIV.

Pennsylvania Archives, Series 2, Vol. XIV,
Chapter: Muster Rolls and Papers Relating to the
Associators and Militia of the County of Bucks, pp. 209

Return of Provisions for part of the Second Regt. of Bucks County Militia commanded by Lt. Col. John Keller, October 3, 1781.[117] In 1783 the Bucks County Militia is listed:[118]

---

442   ASSOCIATORS AND MILITIA.

(c.) I do hereby certify that in the month of August Anno Domini, 1782, I did .Agree with William McHenry Esquire, one of the Sub Lieutenants of the county of Bucks to pay him the sum of Five pounds and Ten Shillings in Specie, in full for the Substitute fines of John Rice of the Township of Rockhill (who was then a Soldier of the Pennsylvania Line of Regulars as appears by his Discharge), for the Year 1781, and accordingly paid the said Sum to him and received his receipt for the same in full of the said fine (except the Collectors 'fees), and Ordered the same to be Delivered unto the said Collector, who says that he Returned the said Receipt to the said Sub Lieutenant again in full of the said fine.

ABRAHAM STOUT.

(c.) This may Certify that the Bearer Alexander Hughes acted Ten Days as Adjutant to my Battalion of Bucks County Militia for the year 1782. Given under my hand this 17th Day of March 1783.

JOHN KELLER,
Lt. Coll.

Bucks County, May Ye 12th, 1783.

A Return of Militia Officers elected agreeable to the Militia Law, and now returned to the Supreme Executive Council for Commissions Pr Joseph Hart Lieut. of sd. County. (c.)

Battalion No. 1.

John Kellar, Lieut. Col.
Thomas Long, Mayor. } Field Officers.

Captains.

1. David Spinner.	5. Jacob Shupe.
2. John Freise.	6. George Hineline.
3. Abra Kickline.	7. Jacob Bishop.
4. John Barkley.	8. Moness Yost.

Lieutenants.

Peter Shull.	Saml. Wilson.
Wm. Hickenbottom.	John McFall.
Adam Magle.	Henry Blyer.
Henry Smith, Jun.	Henry Herring.

COUNTY OF BUCKS.   443

Ensigns.

Christian Millar.   Solomon Leibgib.
Theophilus Foulk, Jun.   Jacob Shank.
Jacob Waggoner.   John Henry.
Peter Ruth.   Henry Berson.

Battalion No. 2.

James McMasters, Lieut. Col. ⎫
Gayno Edams, Major.   ⎬ Field Officers.
                             ⎭

Captains.

1. Jno. Hunter.   5. Daniel Hogland.
2. Joseph Hart.   6. Garret Dungan.
3. William Walker.   7. John Vanpelt.
4. *Simon Venasdallen.   8. John Jamison.

Lieutenants.

James Torbet.   Joseph Vanpelt.
John McDole,   Thos. Dungan, Jun.
Wm. Richey.   John Morton.
John Crosedale.   Wm. Walker.

Ensigns.

John Davis.   Joseph Banes.
Harman Vansant.   Jessey Dungan.
Alexr. Long.   Benjn. Buckman.
Isaac Wynkoope.   Robert Jamison.

Battalion No. 3.

Robert Robinson, Lieut. Col. ⎫
Wm. Kennedy, Major.   ⎬ Field Officers.
                             ⎭

Captains.

1. Nathan Evens.   5. William Hines.
2. Wm. McHenry.   6. William Erwin.
3. Robert Gibson.   7. John Thomas.
4. Thos. Sebring.   8. Mathew Greer.

444 ASSOCIATORS AND MILITIA.

Lieutenants.

Josiah Lunn.
Nicholas Gares.
George Geats.
Garret Cavender.

Thomas Stewart.
Ludwick Worman.
Adam Barr.
Evan Griffith.

Ensigns.

Joseph Wilson.
Henry Wisel.
James Nuckiman.
Joseph Coryell.

Isaac James.
John Shoop.
Samuel Simpson.
James Ledom.

Battalion No. 4.

Augustine Willet, Lieut. Collonel. }
Joshua Vanhorn, Major. } Field Officers.

Captains.

1. John Harrinson.
2. Amos Shaw.
3. Daniel Thompson.
4. Michael Gregg.

5. Robert Patterson.
6. Abr. Johnston.
7. Richard Stillwell.
8. Joseph White.

Lieutenants.

Isaac Johnston.
James Shaw.
William Kinsey.
James McMicken.

John Edgar.
Isaiah Vanhorn.
Philip Slack.
Lewis Rue.

Ensigns.

Jessey Severns.
Daniel Bunting.
Dennis Dailey.
Thos. Huddleston.

Charles Broadnex.
Abner Buckman.
Danl. Anderson.
Richard Rue.

I do hereby Certifie that the above and foregoing is a just and true return, to the best of my Knowledge & belief.

JOSEPH HART, L. B. C.

Commissions made out and dated 1st May, 1783.
Forwarded to Bucks Coy. by Colonel Wall.

George Emig's Later Enlistment

George is listed as 4th Class in 1st company, 2nd Battalion and he "did not go on tower" for period 1780-1783.[119]

EMIG, GEORGE

BUCKS
Lieutenancy

Company   1ST

Remarks: DID NOT GO ON TOWER
Authority: Unit Muster Roll for the period   (1780-83)

|Certified   Dated   N.D.   Muster Fines &

"Military Accounts: Militia," Records of the Comptroller General, at D. P. R.

THE BASIC RECORD DOES NOT PROVE ACTIVE DUTY.

MA B-10M.

Inactive Duty
Militia

Rank
2ND
County: Battalion
Class   4TH

Pennsylvania State Archives; ARIAS; the Archives Records Information Access System located at: http://www.digitalarchives.state.pa.us/index.asp; Revolutionary War Military Abstract Card File, Emig, George

Henry Amick's Enlistment

Henry Amick [listed as Emig] is listed as number 50 on the muster roll dated October 11, 1781 of Captain Manus Yost's Company of the First Regiment of Foot in the service of the United States, Col. John Keller commanding, First Class of Bucks County Militia of the State of Pennsylvania. Also listed are Henry's cousins: Daniel, Henry and Jacob Nicholas.[120] Henry Amick [Emig] is listed as "Henry Amick" in the Daughters of the American Revolution Patriot Index. His documentation was submitted by Barbara Nichols.[121]

Two cousins, Christopher and Henry Keller served as privates and brother-in-law John Niemand was the drum and fifer.

The battalion was in service during the fall of 1781. Provision returns show 10 field and staff officers, eight companies, 677 men. Muster rolls of only three companies survive today.[122]

Emig, Henry

Inactive Duty Militia

Lieutenancy .... Bucks ....

Rank 2nd

County, Battalion ....

Company 1st

Class ....

Remarks: .... for Casper Burger ....

Authority: Unit Muster Roll for the period .... 1781 ....

[Certified .... Dated Oct. 4, 1781 .... Muster Fines £ .... A(5) V, pp. 430-3

"Military Accounts: Militia," Records of the Comptroller General, at D. P. R.

THE BASIC RECORD DOES NOT PROVE ACTIVE DUTY.

MA 0 10M

Henry Amick [Emig] from Bucks County is listed in the 1st Company of the 2nd Battalion on October 4, 1781 serving "for Casper Burger."[123] Casper Burger is listed on the tax rolls of Haycock Township, Bucks County in 1782 as a "weaver" with no land and two horses.[124]

Henry Emig from Bucks County is listed in Colonel John Keller's 1st Regiment of Foot in Captain Manus Yost Company 1st Class on a muster roll of October 11, 1781 with duty "Service of the United States."[125]

From *Pennsylvania Archives,* Fifth Series Volume V page 426-427 it states:

[Page #]   426   ASSOCIATORS AND MILITIA.

Muster Roll of Captain Manus Yost's Company of the First Regiment of Foot, in the Service of the United States, Commanded by Colonel John Keller of the First Class of Bucks County Militia, of the State of Pennsylvania.

Captain, Manus Yost
Commissioned Lieutenant, Adam Magel
Ensign, Samuel Wilson

	Appoint	Remarks
	Sergeants	
1. Peter Myers		
2. John Henry		on Guard
3. Robert McEntire		
	Corporals	
1. Yost Mills		
2. Jacob Bernet		
3. Jared Ervin		
	Drum & Fifer	
1. John Niemand		
2. Philip Daron		

Privates	Enlisted
1. Nicholas Rudy	Sept. 24, 1781,
2. Henry Hertsel	
3. Michael Groman	
4. Benjamin Stine	
5. James Muckelroy	
6. Philip Smith	
7. Adam Sharer	
8 Leonard Geiger	
9. Henry Keller	
10 George Nicely	
11. John Hinkel	
12. John Hoover	
13. Christopher Yeller	
14. Bastian Bmng	
15. Patrick Hines	
16. Philip Detesman	
17. Daniel Althouse	
18. Henry Nicholas	
19. Henry Berson	
20. George Ziegefus	
21. William McNiel	
22. William Diel	
23. John Erhart	
24. Frederick Bremour	
25. Jacob Youngken	
26. Robert Thompson	
27. John Hedrick	

427 [Page #]   COUNTY OF BUCKS
                      Privates   Enlisted   Remarks
  28. Moses Glore
  29. Andrew Wile
  30. Peter Rude
  31. Samuel Bell
  32. Henry Godfrey
  33. David Alshouse
  34. Benjamin Alshouse
  35. Adam Hinkel
  36. Balser Stoneback
  37. Henry Fackendahl
  38. Lott Melone
  39. Henry Good
  40. Jacob Bergy
  41. Henry Smith
  42. George Baron   on Guard
  43. Christopher Beang   Ditto
  44. George Overpeck.
  45. Henry Shoub   on Guard
  46. George Sheffer.
  47. Dewald Gidleman,   On Guard
  48 Henry Koon   on Guard
  49. Daniel Nicholas.
  50. Henry Emig.
  51. John Bennett.   on Guard
  52. Philip Berson
  53. Peter Berson.
  54. Henry Frankefleld   Jun
  55. Daniel Snider
  56. Michael Dritteback
  57. George Wisel
  58. Jacob Nicholas
  59. Philip Steckel
  60. Philip Oyer
  61. Jonathan Dickinson
  62. John Bernet   on Guard
  63. Thomas Anderson   Sept 24 1781
  64. Jacob Richy
  65. Samuel Hart
  66. James Long
  67. Patrick McCarty
  68. William Mellinger
  69. Thomas McCarty
  70. William Harvy
  71. George Black
  72. Peter Iker
  73. George Ziegefus
  74. Jacob Herner
  75. Jacob Renner
  76. John Smith
  77. Adam Shoe
  78. Jacob Anderson
  79. Joshua Jones

426 ASSOCIATORS AND MILITIA.

MUSTER ROLL OF CAPTAIN MANUS YOST'S COMPANY
OF THE FIRST REGIMENT OF FOOT, IN THE SERVICE
OF THE UNITED STATES, COMMANDED BY COLONEL
JOHN KELLER OF THE FIRST CLASS OF BUCKS
COUNTY MILITIA, OF THE STATE OF PENNSYLVANIA.
(c.)

Commissioned { Captain, Manus Yost,
Lieutenant, Adam Magel.
Ensign, Samuel Wilson.

Sergeants.	Appoint.	Remarks.
1. Peter Myers.		
2. John Henry, ...	....	On Guard,
3. Robert McEntire.		
Corporals.		
1. Yost Mills.		
2. Jacob Bernet.		
3. Jared Ervin.		
Drum & Fifer.		
1. John Niemand.		
2. Philip Daron.		
Privates.	Enlisted	
1. Nicholas Rudy.	Sept. 24, 1781,	
2. Henry Hertsel.		
3. Michael Groman.		
4. Benjamin Stine		
5. James Muckelroy		
6. Philip Smith.		
7. Adam Sharer.		
8. Leonard Geiger.		
9. Henry Keller.		
10. George Nicely,		
11. John Hinkel.		
12. John Hoover.		
13. Christopher Keller.		
14. Bastian Brang,		
15. Patrick Hines.		
16. Philip Detesman.		
17. Daniel Althouse.		
18. Henry Nicholas.		
19. Henry Berson.		
20. George Ziegefus.		
21. William McNiel.		
22. William Diel.		
23. John Erhart.		
24. Frederick Bremour.		
25. Jacob Youngken.		
26. Robert Thompson		
27. John Hedrick		

MUSTER ROLL OF CAPTAIN MANUS YOST'S COMPANY
OF THE FIRST REGIMENT OF FOOT—Continued.

Privates.	Enlisted.	Remarks.
28. Moses Glore.		
29. Andrew Wile		
30. Peter Itude.		
31. Samuel Bell.		
32. Henry Godfrey.		
33. David Alshouse.		
34. Benjamin Alshouse.		
35. Adam Hinkel.		
36. Balser Stoneback.		
37. Henry Fackendahl.		
38. Lott Melone.		
39. Henry Good.		
40. Jacob Bergy.		
41. Henry Smith.		
42. George Baron, ...	....	On Guard.
43. Christopher Beang, ...	....	Ditto.
44. George Overpeck.		
45. Henry Shoub, ...	....	On Guard.
46. George Sheffer.		
47. Dewald Gidleman, ...	....	On Guard.
48. Henry Koon, ...	....	On Guard.
49. Daniel Nicholas.		
50. Henry Emig.		
51. John Bennett.		
52. Philip Berson, ...	....	On Guard.
53. Peter Berson.		
54. Henry Frankefield, Jun.		
55. Daniel Snider.		
56. Michael Dritteback.		
57. George Wisel.		
58. Jacob Nicholas.		
59. Philip Steckel.		
60. Philip Oyer.		
61. Jonathan Dickinson.		
62. John Bernet, ...	....	On Guard.
63. Thomas Anderson, ...	Sept. 24, 1781,	
64. Jacob Richy.		
65. Samuel Hart.		
66. James Long.		
67. Patrick McCarty.		
68. William Mellinger.		
69. Thomas McCarty.		
70. William Harvy.		
71. George Black.		
72. Peter Iker.		
73. George Ziegefus.		
74. Jacob Herner.		
75. Jacob Renner.		
76. John Smith.		
77. Adam Shoe.		
78. Jacob Anderson.		
79. Joshua Jones.		

428   ASSOCIATORS AND MILITIA.

MUSTER ROLL OF CAPTAIN MANUS YOST'S COMPANY
OF THE FIRST REGIMENT OF FOOT—Continued.

Privates.	Enlisted.	Remarks.
80. Ludwig Ableback.		
81. John Magel.		
82. George Shoeman.		
83. George Joseph.		
84. Henry Nehs.		
85. Adam Litseberger.		
86. Anthony Simon.		
87. John Charles.		
88. Michael Sloyer.		
89. Michael Kyser.		
90. Jeremiah Clark.		
91. Robert Davis.		
92. Arthur Handerson.		
93. Valentine Rear.		
94. Jacob Sasseman.		
95. Jacob Shank.		
96. William Cambell, Sen.		
97. James Smith.		
Clark Valentine Marsteller.		

October 11, 1781. Mustered then Captain Manus Yost's Company, as specified in the above roll.

SAMUEL STERETT,
M. M. P. M.

PROOF OF THE EFFECTIVES.

	Capt.	Lieut.	Ens.	Serjts.	Corp.	Drum.	Fifer.	Priv.
Pres.,	1	1	1	3	3.	1	1	97
Absent,								
Total,	1	1	1	3	3	1	1	97

I do Swear, that the within Muster-Roll is a true State of the Company, without fraud to the United States or to any Individuaal according to the best of my knowledge.

Sworn before me this thirteenth Day of October 1781.
JOHN LACEY, B. G.

MANUS YOST.

Nicholas Emmick's Enlistment

Nicholas Emmick [listed as Emig], 4th class, was in Captain Wiedner's Company 1st Battalion Berks County on rolls April and May 1785.[126] Henry Emig is also listed as in the same company as 2nd Class. This would be Nicholas Emmick's younger brother.

A CLASS ROLL OF CAPT. WEIDNER'S COMPANY OF APRIL & MAY 1785 NO. 3 OF THE FIRST BATTALION OF BERKS COUNTY COMANDET BY COL. LUTZ

Capten
John Weidner

Leutenant
Christian Bechtel

Ensign
David pontzius

Sergands
Isaac pether
George Kohl
Henry Hottenstein

first class

Christian Bauman.
Michel Franckhauser.
John Gerber.
John Keing.
Henry Wetz.
Jonas Steihl.

Emanuel Becht.
Jacob Nithack.
Christian Gerber.
Fridrick Schweitzer.
Adam Sawel.
Jacob Steihl.

2 Class

John Bauman.
Paul Horney.
Abraham Geman.
John Behr.
Jacob Keblinger.
John Kachel.
Matheis Laub.

Henry Emig.
Michel Jeig.
Jacob Schnauffer.
Joseph Bauman.
Henry Bauman.
John Bauman, John's son.
Fridrich Becht.

3 Class

George Beihm, Juner.
Wendel Bauman.
John Moser.
Peter Schweitzer, juner.
Adam Weidner.

Jacob Kesler.
John Biding.
Andrew Etzel.
Peter Bauman, wets son.
John Schrack.

56   MILITIA ROLLS—1783-1790.

Runumus Wild.
Fridrick Neig.
Lenhant Keblinger.

Henry Lantz.
Marticke Wels.

4 Class

Christian Zigler.
John Laub.
George Zigler.
Fridrick Hoschar.
Philip Wild.
John Hardman.
Nichlos Emig.

Henry Geman.
Jacob Stichler.
Simon Kachel.
Michel Laub.
Peter Geier.
John Becht.
Henry Hoffer.

5 Class

Grafft Velckel.
Jacob Blanckenbiler.
Christian Bauman, wits son.
Philip Remp.
John Zerben, juner.
Philip Biding.
Gottlib Jeiser.
Fridrich Rimschneider.

Christian Bradenstein.
Joseph Dost.
Lenhart Speigelmeier.
John Lewis.
Jacob Bauman.
Stofel Schneider.
Conrad Ruffner
John Wachner.

6 Class

John Frantz.
Henry Gring.
Jacob Eigerd.
Jacob Remp.
Nichlos Moser.
Wiliam Hoschar.

Wiliam Remp.
Peter Eselman, juner.
Andrew Borghart.
Jacob Stein.
Lukes Melone.
John Strunck.

7 Class

Andrew Greiner.
Thomas Lewis.
David Eselman.
Nichlos Getz.
Adam Gramling.
Abraham Kortz.
George Fitterling.

John Maeir.
Abraham Reihm.
James Lewis.
George Ruffner.
Joseph Dickeson.
Simon Blanckenbilen.
Michel Mauera.

8 Class

Michel Fitterling.
Adam Bem.
Jacob Morgen.

Jacob Keing.
Philip Weiss.
John Etzel.

Neighbors in the War

Neighbors of Henry Emig were also active in the war. Andrew Keckline was an auditor of Henry's father's estate.

From *The History of Bucks County, Pennsylvania* by W. W. H. Davis:[127]

> John Keller, Samuel Smith and Andrew Keckline were appointed on September, 1778 to audit and examine the accounts of the administrators of the estate of Henry Amey.

And continues...

> The Keichlines, of Bedminster, not so numerous as they were half a century ago, are descended from John Peter Keichline, who immigrated from Heidelberg, Germany, and settled in this township as early as about 1742. He had three sons, Peter, Andrew, and Charles, all of whom entered the Revolutionary army. Peter, who lived at Easton, as early as 1749, raised a company of riflemen in Northampton and Bucks, for Colonel Miles's regiment, and was in command of it at the battle of Long Island, 1776, where he was taken prisoner. Lord Sterling wrote to Washington that the English General Grant was killed by some of Keichline's riflemen. Andrew was promoted to a majority on the field of Monmouth. Charles, who entered the army later than his brothers, took the oath of allegiance in June 1777. Jacob Keichline, son of Andrew, born in Bedminster, September 8, 1776, and died February 26, 1861, well-known in the upper section of the county, was the landlord of Keichline's tavern in Bedminster 36 years. Andrew and Charles Keichline, were both born in Bedminster, the former being the grandfather of William H. Keichline, Philadelphia. Peter Keichline built the first flour-mill on the Bushkill. Andrew owned and kept a tavern, now a dwelling house, opposite Tohickon church.
> George Piper, the founder of Pipersville, and the ancestor of those bearing the name in that section of the county, was born on the Wissahickon, Philadelphia county, November 11, 1755. He removed to Bedminster about the time he arrived at manhood, and married a daughter of Arnold Lear, of Tinicum. About 1775 he opened a store at Pipersville, and in 1778 he moved into the tavern at that place, which he kept until his

death in 1823. He was an officer in the Continental army, and a colonel in the state militia; and assisted General Paul Mallet Provost to purchase the tract of land on the east bank of the Delaware, on which he afterward laid out Frenchtown, Hunterdon county, New Jersey. Colonel Piper listened to the reading of the Declaration of Independence in front of the state house, Philadelphia, July 4, 1776. The tavern at Pipersville was built by one Bladen in 1759. The sign of the old inn, simply "Piper's tavern," was painted on a board and fastened to the front of the upper porch. It was called Bucks County hotel while Jacob Keichline was landlord, and was only called Pipersville when the postoffice was established, in 1845, and Jacob Nicholson [David Glick*] appointed postmaster.

Andrew Kiechline is listed in the records as a sub-Lieutenant for Bucks County Militia.

After the War

Henry was a miller, inheriting his father's grist and saw mill on Tohickon Creek. His son would later have a powder mill in Virginia and Henry may have had one here as well; learning the trade for supplying the needs of the Revolutionary War.

Henry married Barbara Niemand. Barbara's father, Johannes Niemand came over from Rotterdam on the ship Snow Charlette, John Mason Master, and qualified September 5, 1743.[128] He died in 1768.

Barbara's mother Barbara Niemand remarried Michael Steinbach July 20, 1769. He is listed in Keller's Church record as the son of Christian and Dorothy Steinbach. Michael Steinbach was born in 1746 in Haycock, Bucks County. His father Christian Steinbach arrived in Pennsylvania in 1732 on the ship Pennsylvania Merchant. He was a deacon at Keller's Church in 1751.[129]

> May 25, 1783 Samuel son of Christian Nicola and wife Susanna, Sponsors, Henry Emig and Barbara, [no surname] single.[130]

Henry Emich married Barbara Niemand about 1784; there are no marriages recorded at either Keller's Church or Tohickon Churches from 1774 through 1795. Elisabeth Barbara Niemand was born August 8, 1764 at Haycock and baptized September 20, 1764 at Keller's Church. She was the daughter of John Niemand and Elisabeth Barbara Keller, the daughter of Hierarch Keller. Colonel John Keller was her uncle. John Niemand, Barbara's elder brother married Julianna Emigh, Henry's sister.[131]

Also recorded at the same baptism is: "May 25 1783, Elisabeth daughter of John Nicola and wife Susanna: sponsors Henry Emig, Barbara Emig, single." Samuel and Elisabeth were christened the same day but parents and sponsors are confused in the transcribed record.[132]

George and Henry from 1879 to 1878

In 1779 Bucks County Tax Transcripts Georg Emy is listed owning 250 Acres, 4 horses and 6 cattle. Henry is not listed, the will is still moving through probate.[133] John Keller is listed with 150 acres, Valentine Nicholas with 125 acres and Michael Stonebach (Michael Steinbach), Barbara's stepfather, with 100, George Stoneback with 75, Henry with 75 and Balser with 25 acres. Andrew Keichline is listed with 25 acres. John Keller (Jr.), Henry Nicholas and Christian Nicholas are listed as single men.

Geo. Amy, named spelled differently, is listed in Bucks County Transcripts for 1781 as owning 231 acres, 3 horses and 6 head of cattle.[134] Some of the entries carry professions for the first time. Geo. Nicholas is listed as a nailer, Michael Stoneback as a potter and Balser Stoneback as a wheelwright.

George Amy is listed in 1782 with 230 acres of land, 3 horses and 6 head of cattle.[135] Henry Amy is listed for the first time in 1783 with tax of 15.0. This would indicate that the probate for the older Henry's will had completed, giving Henry title to land. Geo. Amy is listed with tax of 3.17.7.[136]

Geo. Amy is listed in Bucks County Transcripts for 1784 with 231 acres, 2 dwelling houses, 1 outhouse and 8 white inhabitants. Henry is not listed.[137]

Henry Amey is listed as owning 70 acres of land in Haycock Township, Bucks County in 1785 and Geo. Amy is listed as owning 281 acres.[138]

In Bucks County Transcripts for 1786 Geo. Amy is listed with tax of 1.7.8. Henry Amy is listed with tax of 9.8.[139] John Numond is listed for tax of 3.0.

Geo. Amy is listed in the 1787 transcripts with taxes of 1.8.9 and Henry Amy with taxes of 4.0.[140]

	Acres.	Horses.	Cattle.	Servants.
George Emy,	250	4	6	..
George Fulmer,	140	2	4	..
John Frats,	115	2	4	..
Joseph Fulmer,	115	3	4	..
Connard Good,	25	..	3	..
Jacob Good,	140	2	5	..
Jacob Grove's est., f. m.,	45	2	2	..
Gasper Horn,	50	2	3	..
Ludowick Hoffman,	..	..	2	..
Connard Hefler,	100	2	2	..
Alexander Hughes,	50	1	2	..
Peter Heft,	150	2	3	..
John Hoffman,	..	..	..	..
John Hartsel's est.,	100	1	4	..
Patrick Hines,	..	..	2	..
Phillip Haning,	180	4	3	..
John Hart,	50	..	..	..
Isaac Yost,	125	2	3	..
Mawness Yost,	130	2	3	..
Michael Yost,	260	3	8	..
Andrew Kichline,	25	..	..	..
Henry Keller, Jr.,	35	1	3	..
John Keller,	150	3	7	..
Henry Keller, Se'r,	100	1	2	..
Peter Keller,	75	2	4	..
Christopher Keller,	75	1	3	..
Frederick King,	45	2	3	..
Benja. Kinsey,	..	..	1	..
Aaron Klinker,	270	5	8	..
Henry Louks,	50	1	2	..
John Ludwick,	20	2	3	..
Adam Litsbury,	75	2	3	..
John Morrison,	..	6	9	..
Widow Moyer,	100	2	3	..
Vallintine Mostler,	..	1	2	..
Henry Mostler,	150	..	..	..
Peter Moyer,	125	..	..	..
Jacob Mosht,	50	..	..	..
John Mill,	200	2	4	..
Vallintine Nicholas,	125	3	8	..
Ludwick Nuspickle,	45	..	..	..
Jacob Nicholas,	140	2	4	..
John Nicholas' est.,	20	1	2	..
Martin Oyer,	70	2	3	..

176   BUCKS COUNTY TRANSCRIPT—1781.

	Acres.	Horses.	Cattle.	Servants.
Peter Walter, Sen.,	50	2	4	..
Phillip Waggoner,	160	4	6	..
Michael Wisel,	15	..	..	..
Ulrich Weaver,	..	..	1	..
Geo. Wickert,	43	..	..	..
Abram Wambolt,	19	1	3	..
Jacob Wadeknight,	..	..	1	..
John Benner,	100	..	..	..
Connard Shellyberger,	40	..	..	..
M. Wack,	..	3	2	..
M. Neirmire,	60	2	3	..

SINGLE MEN.

John Barnt,	Connard Lyster,
Phillip Barnet,	Henry Lyster,
Michael Blank,	Adam Mogal,
John Ball,	Geo. Mogal,
Christian Benner,	Isaac Morgan,
Ludwick Benner,	Henry Nase,
John Freed,	John Rice,
Jacob Geese,	Jacob Stitsell,
John Grove,	James Smith,
Abram Huntsberry,	Rob't Smith,
Henry Hartsell,	Ludwick Wats,
Jacob Harr,	Peter Wolf,
Jacob Itterly,	John Lambright.
John Kittleman,	

HAYCOCK TOWNSHIP.

	Acres.	Horses.	Cattle.	Servants.
And'w Armstrong,	130	..	..	..
Geo. Amy,	231	3	6	..
Stephen Ackerman,	75	3	6	..
Jacob Allum,	120	4	5	..
Daniel Althouse,	..	3	3	..
Vallintine Albert, weaver,	..	..	2	..

Pennsylvania Archives, Series 3, Volume: XIII,
Chapter: Provincial Papers Proprietary and Other Tax Lists of the County of Bucks for the Years,
1779, 1781, 1782, 1783, 1784, 1785, 1786, pp. 176

HAYCOCK TOWNSHIP.

	Acres.	Horses.	Cattle.	Servants.
Daniel Applebach,	100	2	3	..
Wm. Albert,	100	1	2	..
Vallintine Albert, weaver,	..	1	2	..
Stephen Akerman,	75	3	6	..
Daniel Althous,	..	2	3	..
Geo. Amy,	230	3	6	..
Joel Bryan,	150	2	5	..
James Bryan,	270	2	7	..
Leonard Bidleman,	180	2	9	..
Nicholas Burgar,	74	2	3	..
Casper Burgar, weaver,	..	2	..	..
Abram Bidleman,	..	1	2	..
Henry Coder, mason,	21	..	1	..
Nicholas Carty,	200	3	4	..
Wm. Deal,	150	3	4	..
Eleazer Doan,	150	2	3	..
Michael Deal,	70	1	3	..
Samuel Furman, weaver,	75	..	2	..
Geo. Fulmer, g. m.,	147	2	5	..
Thomas Fell, b'smith,	..	1	1	..
Phillip Tatesman,	29	1	3	..
Yost Fulmer,	116	3	5	..
John Frats, g. m.,	129	3	3	..
Manasah Fretts, tan yard, tanner,	..	..	1	..
Joseph Fratz, f. m..	48	1	2	..
Connard Good,	32	..	3	..
Jacob Good,	100	2	5	..
Connard Hefler,	54	2	1	..
John Hefler,	..	1	..	..
Alexander Hughes, sadler,	90	2	3	..
Phillip Harring,	180	2	5	..
Henry Harring,	..	1	2	..
Michael Harring,	..	..	2	..
Ludwick Hoffman, shoemaker,	..	..	2	..
Gasper Horn,	50	2	3	..
Bostin Horn,	..	..	2	..
Patrick Hines,	..	1	1	..
Marones Jost,	100	3	4	..
Michael Jost,	180	2	4	..

400   BUCKS COUNTY TRANSCRIPT—1783.

SINGLE MEN.

	Amount of Tax.
Jos. Burson,	15 .0
Henry Funk,	1 .0 .0
Wm. Clutsom,	15 .0
And'w Trop,	15 .0
Jacob Schoch,	15 .0
Phillip Overpack,	1 .0 .0
Absolam Thomas,	16 .0
Mich'l Shuman,	15 .0
Jacob Barron,	15 .0
George Overpeck,	15 .0
Dan'l Christine,	15 .0
Benja. Rosenbery,	15 .0
Christian Moyers,	1 .0 .0
Peter Rodrick,	15 .0
Aron Bushkirk,	15 .0
Geo. Miller,	16 .0
John Man, Jun.,	15 .0
Peter Man,	15 .0
Phillip Trop,	
Fardinand Waggoner,	10 .0
George Hess,	15 .0
Peter Erhart,	15 .0

HAYCOCK TOWNSHIP.

	Amount of Tax.
Wm. Albert,	9 .8
Valentine Albert,	3 .0
Dan'l Appleback,	10 .4
Henry Amy,	15 .0
Stephen Akkerman,	1 .7 .3
Dan'l Althouse,	3 .9
Jacob Allom,	2 .1 .4
Geo. Amy,	3.17 .7
And'w Armstrong,	1.16 .8
Nicolas Burger,	14 .0
Gasper Burger,	3 .0
Leo. Bidleman,	2 .8 .2
Joel Bryan,	2 .2 .4

436   BUCKS COUNTY TRANSCRIPT—1784.

	Acres.	Dwelling Houses.	Out Houses.	White Inhabitants.	Black Inhabitants.
Widow Wildonger, ...	50	1	..	6	..
Stophel Segafuse, ...	286	1	..	6	..
John Nolton, ...	..	..	..	8	..
David Wilson, ...	100	1	1	6	..
Samuel Wilson, ...	250	2	2	12	..
Connard Cline, ...	100	1	1	9	..
Jacob Fair, ...	130	1	1	7	..
Stophel Lambing, ...	40	1	1	11	..
Widow Frealy, ...	300	2	2	6	..
Nicholas Houpt, ...	50	1	1	6	..
Jonathan Gregory, ...	129	1	..	9	..
John Woolfanger, ...	130	1	1	8	..
John McCammon, ...	250	1	1	6	..
Daniel Jamison, ...	134	1	1	5	..
Anthony Shumaker, ..	500	2	1	5	..
George Riegle, ...	300	2	'2	5	..
Henry Adams, ...	87	2	1	3	..
Jos. Cole, ...	50	1	..	5	..
Lawrence Pearson, ...	50	1	..	5	..

HAYCOCK TOWNSHIP.

	Acres.	Dwelling Houses.	Out Houses.	White Inhabitants.	Black Inhabitants.
William Albert, ...	100	2	1	9	..
Daniel Appleback, ...	100	1	1	6	..
Stephen Ackerman, ..	75	2	2	9	..
Jacob Allom, ...	120	1	2	11	..
Geo. Amy, ...	231	2	1	8	..
Nicholas Burger, ...	74	1	1	9	..
Leonard Bidleman, ...	180	2	1	11	..
Joel Bryan, ...	150	1	1	19	..
James Bryan, ...	270	2	2	14	..
Nicholas Carty, ...	200	1	1	4	..
Martin Connard, ...	50	2	1	6	..
Wm. Deal, ...	150	1	1	9	..
Michael Deal, ...	74	1	1	8	..
Levey Dennis, ...	80	1	1	3	..

Pennsylvania Archives, Series 3, Volume: XIII,
Chapter: Provincial Papers Proprietary and Other Tax Lists of the County of Bucks for the Years,
1779, 1781, 1782, 1783, 1784, 1785, 1786, pp. 436-439

554   BUCKS COUNTY TRANSCRIPT—1785.

	Acres.	Horses.	Cattle.	Servants
John Trillibough,	100	2	3	..
Christian Traugher, Jr.,	70	2	3	..
Stophel Traugher,	50	..	2	..
Widow Trough,	100	2	2	..
Benja. William,	500	6	8	..
Widow Williams,	100	..	..	..
Samuel Wilson,	200	3	4	..
John Wolfinger,	130	4	2	..
Jacob Young,	125	3	4	..
John Youngan,	200	3	7	..
Jacob Sumpstun,	50	2	3	..
David Stern,	30	1	3	..

UNIMPROVED LANDS.

	Acres.	Horses.	Cattle.	Servants.
Vallintine Houseworth,	36	..	..	..
John Baily,	50	..	..	..
John Sherrid,	50	..	..	..
James Wilson,	150	..	..	..
James Morgan,	250	..	..	..
Michael Youst,	100	..	..	..
Michael Walker,	24	..	..	..
David Marepole,	50	..	..	..
Michael Wormen,	50	..	..	..
Geo. McElroy & Tho's Little,	42	..	..	..
David Wilson,	100	2	4	..

SINGLE MEN.

John Ruse,	Hugh Jamison,
John Rimore,	Jacob Sheveleer,
Samuel Williams,	Henry Frankinfield,
Solomon Woolfanger,	Nicholas Grover,
Amose Loughery,	John Addams.

HAYCOCK TOWNSHIP.

	Acres.	Horses.	Cattle.	Servants.
And'w Armstrong,	130	..	..	..
Geo. Amy,	281	4	5	..

BUCKS COUNTY TRANSCRIPT—1785.   555

	Acres.	Horses.	Cattle.	Servants.
Stephin Ackerman,	75	3	5	..
Jacob Allom,	140	3	7	..
Wm. Albert,	100	2	3	..
Daniel Applebouch,	100	1	4	..
Henry Amey, s. m.,	70	2	2	..
Casper Burger,	92	2	2	..
James Bryan,	290	2	5	..
Joel Bryan,	150	3	5	..
Henry Barnt,	..	..	2	..
Nicholas Carty,	200	3	4	..
Henry Coder,	21	1	1	..
Wm. Deal,	150	3	6	..
Jacob Coder,	..	..	1	..
Eleazer Doan,	130	2	3	..
Levey Dennis,	70	2	2	..
Josiah Dennis, single man,	100	..	..	..
Wm. Dixsey,	..	1	..	..
Martin Eyer,	70	1	5	..
Manassa Frets, tan yard,	14	1	2	..
Joseph Frets, f. m.,	49	2	2	..
Geo. Fulmer, g. m.,	147	2	4	..
Youst Fulmer,	116	3	4	..
Abraham Funk,	30	2	2	..
John Fulton,	1	1	..	..
Jacob Glees,	75	..	1	..
Isaac Gerhard,	130	2	4	..
Peter Heft,	150	4	5	..
Phillip Harring,	180	2	5	..
Michael Harring,	12	1	2	..
Henry Harring,	..	1	3	..
Connard Hefler,	54	3	2	..
John Heflar,	..	..	2	..
Alexander Hughes,	90	2	3	..
Bostin Horne,	50	2	2	..
Casper Horne,	..	..	2	..
Patrick Hynes,	50	1	1	..
John Hartsell,	80	2	3	..
Jonas Hartsell,	70	..	..	..
Christian Hoghman,	..	1	1	..
Henry Heft,	..	..	..	..
Manus Jost,	130	2	4	..
Michael Jost,	100	2	4	..
Peter Keller,	99	2	4	..
Christophel Keller,	104	4	4	..

688   BUCKS COUNTY TRANSCRIPT—1786.

	Amount of Tax.
Abraham Huntsbery,	5 .0
Henry Rosenberry,	5 .0
Dewalt Kittleman,	5 .0
Isaac Morgan,	5 .0
Peter Frank,	5 .0
Jacob Trisback,	5 .0
Adam Deager,	5 .0
Geo. Wisell,	5 .0
Henry Grove,	5 .0
James Smith,	5 .0
John Grove,	5 .0
Geo. Wikle,	5 .0
Amos Richinson,	5 .0
Abraham Dosh,	5 .0
John Nees,	5 .0
Vallintine Refsnider,	5 .0
Sam'l Bechtol,	5 .0

HAYCOCK TOWNSHIP.

	Amount of Tax.
And'w Armstrong,	12 .2
Geo. Amy,	1 .7 .8
Stephin Ackerman,	8 .4
Jacob Allcom,	17 .2
Wm. Albert,	3 .0
Daniel Appleback,	3 .9
Henry Amy,	9 .8
Casper Berger,	7 .6
James Bryan,	19 .3
Joel Bryan,	15 .2
Henry Barnt,	1 .0
Nicholas Carty,	15 .8
Henry Cooder,	2 .3
Jacob Cooder,	9
Wm. Deal,	7 .0
Eleazer Doan,	15 .6
Levey Dennis,	8 .0
Josiah Dennis,	4 .9

Pennsylvania Archives, Series 3, Volume: XIII,
Chapter: Provincial Papers Proprietary and Other Tax Lists of the County of Bucks for the Years,
1779, 1781, 1782, 1783, 1784, 1785, 1786, pp. 688

794   BUCKS COUNTY TRANSCRIPT—1787.

SINGLE MEN.

	Amount of Tax.
Geo. Wisell,	6 .6
David Kulp,	6 .6
Christian Hockman,	6 .6
Jacob Hockman,	6 .6
Peter Homely,	7. .6
Peter Tinsman,	7 .6
Christian Fritz,	6 .6
Jacob Overholt,	6 .6
Henry Stover,	8 .6
Henry Sallady,	7 .6
Daniel Sallady,	6 .6
Henry Fritz,	6 .6
Phillip Harple,	6 .6
Benja. Jovious,	6 .6
Jacob Wissel,	7 .6
Henry Wisell,	6 .6
Robert Morrison,	6 .6
Connard Youst,	8 .6
Matthew Armstrong,	6 .6
John Armstrong,	10 .0
Jacob Landes,	6 .6
Michael Pissor,	7 .6
Christian Stone,	6 .6
Joseph Mitlin,	6 .6
Peter Loux,	6 .0
John Culp,	6 .6

HAYCOCK TOWNSHIP.

	Amount of Tax.
And'w Armstrong,	16 .2
Geo. Amy,	1 .8 .9
Stephin Ackerman,	8.10
Jacob Allom,	15 .8
Wm. Albert,	2.10
Daniel Applebouch,	3.11
Henry Amy,	4 .0
Casper Borger,	7 .4

Pennsylvania Archives, Series 3, Volume: XIII,
Chapter: Provincial Papers Proprietary and Other Tax Lists of the County of Bucks for the Years,
1779, 1781, 1782, 1783, 1784, 1785, 1786, pp. 794

Henry sold his father's land to Jacob Lydey (Lindley) Jr. of Franconia, Montgomery County on June 12, 1786 and signed by Henry Emig, Barbara his wife, and Frederich Premour and Catherine his wife (Henry's mother and stepfather). Barbara Emigh, being of full age, and Catherine, being the mother of Henry Emigh, were "secretely and apart examined and the contents made known to them they voluntarily consented". The property: "Land in Haycock, beginning at a Black Oak sapling being also a corner of John Mills land --- by land of Henry Yonkon—land of John Doan."[141]

An Indenture is a deed or contract and for deeds recorded in the county clerk's office. Once land has a recorded patent ownership is transferred by an indenture.

372

Premises or any Part thereof by them or under them or either of them shall and
will **Warrant** and forever Defend by these presents *In Witness* whereof
the said Parties to these presents have Interchangeably Set their Hands and Seals
hereunto Dated the Day and Year first above written

Sealed and Delivered in the presence of us }   Abraham Schleiffer (seal)
John Davis Jun.r John Davis ──── }   Catharina Schleiffer (seal)

Received on the Day of the Date of the within written Indenture of the
within named Andrew Schlichter the Sum of two Hundred and Seven pounds
and ten Shillings lawful Money of Pennsylvania in Specie it being in full
of the Consideration Money within mentioned I say Received for me
Witness present at signing John Davis Jun.r John Davis) Abraham Schleiffer

The tenth Day of June Anno Domini 1786 before me John Davis Esq.r one of the
Justices of the Court of Common Pleas for Bucks County came the above named
Grantors Abraham Schleiffer and Catharina his Wife and acknowledged the
above written Indenture to be their Act and Deed and desired the same may be
Recorded as such as the Law directs; the said Catharina voluntarily thereunto
consenting she being of lawful Age and apart from her Husband examined of
the Contents thereof first made fully known unto her *Witness* my hand &
Seal on the Day and Year first above written   Jn.o Davis (seal)

Recorded June 13.th 1786

This Indenture made the twelfth Day

of June Anno Domini One Thousand Seven Hundred and Eighty six *Between*
Henry Emigh of Haycock Township in the County of Bucks and State of Penn-
sylvania Yeoman and Barbara his Wife and Frederick Primore of the County
aforesaid and Catharine his Wife of the One Part. And Jacob Lyday Junior of
Franconia in the County of Montgomery and State aforesaid of the other Part.
Whereas Henry Emigh Sinor late of y.e Township of Haycock afors.d dec.d was
in his lifetime and at the Time of his Decease Possessed of several Tracts Lots or Pieces of
Land Contiguous together Situate lying and being in Haycock Township afors.d
Containing in the whole One Hundred and Ninety four Acres which s.d several Lots
of Land was Convey'd and Confirm'd unto him the s.d Henry Emigh Sin.r by two
several Patents each bearing Date on the 22.d Day of February 1776 which s.d
Patents are Recorded in Patent Book in Philad.a AA Vol. 15 pages 635 and 636 relation being thereunto had more fully and at large will appear &c. And being so seiz'd
thereof he Dyed Intestate leaving a Widow and Seven Children and Some time
afterwards a Writ of Partition being Issued out of the Orphan's Court held at Neus-
town in and for the County of Bucks at March Term 1784 to Samuel Dean Esq
then High Sheriff of the County of Bucks commanding that the said Sheriff
with

Bucks County, Pennsylvania Deeds, Book 22 (12 June 1786) pp. 372-74

373

with twelve lawful Men of his Bailiwick would View the Lands the Lands & Premises late of Henry Emigh deceased and Partion thereof make And the Sheriff aforesaid in Obedience to the Court and by Virtue of the said Writ in his own proper person on the 15th Day of April A.D. 1786 taking with him the twelve men of his Bailiwick caused the above One Hundred and Ninety four Acres of Land to be valued at the Sum of Six pounds and ten Shillings for Acre a return of which was made unto the Court by the said Sheriff at June Term following and Henry Emigh the Intestates eldest Son (and Party to these presents) appearing in Court the Lands were Adjudged unto him upon the above Valuation (by the s'd Court) he paying unto his Brothers and Sisters their respective Shares according to the Laws of this State and also paying his Mothers Dower annually unto her &c. **Now this Indenture witnesseth** that the said Henry Emigh and Barbara his Wife and Fredrick Rumore and Catharine his Wife for and in Consideration of the Sum of Seven Hundred Pounds Lawful Current Money of Pennsylvania to them in Hand paid by the said Jacob Lyley at or before the Sealing and Delivery the Receipt of which is hereby acknowledged and thereof they do acquit and forever Discharge the said Jacob Lyley his Heirs and Assigns by these Presents **Have** Granted, Bargained, Sold, Aliened, Released, Convey'd and Confirmed by these presents they the said Henry Emigh and Barbara his Wife and Fredrick Rumore and Catharine his Wife **Do** Grant, Bargain, Sell, Alien, Release, Convey and Confirm unto the said Jacob Lyley his Heirs and Assigns a certain Tract or Parcel of Land Situate, Lying and being in the Township of Haycock aforesaid **Beginning** at a Black Oak Saplin being also a Corner of John Mills's Land thence extending by the same South Forty two Degrees West Twenty one Perches and one tenth to a White Oak Tree and North Sixty six Degrees West Fifty perches and then tenths to a Hickory Stump for a Corner and North Eleven degrees West Fifty two perches and Seven tenths of a perch to a heap of Stones thence North thirteen Degrees and a half West by Land of Henry Yonker one Hundred perches to a heap of Stones thence by Vacant Land North Seventy Seven Degrees and a half East Eighty four perches and Seven tenths of a perch to a heap of Stones thence by Land of Eaases Doan South three Degrees West one Hundred and Seventy six perches and five tenths to the place of Beginning Containing Sixty four Acres of Land (be the same more or less) which s'd Described Land is part of the above mentioned One Hundred and Ninety four Acres which was possessed by Henry Emigh Senr in his life time **Together** also with all and Singular the Buildings Improvements, Woods, Ways, Waters, Water Courses, Rights, Liberties, Privileges, Advantages, Hereditaments and Appurtenances whatsoever unto the said Described Piece of Land belonging or in any wise appertaining thereto. And the Reversion and Reversions Rents Issues and Profits thereof **To Have and to hold** the said Tract of Land Hereditaments and Premises hereby Granted or mentioned to be Granted with the Appurtenances unto the said Jacob Lyley his Heirs and Assigns to the only proper Use and Behoof of him the said Jacob Lyley his Heirs and Assigns forever

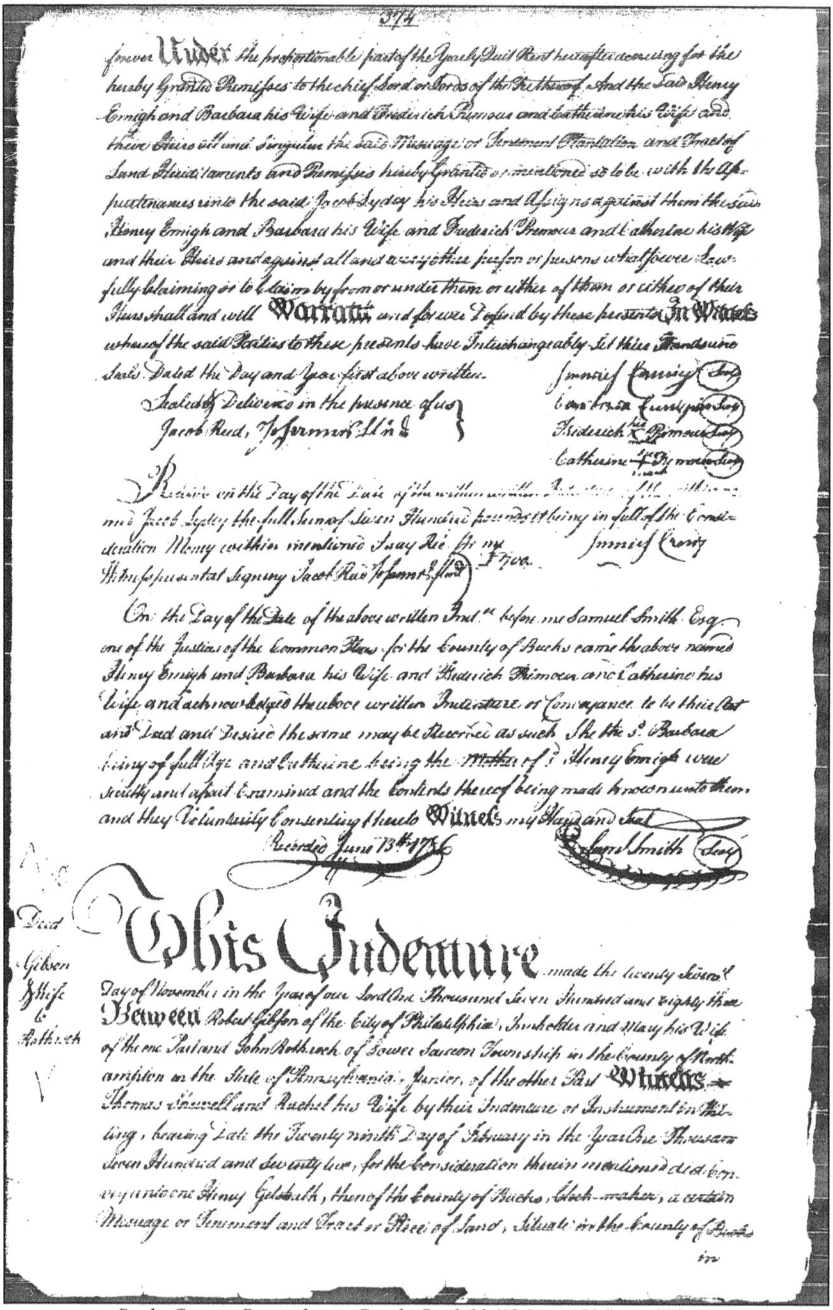
374

forever Under the proportionable part of the Yearly Quit Rent hereafter accruing for the hereby Granted Premises to the chief Lord or Lords of the Fee thereof. And the said Henry Emigh and Barbara his Wife and Frederick Rimour and Catherine his Wife and their Heirs all and Singular the said Messuage or Tenement Plantation and Tract of Land Hereditaments and Premises hereby Granted or mentioned so to be with the Appurtenances unto the said Jacob Sydey his Heirs and Assigns against them the said Henry Emigh and Barbara his Wife and Frederick Rimour and Catherine his Wife and their Heirs and against all and every other person or persons whatsoever Lawfully Claiming or to Claim by from or under them or either of them or either of their Heirs shall and will Warrant and forever Defend by these presents. In Witness whereof the said Parties to these presents have Interchangeably Set their Hands and Seals. Dated the Day and Year first above written.

Sealed & Delivered in the presence of us
Jacob Reed, Jo[illegible]

Henry Emigh (Seal)
Barbara [illegible] (Seal)
Frederick his X mark Rimour (Seal)
Catherine her X mark Rimour (Seal)

Received on the Day of the Date of the within written Indenture of the within named Jacob Sydey the full Sum of Seven Hundred pounds it being in full of the Consideration Money within mentioned I say Rec'd for me
£700.
Henry Emigh
Witness present at Signing Jacob Reed Jo[illegible]

On the Day of the Date of the above written Ind.re before me Samuel Smith Esq. one of the Justices of the Common Pleas for the County of Bucks came the above named Henry Emigh and Barbara his Wife and Frederick Rimour and Catherine his Wife and acknowledged the above written Indenture or Conveyance to be their Act and Deed and Desired the same may be Recorded as such She the s.d Barbara being of full Age and Catherine being the Mother of s.d Henry Emigh were secretly and apart Examined and the Contents thereof being made known unto them and they Voluntarily Consenting thereto Witness my Hand and Seal
Recorded June 13th 1786
Samuel Smith (Seal)

Deed Gibson & Wife to Rothrock

This Indenture made the twenty Seventh Day of November in the Year of our Lord One Thousand Seven Hundred and Eighty three Between Robert Gibson of the City of Philadelphia, Innholder and Mary his Wife of the one Part and John Rothrock of Lower Saucon Township in the County of Northampton in the State of Pennsylvania, Junior, of the other Part Whereas Thomas Sewell and Rachel his Wife by their Indenture or Instrument in Writing, bearing Date the Twenty ninth Day of February in the Year One Thousand Seven Hundred and Seventy two, for the Consideration therein mentioned did Convey unto one Henry Gilsbath, then of the County of Bucks, Clock-maker, a certain Messuage or Tenement and Tract or Piece of Land, Situate in the County of Bucks in

Bucks County, Pennsylvania Deeds, Book 22 (12 June 1786) pp. 372-74

Henry Amey and wife Barbara sold to John Mill on October 5, 1786 two tracts of land containing one hundred and thirty acres. The first tract called "Einbeck" and the second tract called "Embden" sold for eight hundred forty five "good gold, silver and coined money". It also stated that "John Mill "shall have liberty and privilege to take the stream of water out of the tale race of the Amey Grist Mill, so as to do no damage to the said mill." And continues: "for the use of watering meadow or any other use or purpose that he the said John Mill his heirs or assigns may see fit to put to use".[142] This was the 1765 patent land of Henry's father.

Henry, first son of Henry and Barbara Emig was born in Haycock, January 13, 1788 and baptized March 9, 1788 at Tohickon Church with Henry Laux & Barbara sponsors. The Emig name was spelled Oehmie in this record.[143]

Jacob Emig, second son of Henry and Barbara was born in Pennsylvania in 1789 but no record was found of baptism. He may have been born along the Great Wagon Road when the family moved.[144] 43rd Western District, Nicholas County, Virginia lists Jacob Amick, family #321, age 62, born in PA. Occupation – farmer with real estate valued at three hundred dollars.[145]

May 20, 1790 Henry Emigh and wife Barbara of Haycock conveyed to Michael Steinbach (Barbara's stepfather) of Haycock, forty-six acres of land on the Tohickon Creek and the road leading to Bethlehem for two hundred fifty pounds. The deed lists all previous owners to the original patent made out to John Henry Schoube, July 7, 1766 and recorded in *Patent Book D 2nd*, vol. 6 p. 210. "the two tracts above mentioned taking in the whole forty-six acres of land, of which two separate tracts Henry Keller was lawfully seized....Whereas: William Roberts, Esq., High Sheriff of the county of Bucks by his deed bearing date Twenty Nine Dec 1786, reciting as therein is at large recited did grant forty six acres and confirm the above two described pieces or tracts containing forty six acres there to belonging to Henry Emig, his heirs and assigns as...acknowledged in open court in Newtown by the said Robert high sheriff...and intended to be recorded."[146] This 1790 citation is the last mention of Henry in Bucks County.

Bucks County, Pennsylvania Deeds, Book 25 (1790) pp. 457-459

Bucks County, Pennsylvania Deeds, Book 25 (1790) pp. 457-459

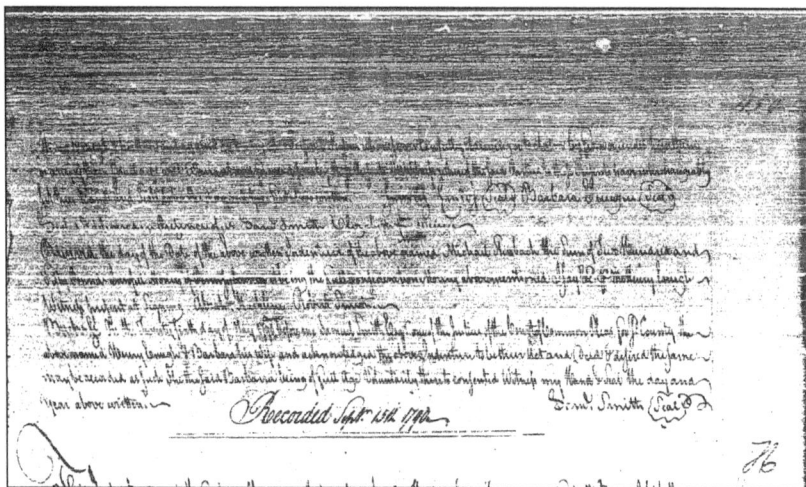

Bucks County, Pennsylvania Deeds, Book 25 (1790) pp. 457-459

Henry Keller had purchased the two tracts of land from John Drach and Eve his wife on August 28, 1780 for consideration "therein mentioned". The High Sheriff granted the forty-six acres to Henry Emigh, as Barbara's husband when Henry Keller died ("seized" meaning owning the land).

The deed was signed by Henry Emigh and Barbara Emigh on May 20, 1790 in the presence of Samuel Smith and Elizabeth Weise. The deed was recorded September 15, 1790 and witnessed to receipt by Abraham Kechlien and Robert Smith.

Barbara Emig's grandfather, Henry Keller, is mentioned in the preceding deed. He died in October 1782; and his will was probated November 4, 1782, at Doylestown, Bucks County. Barbara's mother Barbara (Keller) Niemand, now married to Michael Steinbach, received forty-three pounds as her share "as daughter of Henry Keller".[147]

Be it remembered that on the 15th day of November 1782 the within written last Will & Testament of Henry Heller dec'd was duly proved, when Letters testamentary were granted to John Heller, being for them named, he being first solemnly sworn well & truly to administer the Goods & Chattels, Rights & Credits of the s'd Deceased, also to exhibit into the Register's Office for the said county, within one Month from the above Date, a true Inventory and reasonable Appraisement of the same, and within twelve Months, or when thereunto lawfully required, to render a just Account of his whole Administration. In Testimony whereof I have hereunto set my Hand and the Seal of said Office the Day & Year abovesaid

John Heir & Reg'y

Be it remembered that I, Alexander Brown of the Township of New Brittain in the County of Bucks in Pennsylvania Yeoman, being considerably advanced in age and somewhat weak & infirm of Body, but of Sound & disposing Mind & Memory (Thanks be to God for the same) knowing the Uncertainty of time here and that it is appointed for all Men once to die have thought proper to make & publish this my last Will & Testament in Writing in Manner & Form following (that is to say) First & principally I recommend my Soul to God who gave it, and my Body to the Earth to be buried in a decent & Christian like Manner at the Discretion of my Executors hereinafter named, and as to such worldly Estate as it hath pleased the Lord to bless me & bestow me in this Life, and which I have not otherwise disposed of already I give devise & dispose thereof as follows:

First I Will that all my just Debts & funeral Expenses be fully paid & discharged

Secondly I give & bequeath to my beloved Wife Esther Brown my best Bed & Furniture all my wearing Apparel, my best Looking Glass and fifty pounds in Money. And twenty Pounds in Goods & Chattels to be taken as she shall chuse, and taken at the Appraisement Price to her, her Heirs & Assigns forever. Also give & bequeath to my said Wife during her natural Life, my great Bible and ...

Bucks County, Pennsylvania, *Register of Wills*, 1782, Estate #1756

Bucks County, Pennsylvania, Register of Wills, 1782, Estate #1756

The Keller Family

Barbara was descended from the Keller family and her uncle was Colonel Keller.

Keller Family Tree

Heinrich KELLER (1708 – 1792)
+Juliana KLEINDINST (1711 – 1785)
    Johan John Peter KELLER (1729 – 1738)
    Johanes "John" KELLER, Colonel (1732 – 1794)
    +Maria Margaret DRACH (1732 – 1794)
        John "Adam Peter" KELLER (1756 – 1813)
        +Maria Margaret BARNET
        Elizabeth KELLER (1758 -)
        +Peter DURANF (- 1771)
        +Jacob GOOD
        Henry KELLER (1760 – 1840)
        +Magdalena NICOLA (1776 – 1825)
        Anna Catherine "Barbara" KELLER (1761 – 1808)
        +Abrahan KACHLINE (1753 – 1837)
        Jonathan "John Adam" KELLER (1762 – 1850)
        +Elizabeth
        John Conrad KELLER (1764 -)
        Mary Anna "Magdalena" KELLER (1768 -)
        +John OTT(1767 -)
        Michael KELLER (1774 -)
        +Anna
        John Jacob KELLER (1777 -)
    Anna Margretha "Margaret"KELLER (1735 – 1767)
    +Solomon GRUVER (GRUBER) (1735 – 1811)
        John GRUVER (1757 -)
        +Anna Maria BERGE
        Elizabeth Barbara GRUVER (1762 -)
        +Christian STONE (Stien) (1760 -)
        Philip Heinrich GRUVER (1758 – 1795)
        +Elizabeth BERGER (1760 – 1798)
        John Peter GRUVER (1764 – 1811)

Keller Family Tree

Continued...
     Maria Elizabeth KELLER (1737 – 1778)
     +Philip STEVER, Captain (1737 – 1808)
         Barbara Elizabeth STEVER (1757 -)
         +George SHEFFER
         Margaret STEVER (1759 – 1769)
         Henry STEVER (1761 – 1769)
         Unknown (1762 -)
         Adam John STEVER (1764 – 1769)
         George John STEVER (1766 -)
         Juliana STEVER (1768 – 1769)
         John Adam "John" STEVER (1772 -)
         Michael STEVER (1774 -)
         Elizabeth STEVER
     Elizabeth Margaret Mary "Eliz" Barbara KELLER (1739 -)
     +John NIEMAND (- 1768)
         John NIEMAND (1761 -)
         Philip John NIEMAND (1762 -)
         Elzabeth Barbara NIEMAND (1764 -)
         +Henry AMICK (1762 – 1830)
         Peter John NIEMAND (1766 – 1816)
         Barbara STEINBACH
     +Michael STEINBACH (1746 – 1803)
         Elizabet STEINBACH (1770 -)
         Mr. GIER
         Christopher STEINBACH (1772 -)
     Anna Maria KELLER (1742 – 1814)
     +Johann Adam LITZENBERGER (1738 – 1812)
         Juliana LITZENBERGER
         John LITZENBERGER (1770 -)
         Maria Catherina LITZENBERGER (1774 -)
         +Henry APPEL
         John Peter LITZENBERGER (1778 -)
         Maria Philippina LITZENBERGER (1778 -)
         John LITZENBERGER (1781 - 1806)
         Wilamina LITZENBERGER (1782 – 1812)
         +Daniel BARTHOLOMEW
         +William SINE
         Solomon LITZENBERGER (1784 - 1857)
         +Susanna "Rebecca" KODER (1790 – 1845)

Keller Family Tree

Continued...
Johan Henrich "John Henry" KELLER (1745 – 1748)
Peter Johan John KELLER (1747 – 1830)
+Shibella "Sybil" FUNK (1750 – 1776)
Catherine KELLER (1772 -)
Barbara KELLER (1775 -)
+Maria Elizabeth WIMMER (1758 – 1786)
Elizabeth KELLER (1776 -)
Peter KELLER (1782 – 1862)
George KELLER (1783 – 1878)
+Elizabeth KACHLINE (1790 – 1868)
+Catherine APPEL
Mary KELLER
Unknown KELLER
Unknown KELLER
Jacob KELLER (1787 -)
John Henry KELLER (1789 – 1794)
Henry KELLER (1793 -)
+Catherine Appel (1795 -)
Anna Catherine KELLER (1794 -)
Maria "Mary" KELLER (1796 -)
Elizabeth KELLER (1797 -)
Lydia KELLER (1814 -)
Dorothea "Martha" KELLER (1749 – 1816)
+Johann Henrich "John Henry" STEINBACH (1750 – 1795)
Michael STEINBACH (1773 -)
+Maria SPRINGER
Christian STEINBACH (1775 – 1777)
Christain STEINBACH (1778 – 1779)
Anna Maria "Mary" STEINBACH (1780 -)
+Thomas BOND (1776 -)
John STEINBACH (1782 – 1864)
+Elizabeth TRISTLE (1786 – 1868)
George STEINBACH (1783 -)
Jacob STEINBACH (1785 -)
Johan George STEINBACH (1789 – 1847)
+Catherine (1789 – 1890)
Elizabeth STEINBACH (1792 -)

Keller Family Tree

Continued...
      Christopher KELLER (1751 – 1820)
      +Anna Margaretha "Margaret" DRACH (1759 – 1811)
            John KELLER (1781 – 1842)
            +Maria "Mary" BERNDT (1783 – 1873)
            Henry KELLER (1783 – 1831)
            +Elizabeth Catherine FOX (1792 – 1863)
            Michael KELLER (1786 – 1853)
            +Sara "Hannah" WIMMER (1800 – 1874)
            Elizabeth KELLER (1788 – 1900)
            +Abraham WAMBOLD (1786 -)
            Anna Catherine KELLER (1790 -)
            +Joseph STEELEY (1779 – 1817)
            +unknown ALGARD
            Samuel KELLER (1792 – 1864)
            +Elizabeth KULP (1794 – 1875)
            Joseph KELLER (1794 – 1877)
            +Maria "Anna Mary" APPLEBACH (1798 – 1876)
            Sara KELLER (1797 -)
            Daniel KELLER (1802 – 1833)
            +Elizabeth
      Henrich "Henry" KELLER (1755 -)
      +Margaret [HINKLE] LAUDENSLAGER
            Henry KELLER (1780 -)
            +Sarah
            Michael KELLER (1780 -)

A brief history of the Keller family is found at http://www.kellerkin.com/ and is included here. Although citations are not listed most of the facts are consistent with the citations appearing elsewhere in this document.[148]

> Henry of Heinrich Keller arrived in Philadelphia on the good ship "Glasgow" September 9th, 1738. From the records of Keller's Church, we have the following: "Heinrich Keller was born January 9th, 1708 and died October 18, 1782, his father's name was Wilhelm Keller and his Mother's name was Gertraut, in Weierbach, out of Naumburch, Braden. and came to America September 9th, 1738. On the 20th of October,

1728, he married Juliana, born in 1711: her Father's name was Peter Kleindinst and Mother's name Anna Maria, also out of Weierbach, Naumburch. Her Father held an Office there."

Their eldest child Peter died within a week of their landing and seven others were born to them in Pennsylvania.

After Henry (Heinrich)'s arrival, the first record of him as a landholder was in 1750, when he purchased of Thomas and Richard Penn 150 acres in Bedminster township, on the northwest side of the Ridgeroad. This tract he conveyed to Michael Yost in 1752. His residence at that date as shown by the deed was Bedminster. In the year 1734, a tract of 300 acres on the north side of the Tohickon, in Haycock township, was sold to Henry (Heinrich) Keller on May 10, 1757.

On November 05, 1754, Henry (Heinrich) Keller obtained a warrant for the survey of 21 acres and 136 perches at the northwest corner of the above tract and the draft of survey, on file at Harrisburg, shows that the Davis tract was then in the tenure of Henry (Heinrich) Keller. It is therefore probable the Henry (Heinrich) Keller took possession of the tract soon after his sale of his Bedminster land in 1752, under an agreement to purchase that was not completed until the date of the over the Tohickon into Bedminster township at two or three points, caused by curves of the creek. Of this tract of 300 acres purchased of Davis, Henry (Heinrich) Keller and Juliana, his wife, 1772, conveyed about 225 acres in three practically equal tracts to their sons Henry, Peter and Christopher. His son John, had purchased a large tract adjoining his father in 1772 of David Graham. Henry (Heinrich) Keller was a man of prominence in his community. He was the first constable of Haycock Township, and was frequently named by the Court or selected by the parties to assist in the settlement of estates.

He is buried beside his wife, Juliana, in the graveyard at Keller's Church. His will, dated January 23, 1782, probated November 1, 1782, devises to his wife "my dwelling house together with all other buildings as it is mentioned in a certain article between Peter Keller and Christopher Keller, together with all incomes of my four sons, that is to say, John Keller, Peter Keller, Christopher Keller, and Henry Keller, as it is mentioned in a certain article of agreement [together with her personal goods and his personal estate] and 100 pounds shall stand upon interest if she should want it, ... all this she shall have so long as she remain my wife. " To his four sons he devises 75 pounds each and to his five daughters 50 pounds each.

The first place of worship in Bucks County was at the Tohickon Church, and dates back to 1743. It was called Keichlines Church, as he is reported to have given the land on which the first building, a log structure, was built. This building, also used as a school house, was replaced by a stone building by 1766. By 1749 the church was a union church - that is, it housed two congregations. One was the Lutheran congregation, the other a German Reformed congregation. The first full time Reformed minister was Jacob Riesz.

Melchoir Muhlenburg sent them a catechist in 1751 named Lucas Rauss. Under his supervision the church began to grow. A warrant for land for the erection of a church building was taken out. The survey is dated 5 November 1752. [However, the patent for this land was not issued until 5M ay 1857.] Henry (Heinrich) Keller was one of the active leaders in the development of this church. His farm was opposite the present Upper Bucks Technical School. The first church was made of logs. Keller's Church was a union church as well. It's sister congregation was Solomon's Reformed Church. The two churches separated now, alternated services on Sunday mornings and afternoons. The church in the community was a unifying organization for the people of the area. It offered its congregation reassurance - a time to see relatives and neighbors - and a time to hear a word of hope. Politics did enter into the church - the various ministers told the people what their faith expected of them at the time of the Revolution.

Henry (Heinrich) was the chief founder of Kellers' Church in 1746. He purchased a large tract of land extending across the Tohickon Creek into Haycock Township and lived there until his death. He was one of the trustees who, on July 28, 1751, secured title to the twenty-acre tract upon which the first church, known as "Kellers," was erected; and he was one of the elders and trustees of that church until he died.

During the Revolutionary struggle, his eldest son, Colonel John Keller, was one of the most prominent men of his nationality in Bucks County. He was a member of colonial assembly in 1776, and in the same year a delegate to the first constitutional convention, and in 1778 was a member of the supreme executive council. In 1784, he was again returned as a member of the Supreme Executive Council. At the organization of the Bucks county militia in 1776, he was commissioned lieutenant-colonel of the Third Battalion, and in 1780 was assigned to the command of the Second Battalion. His Battalion was in active service during the greater part of the war. His brothers Christopher and Henry, and his brother-in-law Philip Stever, were also in the service, Christopher as an ensign in the Fourth Battalion where he participated in the Battle of Long Island, and Henry as a captain under Colonel Keller.

The Pennsylvania Constitutional convention which John Keller attended took place in late June, the new convention representatives met in Philadelphia and by July 8 elected delegates to write a new state constitution. The constitution was proclaimed by the Convention on September 28, 1776. It is considered the most democratic in America. It was authored by Timothy Matlock, Dr. Thomas Young, George Bryan, James Cannon, and Benjamin Franklin. The constitution made Pennsylvania a Commonwealth. The Constitution proclaimed in detail the rights of citizens and expanded the voting franchise to all tax paying free men.[149,150,151] The constitution was opposed by John Adams, Thomas Jefferson and James Madison for having a single chamber leading to a weakened and divided state.[152]

Tavern at Kellersville, Bucks County.
Taken 2007

Grave of Heinrich Keller, born 1708 died 1782
Keller Church Graveyard, taken 2007

Grave of John Keller
Keller Church Graveyard, taken 2007

Grave of Christopher Keller, born 1751 died 1890
Keller Church Graveyard, taken 2007

Grave of Michael Keller, born 1786 died 1852
Keller Church Graveyard, taken 2007

The Nicholas Family

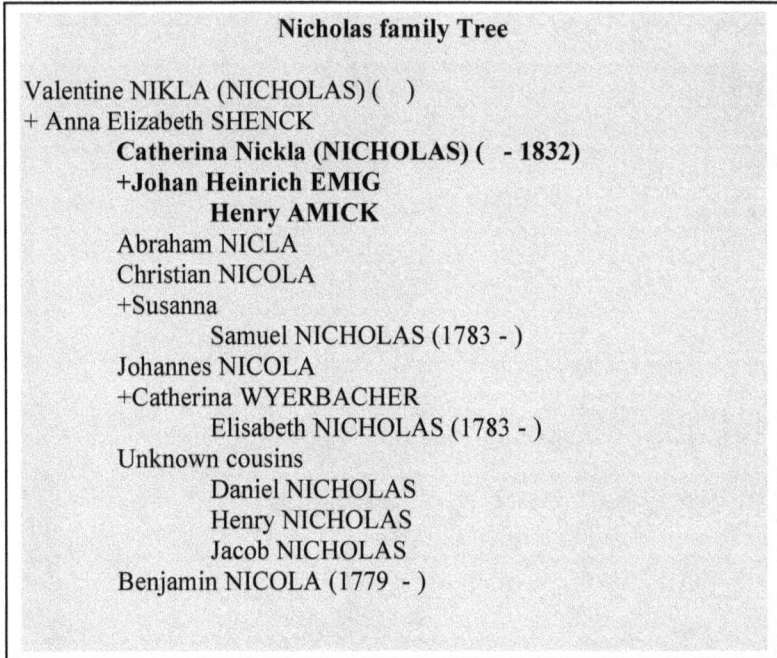

Nicholas family Tree

Valentine NIKLA (NICHOLAS) (   )
+ Anna Elizabeth SHENCK
    Catherina Nickla (NICHOLAS) (- 1832)
    +Johan Heinrich EMIG
    Henry AMICK
    Abraham NICLA
    Christian NICOLA
    +Susanna
        Samuel NICHOLAS (1783 -)
    Johannes NICOLA
    +Catherina WYERBACHER
        Elisabeth NICHOLAS (1783 -)
    Unknown cousins
        Daniel NICHOLAS
        Henry NICHOLAS
        Jacob NICHOLAS
    Benjamin NICOLA (1779 -)

Catherina Nickla was Henry Amick's mother.   Catherina's father was Valentine Nikla and her mother Anna Shenck. The name is variously spelled Nikla, Nicholas or modern spelling Nichols. Several of the Nikla cousins fought in the Revolutionary War with Henry.

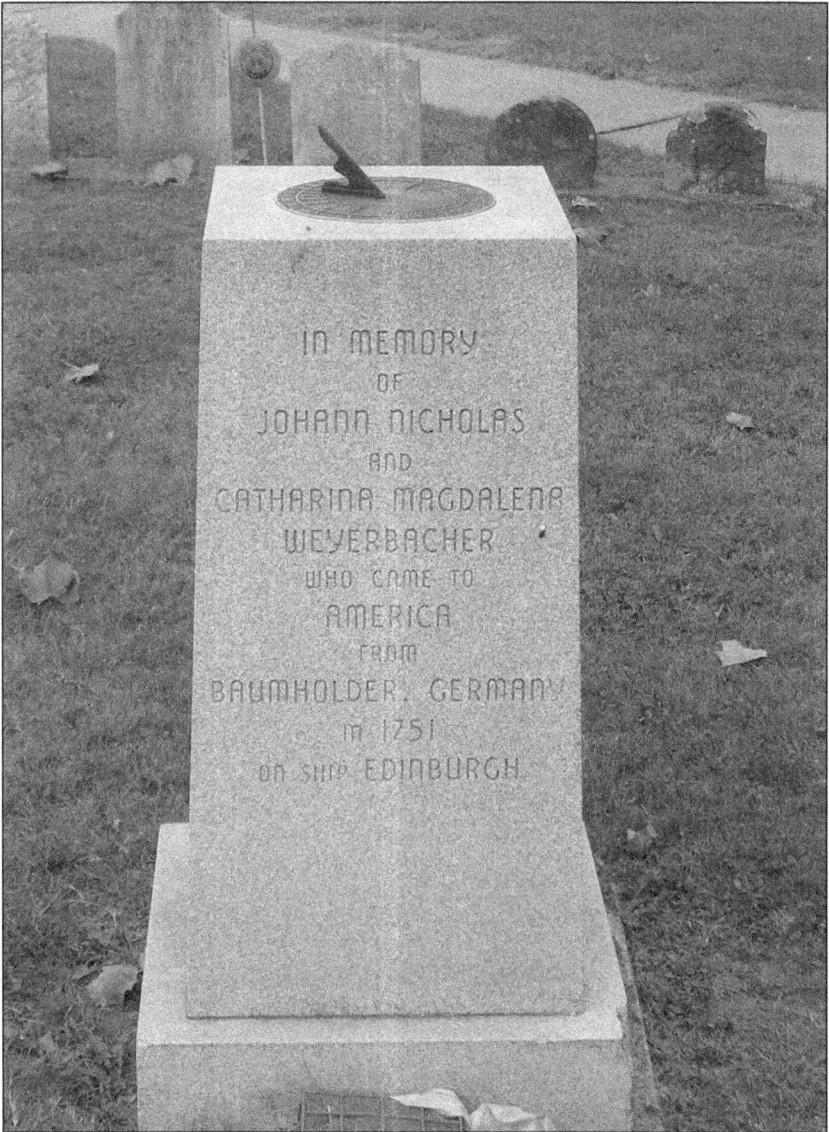

Memorial to Johann Nicholas and Catherina Wyerbacher
located at the Trinity Union Church graveyard, Springfield Township

Grave of Valatine Nichola
Note that the red and gray local sandstones do not weather well
Keller Church Graveyard, taken 2007

Henry Nickel
located at the Trinity Union Church graveyard, Springfield Township

Grave of Benjamin Nichola, 1779
Keller Church Graveyard, taken 2007

Grave of Jacob Nichola
Keller Church Graveyard, taken 2007

Grave of Joseph Nicholas, born 1831 died 1832
Keller Church Graveyard, taken 2007

Grave of Catherine Nicholas, daughter of Daniel and Catherine, born 1813 died 1838
Keller Church Graveyard, taken 2007

Grave of Emeline Nicholas, daughter of Daniel and Catherine, born 1818 died 1838
Keller Church Graveyard, taken 2007

The Steinbach Family

```
Steinbach Family Tree

Leonard STEINBACH
+Apolonia
        Christian STEINBACH (1710 – )
        +Anna Dorothea SCAFER (1708 – )
                Christan Ulich STEINBACH (1732 – 1732)
                Micheal STEINBACH (1734 – 1746)
                Christian STEINBACH (1736 – 1746)
                John Jacob STEINBACH (1739 – 1746)
                John George STEINBACH (1740 - )
                John Balthaser STEINBACH (1742 - )
                Maria Barbara STEINBACH (1744 – 1744)
                Micheal STEINBACH (1746 - 1814)
                +Elisabeth Barbara (KELLER) NIEMAND
                        Elisabeth STONEBACK (1770 – 1813)
                        Christopher STONEBACK (1772- 1821)
                John Henry STEINBACH (1750)
```

Christian Steinbach and wife Dorothea immigrated from Rublingen, Langenburg, Hoheloh arriving in Pennsylvania September 11, 1732 on the ship *Pensilvania Merchant*, John Stedman, Master.[153]   Christian and Dorothea settled in the unorganized district that now comprises Haycock Township receiving a land warrant of 100 acres in Bucks County surveyed June 20, 1744.[154] Son Micheal was a deacon at Keller's Church in 1751. Michael married the widow Elisabeth Niemand on May 23, 1769 at Keller's Church.[155] Michael Steinbach, now in English records as "Stoneback" is listed in Captain Stever's Company, Bucks County Militia with Andrew Kechlien, Esq., listed as sub-Lieutenant.[156]

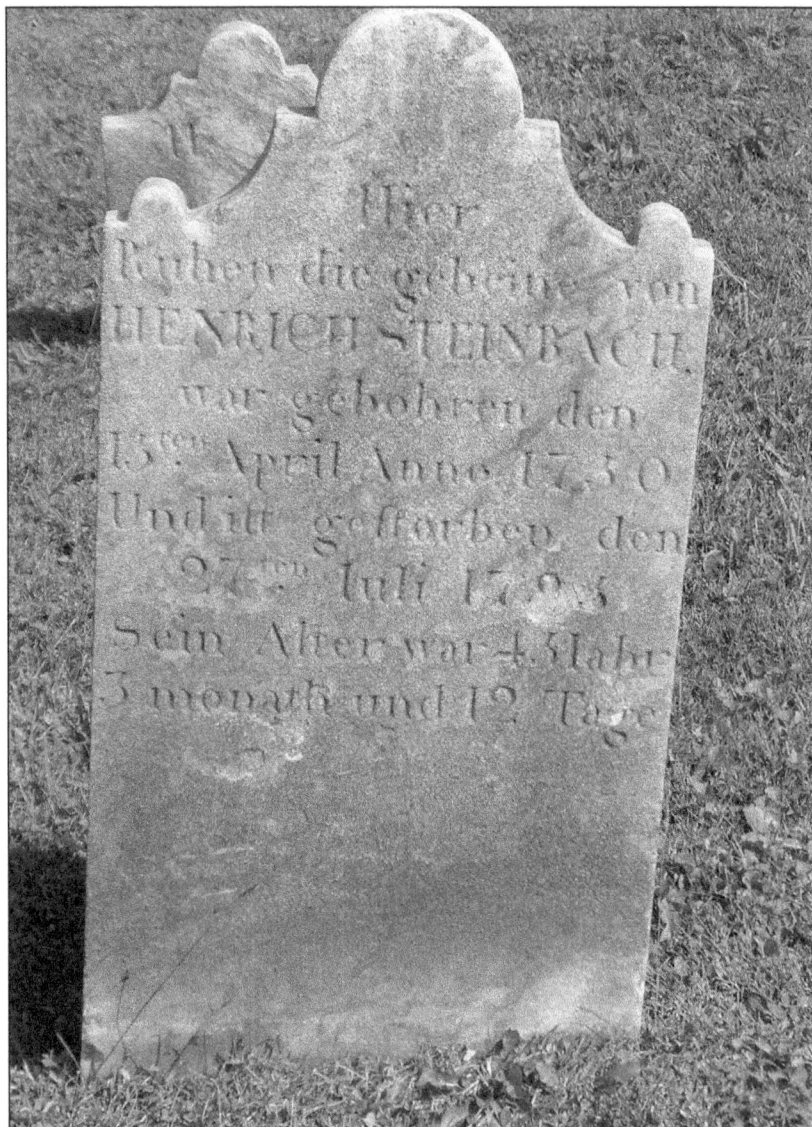

Grave of Henrich Steinbach, 1730 - 1796
Keller Church Graveyard, taken 2007

Grave of Dorothia Steinbach, died 1816
Keller Church Graveyard, taken 2007

The George Emig/Amey Family

George Emig/Amey Family

Johan Georg EMIG (1751 – 1829)
+Anna Margaretha LERCH (1754 – 1829)
      George EMIG (1774 -   )
      Anna Maria EMIG (1778 – 1805)
      Johannes EMIG (1779 – 1849)
      Samuel EMIG (1782 -   )
      Petrus EMIG (1784 -   )
      Anthony EMIG (1789 – 1842)
      Joseph EMIG (1793 – 1842)
      Catharine EMIG (1795 -   )
      David EMIG (1798 -   )
      Magdalena EMIG (1800 -   )

See the previous section on Henry and Georg Emig for the Haycock Township tax records after the war.

Grave of Johannes Emig, 1779 - 1819
Trinity Lutheran Church Graveyard, Springfield Township
Taken 2007

Grave of Joseph Amey, 1793 - 1842
Trinity Lutheran Church Graveyard, Springfield Township
Taken 2007

Grave of Levi Amey (1805-1877) and to the right daughter Amelia (1849- 1866),
to the left not shown wife Christina
Trinity Lutheran Church Graveyard, Springfield Township
Taken 2007

Grave of Saloma Amey
Trinity Lutheran Church Graveyard, Springfield Township
Taken 2007

Berks County Emmicks

There are other Henry Emigs living in Pennsylvania at the same time as Henry Amick. Henry Emig, Nicholas Emmick's brother, is listed in the 1790 Cumru census as head of household with two males under sixteen and two females.[157] Henry Emig did not appear in the Cumru census of 1800.[158] Cumru was settled by Germans on the road heading west.[159]

There are also citations for baptism for Henry Emig's children:[160]

1778, Aug. 30   Maria Margareth, daughter of Henry Emig. Sponsors, Nicholas Lerch and wife Elizabeth.
1780, Aug. 13   Elizabeth Magdalena, daughter of Henry Emig. Sponsors, Christian Young (Iung) and wife Elizabeth Magdalena

There are still Emig's living in Berks County:

Emig, Dorothy D.
[Source: *Hamburg Area Item*, December 18, 2002. Submitted by: Nancy McD.]

> Services were held in the Bean Funeral Home, Sinking Spring, for Dorothy D. Emig, 82, formerly of Jeffrey Road, Bern Township, who died Dec. 7 in Mifflin Court, Cumru Township, where she had resided over three years. Burial was in Forest Hills Memorial Park, Reiffton. She was predeceased by her husband, G. Robert Emig, who died June 10, 1989. Born in Auburn, N.Y., she was a daughter of the late Eugene and Bertha (Kropacek) Drew. Until retiring in 1985, she was employed as vice president of Robert Emig Products Inc., Reading, for 40 years. She was a member of Bausman Memorial United Church of Christ, Wyomissing. Surviving are a son, Lawrence D. Emig, Cumru Township; a daughter, Cynthia J. (Emig) Miller, Bern Township; and four grandchildren.

Clippings from the *Reading Eagle*, October 24, 1941

> Berks County Soldiers Depart for Training. New Cumberland Reception Center lists Donald E. Emig, 1515 N. 15th St.

Daniel Boone in Berks County

The Boone family were Quakers and were subject to persecution in England. They emigrated to "Penn's Woods" as a haven where they could worship as they pleased. The family first settled outside Philadelphia near Gwynned.

The Bertolet House was built in Oley between 1737 and 1750 and moved to the Daniel Boone Homestead in 1968, it is representative of the period dwellings in Berks County, Pennsylvania of the period

Squire Boone married Sarah Morgan in 1726. She was a Welsh Quaker girl whose family was prominent in the Gwynned Meeting in Bucks. During the first ten years of their married life Squire and Sarah lived in a stone house on the bank of the Neshaminy Creek near the town of Chalfont, in Bucks County. In 1730 they moved to Oley Valley in Berks County not far from the Schuylkill River. With the help of his neighbors, Squire Boone built a log cabin on a stone foundation. He built his cabin over a spring so that water would be readily available, and in order to provide a cool place for perishable food, safe from marauding Indians and wild animals. They lived at the Berks County Homestead until 1750, when they migrated to the Yadkin Valley, South Carolina. Later owners built a stone house on the site which is still standing to this day.

Daniel, the sixth of twelve children, was born on November 2, 1734. It was during the fourteen years of his youth in Pennsylvania that Daniel began to develop his skill as a woodsman.

The Boone homestead is very close to Cumru Township and Nicholas Emmick's home. Some of the buildings found there are of the same period and would be similar to the general construction used at the time.

You can find out more about the Daniel Boone homestead in Berks County at: http://kyky.essortment.com/travelhistorica_rnit.htm.

The Second Generation out to Virginia

Henry Amick and wife Barbara sold to John Mill on October 5, 1786 two tracts of land containing one hundred and thirty acres. Henry Amick and wife Barbara sold the land before 1790 and moved to Virginia. They settled in the Brandywine region of Pendleton County on the slopes of the Shenandoah Mountains north of Franklin near the old sink hole. In 1793, forty acres were surveyed for Henry Amick and Nicholas Emmick lying in the forks of Mill Run Gap between lands of Sophia Propst and Emmick's land. Nicholas was Henry's cousin, a son of Philip Emig. Nicholas Emmick later left Pendleton County and moved to Kentucky.

The second generation family…

```
┌─────────────────────────────────────────────────────────────────┐
│                                                                   │
│                  Family Tree Second Generation                    │
│                                                                   │
│  Johan Heinrich EMIG (1737/1739 – 1777)                           │
│  +Anna Catharina NICOLAS (1739/1740 – 1832)                       │
│          Henry AMICK (1762 – 1830)                                │
│          +Elisabeth Barbara NIEMAND (1764 – 1810)                 │
│                  Elisabeth AMICK (1784 – 1800)                    │
│                  Henry AMICK (1788 –    )                         │
│                  Jacob AMICK (1789 – 1869)                        │
│                  John the Miller AMICK (1790 – 1846)              │
│                  Mary AMICK (1797 –    )                          │
│                  Barbara AMICK (1799 –    )                       │
│                  Elizabeth AMICK (1800 – 1856)                    │
│                  Reuben AMICK (1805 –    )                        │
│                  Elias AMICK (1808 – 1881)                        │
│          Catherine                                                │
│                  Christina AMICK                                  │
│                  Catherine AMICK                                  │
│  Johan Philip EMIG (1745 -   )                                    │
│  +Barbara HAHN)                                                   │
│          Nicholas EMMICK (1766 – 1836)                            │
│          +Catherine Hertzel (1769 – 1793)                         │
│                  John Nicholas AMICK                              │
│                  Sally                                            │
│                  Anny                                             │
│                  Betsy                                            │
│          +Susanna SMITH (1777 – 1833) second wife                 │
│                  Mary EMMICK (1797 - )                            │
│                  Jacob EMMICK (1799 – 1850)                       │
│                  Elizabeth EMMICK (1803 – 1830)                   │
│                  Katherine EMMICK (1805 - 1834)                   │
│                  George EMMICK (1811 – 1886)                      │
│                  Allettia EMMICK                                  │
│                  Eliza Jane EMMICK                                │
│                  Nancy EMMICK (1819 - 1859)                       │
│                                                                   │
└─────────────────────────────────────────────────────────────────┘
```

Western Pennsylvania was settled by Pennsylvania Dutch and Scots-Irish. Early on, German immigrants in eastern Pennsylvania started feuding with the Quaker authorities in Philadelphia. This is why they settled the back country and are known as the Pennsylvania Dutch. Catholic Scots and Irish immigrants joined them, chased out of Philadelphia by the Quakers, who complained that one Irishman was more trouble than fifty Englishmen.

It appears that Henry Emig/Amick began moving south from Bucks County about 1790. He is not found in the Pennsylvania census and there was no census in Virginia for that year. It is likely that Henry knew Michael Propst through his wife Anna Maria Keller. Anna Maria was the widow of Peter Keller. The relationship to the Bucks County Kellers is not known. Michael Propst arrived from Germany on the same ship as the York Amick family line and this may be the relationship. The Propst had been making powder and the draw of good work and the push of Quaker laws may have motivated Henry Amick to move.

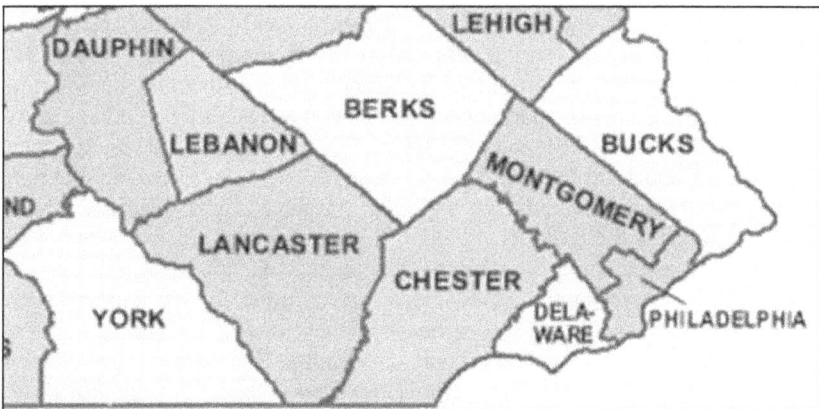

Pennsylvania Counties

The Whiskey Rebellion

Whiskey was an important trade good because it was easier to transport over the mountains than corn or grain. Whiskey became a cash crop in exchange for goods when cash was in short supply.

German distillers near Philadelphia sold Washington's quartermasters "wudka", rye was used for vodka in Germany. Washington's troops drank Old Man Rye at Valley Forge and everywhere they went. When the farm distillers moved to the Allegheny, they made what they already knew how to make. Stored in oak barrels, it became known as "Monongahela Rye." Many of these immigrants sought religious freedom, and formed small community churches, with mills and distilleries. Samuel Bechtel, a Mennonite settler in 1776 built a self-contained flour mill, blacksmith shop, and distillery. Mennonite Abraham

Overholt established a mill and distillery in 1810. Elijah Craig was a Baptist minister with a mill and a distillery.

The immigrants from Germany, Scotland, Ireland, and Switzerland had no scruples against moderate drinking and brought experience and skills in the distilling of alcoholic liquor. Whiskey distilling, and occasionally brewing, on a small scale was fairly common among the settlers in the pioneer communities of colonial and later days, particularly in Pennsylvania and into the Allegheny Mountains. Tradesmen expected a drink as part of wages. Soldiers received four drams per day.

To pay for the revolution, the Continental Congress put a tax on whiskey distilling. The Government had levied a tax on strong drink in 1791. The debate on the tax occurred in 1790, and with its potential passage and impact to daily lives, many Pennsylvania Germans began moving into the wilderness where government involvement and oversight would be more difficult. The frontiersmen considered the tax a scheme to pick the pockets of the poor as it taxed the frontier farmer's staple crop. Already distrustful of national authority, the farmers openly rebelled. The stubborn Dutch settlers refused to pay. To restore order during the "Whiskey Rebellion" of 1791-1794, Washington sent 6,000 troops of the Continental Army to quell the uprising. In 1794, in the four western counties of Pennsylvania, vigilantes grew increasingly violent and blew up the stills of those that paid the tax and even threatened an attack on Pittsburgh. On August 7, 1794, President Washington called out 12,000 militiamen from Virginia, Maryland, Pennsylvania and New Jersey to suppress the rebellion. Under the command of General Henry Lee the force marched from Harrisburg across the Alleghenies but met no opposition.[161] To save the government further troubles with the stubborn Dutch, Washington agreed to pardons if they moved to the Allegheny Mountains which at that time was part of Virginia. The settlers were offered land if they would build a house and raise 60 acres of corn. The tax turned the Allegheny Dutch farmers into staunch Anti-Federalists for generations.

Although it occurred several years after Henry and Nicholas left, Fries Rebellion of 1798 shows the reaction of the local German population around Haycock Township to the Federal Governments taxation. This time the tax was levied on each fireplace in a home in order to raise funds in preparation for war with France. In eastern Pennsylvania, the tax assessors were largely Quakers and Moravians who had abstained from Revolutionary participation and were recruited by the administration of John Adams to levy taxes against their patriot German Reformed and Lutheran neighbors. The House Tax was a reincarnation of the hated "Hearth Tax" in Germany.

The Confrontation, Enoch Roberts' Tavern in Quakertown near the Emig homestead in Haycock Township. March 6, 1799

John Fries became a leader of the opposition to the tax and in 1798 he began to lead a band of about 60 armed men around the countryside near Quakertown and Milford. At Roberts' Tavern several of the tax collectors where attacked. After raising troops the government captured Fries and put down the rebellion.

The Emig families were distillers of rye whiskey prior to the Revolution on their homesteads in Bucks County. Old Henry Amick and wife Barbara sold the land in Bucks County in 1790 and moved to Germany Valley Pendleton County, Virginia with their family.

Emigration routes were well known at the time and before the Revolutionary war Germans were moving into the Shenandoah Valley. From Tindal and Shi[162]: "...Germans filtered southward along what came to be called the Great Philadelphia Road, the primary internal migration route during the colonial period. It headed west from the port city, traversing Chester and Lancaster counties, and turned southwest at Harris' Ferry (now Harrisburg), where it crossed the Susquehanna. Continuing south across western Maryland, it headed down the Shenandoah Valley of Virginia, and on into the Carolina and Georgia backcountry. Germans were first in the upper Shenandoah Valley."

The "Ohio Path" was a name given to several paths that went from Delaware through Pennsylvania to the Forks of the Ohio River. The path went from Bethlehem to Oley called the "Oley path," and onto Lititz and Lancaster in Lancaster County, Middletown and Harris's Ferry (Harrisburg) in Dauphin County. Then the "Raystown Path" (now Bedford) went from Carlisle, Cumberland County, on to Shippensburg, Franklin County, and to Raystown, Bedford County and continued to Sannopins Town at the Forks of the Ohio.[163]

From Raystown the "Warrior's Path" follows present-day US 220 to Cumberland, Maryland and the Potomac River. The South Branch of the Potomac River, near Ft. Cumberland, flows south into Virginia (now West Virginia).

The family moved out to the Allegheny Mountains about the time of the Whiskey Rebellion and the family name changed the spelling to Amick. Nicholas Emmick and his family also moved to Pendleton County. The Amicks, Propsts, Pitsenbarger, Eyes and Nichols made one extended family in Germany Valley. The Propsts had lived in the valley for generations before the Revolutionary War. The Amicks, Nichols, Eyes and Pitsenbarger joined them from Pennsylvania after the war.

Here working with the Propst and Nicholas families the Amicks made black powder and built roads. The Nicholas', sometimes known as Nichols, were road contractors and supervisors. The biggest consumer of black powder at the time was the construction of the B&O Railroad line over the Alleghany Mountains. Old Henry's son John was known as John "the miller' to distinguish him from the other Johns in the family. He ran the powder mill. The Propst family also made powder. Jacob Sr., another son of Old Henry, worked powder on the roads setting charges. The Nicholas brothers supervised the work and the whole extended families were in road construction.

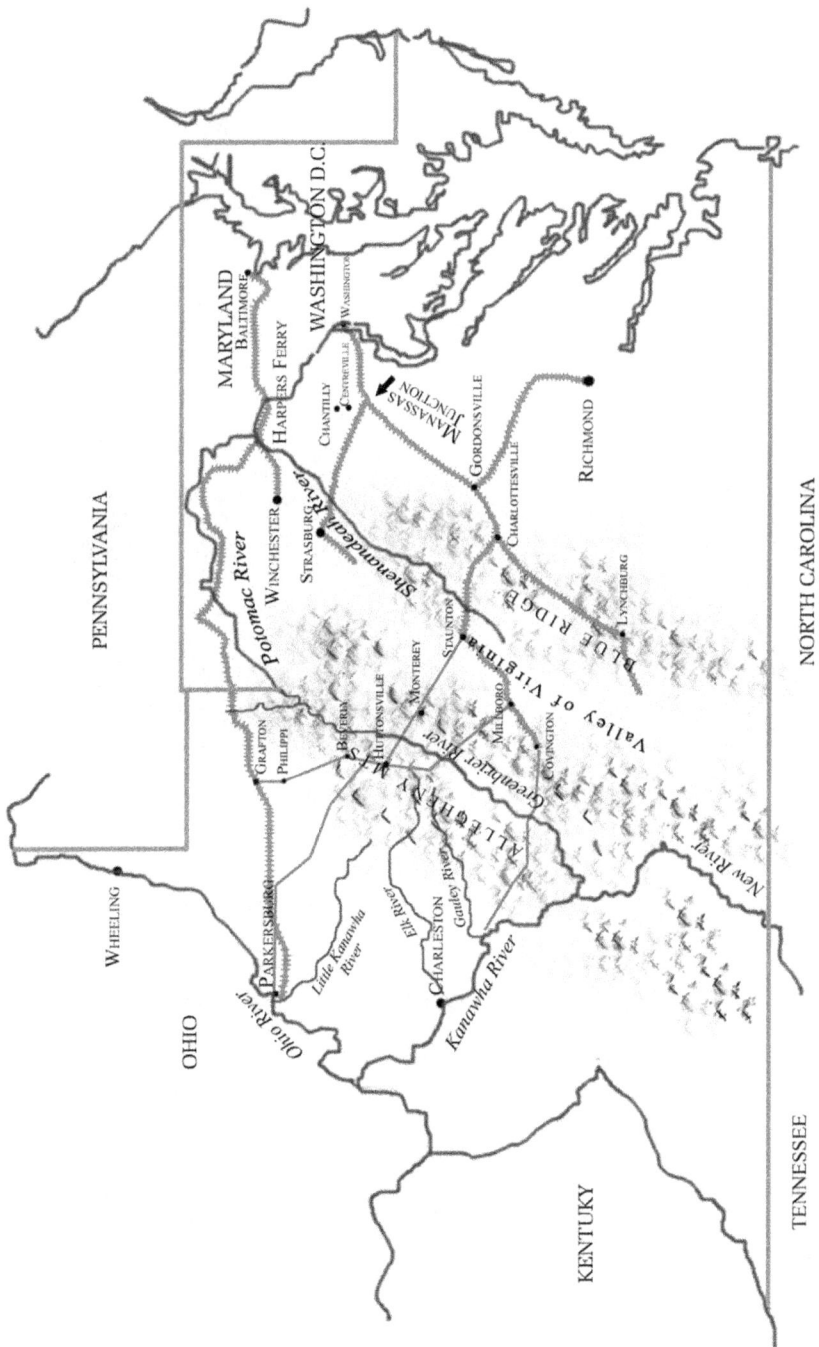

The Family in Pendleton County

Looking over the rolling hills of the South Branch Potomac Valley from Shenandoah Mountain, taken 2007

It appears that Nicholas Emmick went first to Virginia and settled in Rockingham County near Pendleton County. Louise Emmick Reithel, in her work on Nicholas Emmick cites *The 1787 Census of Virginia*, Vol. 1, pg. 639 stating:[164]

> The 1787 Census of Virginia was compiled from Taxpayer Records. This Census lists Nicholas Ameigh on Tax Lists 'A' living in Rockingham County, Virginia, in the District of Commissioner Reuben Moore. He and his family remained in Rockingham County for a few more years.

Henry Amick [spelled Ame and Emick in these records] settled in the Brandywine region of Pendleton County on the slopes of the Shenandoah Mountains and is listed in land records of November 1791.

Road marker outside Franklin Court House, taken 2007

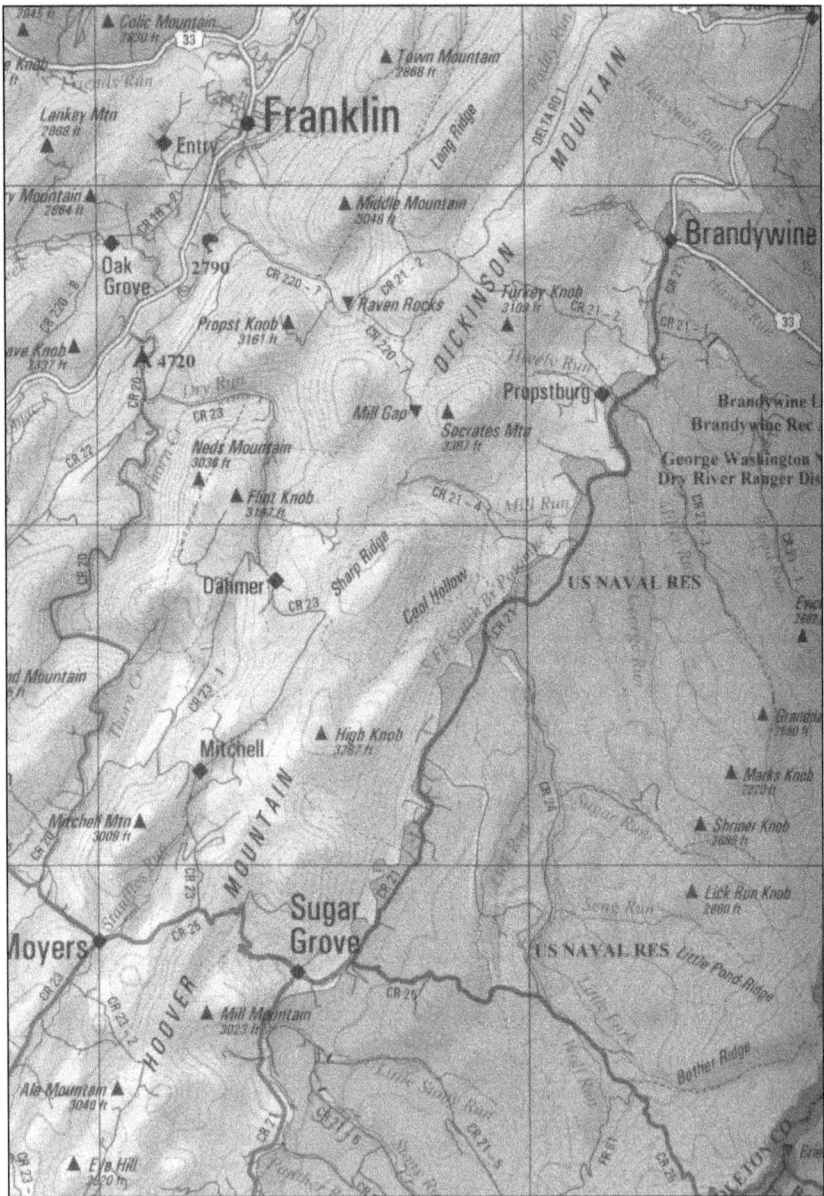

Current Map of Franklin Area; West Virginia Atlas & Gazetteer, DeLorme; page 48

Henry Ame resident of Pendleton County dated 3 Nov. 1791 reads:[165]

> ...indenture made the third day of November, One Thousand
> Seven Hundred and Ninety One between Philip Echart and his
> wife of the county of Pendleton of one part and Henry Ame of
> the said county of the other part. Witnessed that the said
> Philip Echart for and in consideration of the sum of Twenty
> Pounds current money of Virginia to him in hand paid doth
> Bargain & Sell unto the said Henry Ame and to his heirs and
> Assigns a certain tract of land containing One Hundred and
> Three acres by survey Bearing date the Fourth day of April
> One Thousand Seven Hundred and Eighty-Three, lying and
> being in the county of Pendleton on the mountain between the
> South Fork and the South Branch of Potomac at a place called
> the Sink Holes and bounded as follows:
> Beginning at a chestnut near a line of Henry Stone and
> running thence South Sixty Three (63) degrees East Forty (40)
> Poles to a Hickory and white Oak...

153

Together with all its Appurtenances to have and to hold the said Land with its Appurtenances to the said George Reynolds and to his heirs to the Sole Use and Behoof of the Said George Reynolds & his heirs forever. And the said John Davis and William Smith for themselves and their heirs doth Covenant with the said George Reynolds and his heirs in behalf of the said Abraham Smith and his heirs the said Land with all its Appurtenances unto the said George Reynolds and his heirs against all persons whatsoever and will forever Warrant and defend. In Witness whereof the said John Davis and William Smith have hereunto Subscribed their names and Affixed their Seals the day and year above written.

Signed Sealed and delivered }
in Presence of   }   John Davis (Seal)
                   Wm Smith (Seal)

At a Court held for Pendleton County November the [ ] 1791. This Indenture of Bargain & Sale from John Davis and Wm Smith Executors of Abraham Smith decd. to George Reynolds was acknowledged by Gawen Hamilton Attorney in fact for said Executors and Ordered to be recorded.

Test   Gawen Hamilton

This Indenture made the third day of November One Thousand Seven hundred and ninety one Between Philip Stewart and his wife of the County of Pendleton of the one part and Henry Amee of the said County of the other part Witnesseth that the said [ ] for and in consideration of the Sum of Twelve Pounds current Money of Virginia to him in hand paid doth Bargain & Sell unto the said Henry Amee and to his heirs and Assigns a certain Tract of Land Containing One Hundred and thirteen Acres by Survey Bearing date the fourth day of April One thousand Seven hundred and Eighty three Lying and being in the County of Pendleton on the Mountain between the South fork and the South Branch of Potomack at a place called the Sink holes and Bounded as followeth (Viz) Beginning at a Chesnut near a line of Honey Stones and running thence South Sixty three degrees East forty Poles to a Mineral and white oak near said Stones thence North Twenty two degrees East Sixty Six Poles to a White Oak North Seventy one Degrees East Ninety two Poles to a Chesnut North forty five degrees East forty four Poles to a Chesnut North thirty degrees East Eighty two poles to a Black North twelve degrees west forty six poles to a Spanish Oak North Thirty eight degrees West forty three Poles to a white oak

154

on the top of the Mountain South thirty five degrees West
three hundred and fifteen Poles to the Beginning &c &c &c
Together with all its Appurtenances to have and to hold the said
Tract of Land with its appurtenances unto the said Henry
Arne his heirs and Assigns to the Sole use and behoof of him
the said Henry Arne his heirs and Assigns forever. And the
said Philip Echart and his Wife for themselves and their heirs
doth Covenant with the said Henry Arne and his heirs and
Assigns that they the said Philip Echart and his Wife and
their heirs the said Land with the Appurtenances unto
the said Henry Arne and his heirs and his heirs and
Assigns against all persons whatsoever will warrant and
forever defend In witness whereof the said Philip Echart
and his wife have hereunto Subscribed their hands and
Affixed their Seals this day & year above written

     Philip ☓ Echart (Seal)
      mark
     Barbara ☓ Echart (Seal)

At a Court held for Pendleton County Nov 7. 1791. This
Indenture of Bargain & Sale from Philip Echart and Barbara
his Wife to Henry Arne was Acknowledged by the said Philip
She the said Barbara being privily examined as the Law directs
and Ordered to be recorded Test

     Gawin Hamilton

This Indenture made the fourth day of June In the
year of our Lord One thousand seven hundred and eighty
three between Nicholas Seman and Margaret his wife of the
County of Augusta of the one part and Michael Seman of
the County aforesaid of the other part Witnesseth that the
said Nicholas and Margaret Seman for and in consideration
of the Sum of five Shillings Current Money of Virginia to them
in hand paid by the said Michael Seman at or before the sealing and Delivery of these presents the Receipt whereof they do
hereby acknowledge and thereof doth release acquit and discharge
the said Michael Seman his heirs and Assigns by these pres-

Deeds of Pendleton County, Virginia (now West Virginia), Book I (1791) p. 154

Map of present day West Virginia
Note area of Franklin in center near Brandywine,
Greenbrier and Nicholas are also visible to the lower right

In Morten's *History of Pendleton County, West Virginia* Henry is listed as "German, coming before 1795, living near Dahmer Post Office."[166]

Emick -- German - before 1795 - near Dahmer Post Office

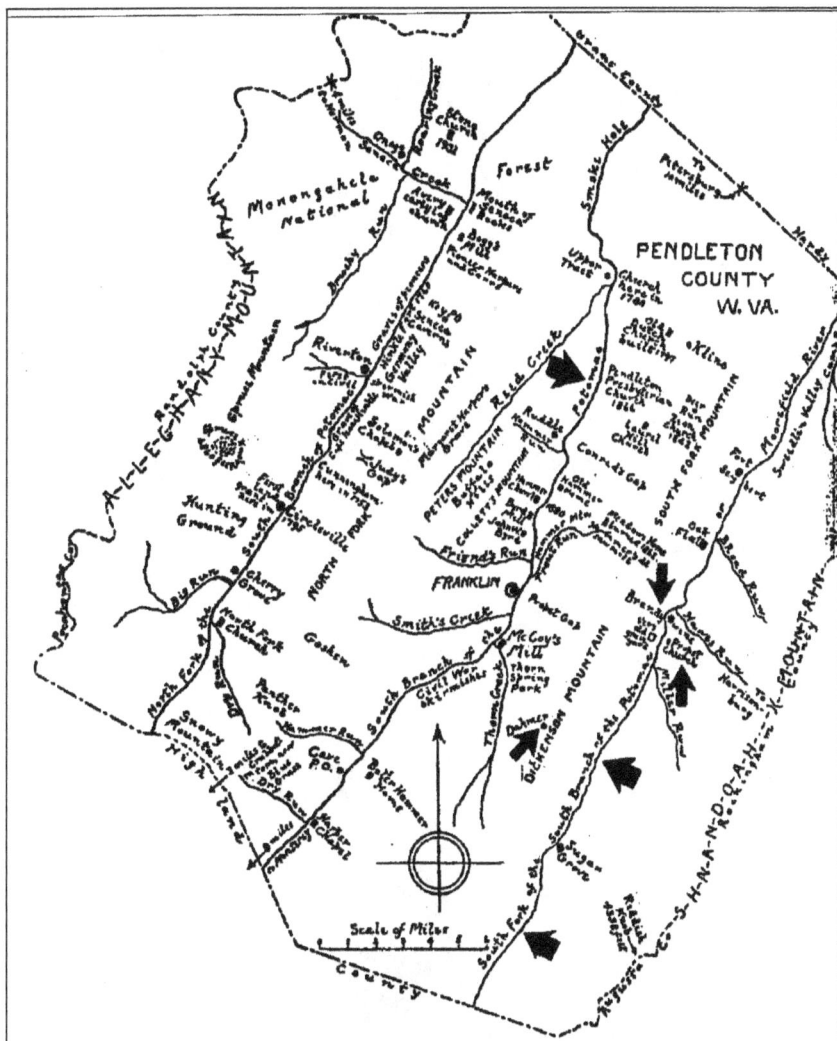

Pendleton County, (now) West Virginia
Notes sites important to Amick Family History indicated by arrows.
Copy by Barbara Nichols

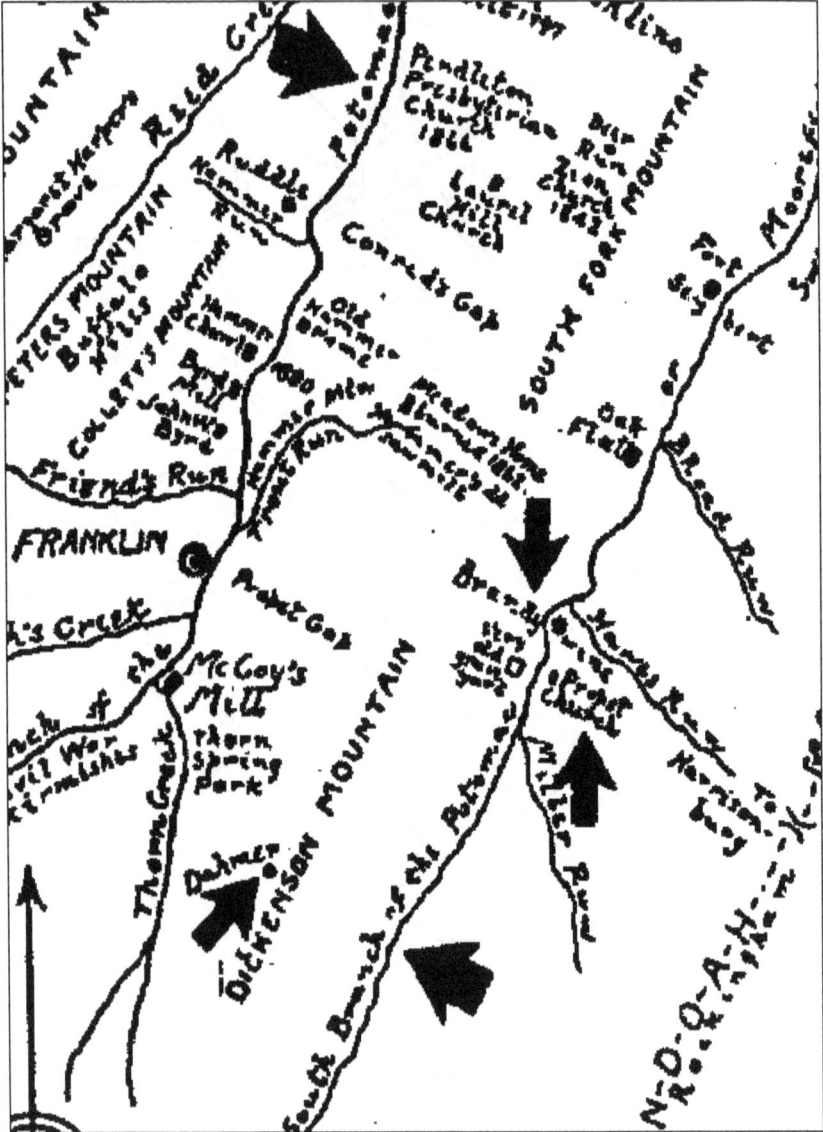

Close up of Pendleton County, (now) West Virginia
Notes sites important to Amick Family History indicated by arrows.
Copy by Barbara Nichols

Franklin West Virginia Amick Homestead

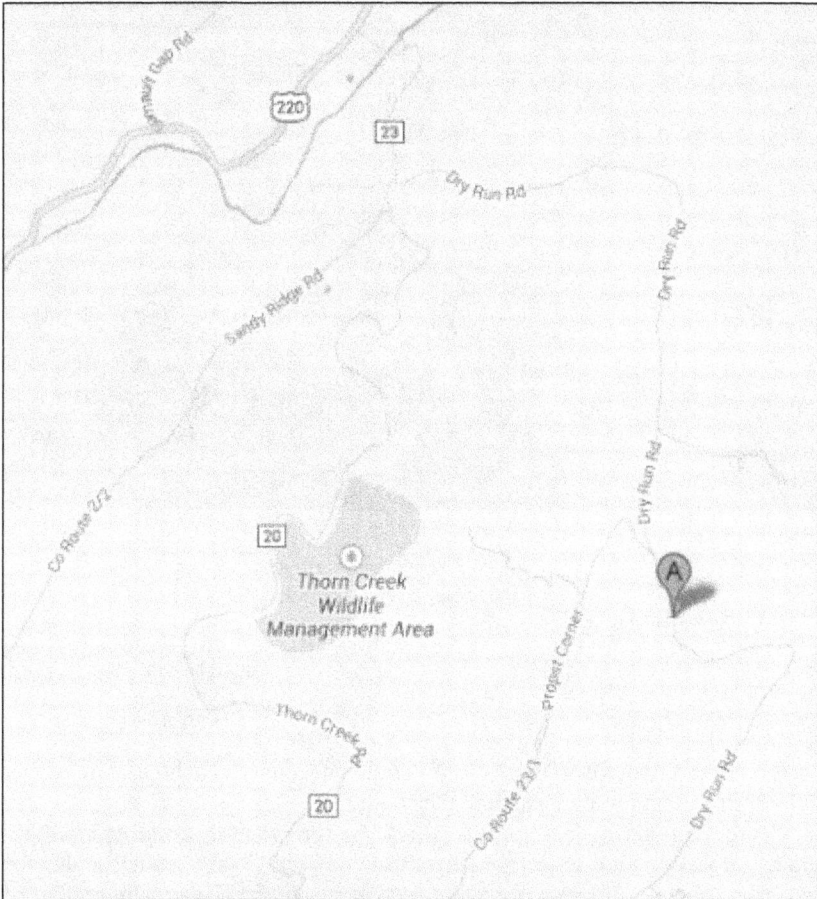

Map of Present day, Pendleton, West Virginia
Note Dahmer south of road (bottom of map)
Amick Homestead is across the road from Dahmer toward the east
Note Propst Corner Road

The Amick homestead is near Dahmer on the map above and Propst Church is near Brandywine on Highway 21. John Arvin Dahmer lived on the farm bordering our Henry Emig/Amick and knew the location of the grave site of Henry and Barbara (Niemand) his wife. Barbara Nichols had a marker put on the spot and the original stone marker is now in the Pendleton County Historical Society. The farm has since been sold to the Munns. Johnny Dahmer told stories about the powder mill on the Thorn at the time period of the War of 1812. Johnny Arvin Dahmer has now passed away.

Dahmer Farm

New Munn log cabin

Old Pitsenbarger farm (now Munns)

Amick homestead

Henry Amick's grave

Randolph County is to the west of Pendleton County. Nicholas, Greenbrier and Fayette Counties are located to the south.

George Smith in *The Church Book for the Propst Congregation* has additional information on early settlers in Pendleton County near Brandywine including history of Hans Michael Propst from the Palatinate region of Germany.[167]

Johnny Arvin Dahmer, the county Historian, in a letter to Barbara Nichols writes:

> 15 May 1984
> Henry owned a lot of land in Pendleton county north of Franklin in the area referred to as Dahmer and Sugar Grove. Henry Amick first settled in the Brandywine Gap area on South Fork Mountain near the Sink Hole in what Gilbert Pitsenbarger referred to as the Old Amick Place. I (John Dahmer) know about where it was. That is, where the house stood. You would enjoy the nice view from this mountain

once called Sink Hole Mountain. A lot of people know it today as Hyers Mountain. I often wondered where they got their water from, as the land is rich limestone soil.[168]

A small Amick grave site with a new marker from descendants was tended by John Dahmer. The current maps show Dahmer and Sugar Grove south of Franklin.

Henry Amick [Henry, Georg] has the spelling Emich in the following records. Henry Emich, October 1793 had sixty acres surveyed described as land lying in the mountains between the South fork of the South Branch of the Potomac, and the Black Thorn and adjoining his land in the Sink Holes.[169]

November 27, 1793 twenty-seven acres surveyed for Nicholas Emich lying on the head of Mill Run Gap, a west branch of the South Fork and joining on the east side of his land.[170]

November 27, 1793, forty acres surveyed for Henry and Nicholas Emich lying in the forks of Mill Run Gap between lands of Sophia Propst and Emick's land.[171]

Louise Reithel in her work on Nicholas Emmick also noted the purchase of land in Pendleton by Nicholas. She states:[172]

> Pendleton County, Virginia, was next-door to Rockingham County, and Nicholas, listed as Nicholas Emick, purchased ninety acres of land on 16 July 1793.(3) This land was in the region of the Allegheny Mts. Between South Branch (of the Potomac river), and South Fork at the head of Mill Run Gap near Dahmer Post Office. In 1796, Nicholas Emick purchased another 27 acres of land at Mill Run Gap next to his previous land purchase. (4) On (20 June 1863, the state of West Virginia was formed and Pendleton Co. became a part of the new state.)
>
> Henry Emick/Amick was already living in Pendleton County, Virginia, as he had purchased land there in 1791. (5) He was the son of Henry Emick/Emig/Amey/Amick, Sr. of Bucks County Pennsylvania. (6) Henry Amick, Jr. owned land at Mill Run Gap, Black Thorn, South Fork, Dry Run and Swadley's Run in Pendleton County VA. (See Sims Index to Land Grants in West VA.)
>
> On 30 March 1796, Henry and Nicholas Emick together purchased forty acres of land at Mill Run Gap near South Fork. (7) This joint purchase brought their farms together, and made them connected at Mill Run Gap.

References:

(4) Sims Index to Land Grants in West Virginia, pg. 598.
(5) Sims Index to Land Grants in West Virginia, pg. 598.
(6) Bucks County, PA. Births, Keller's Lutheran Church, pg. 83, compiled by John T. Humphrey.
(7) Land Grants in West VA., State Auditor, Land Dept. Office, Bk. 1, pg. 260, Charleston, West VA.

Dry Creek looking downstream from Road 23 just up from the McCoy Mill, taken 2007

Coming from Franklin on road 23 you come to the gate on the left to the Munn property. This is
the site of the Pitsenbarger homestead, neighbors of Henry Amick, taken 2007

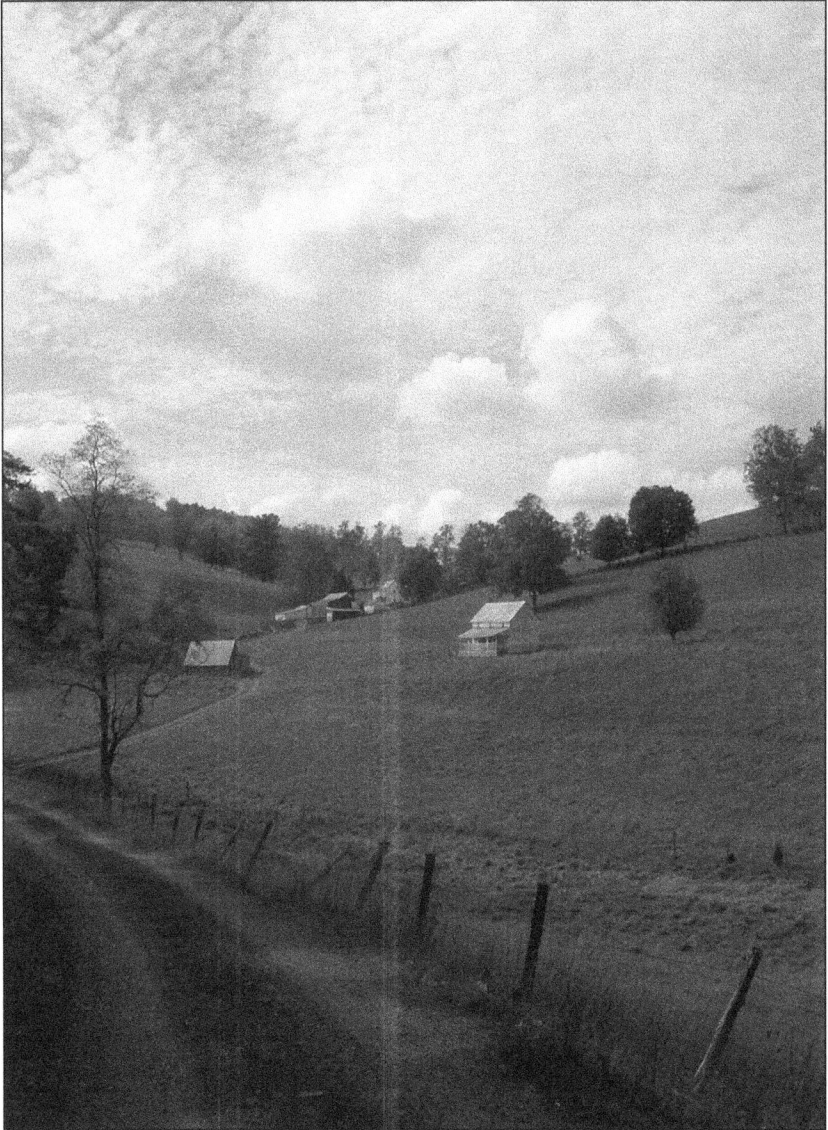

Past the Munn farm on road 23 is Dahmer on the right of the road
(Going south from Franklin). Dahmer is an old post stop with only a few buildings,
taken 2007

Going past Dahmer heading south before the right turn in the road is a
small wooden building in the field to the right.
Across the road to the north is the Amick Homestead. Taken 2007

Looking toward Amick Knob is the gate from the road into the pasture of the old Amick
Homestead. Across the road to the north is the Amick Homestead. Taken 2007

Cross the first of three fields, in the second field is the old Pitsenbarger graveyard. Taken 2007

Looking back south on the old road to the homestead now nearly obscured. This is near the Pitsenbarger graveyard. Note the stacked stones and trees lining the old roadway. Taken 2007

Amick Knob with depression in foreground the old homestead,
Photo taken 1984 by Robert Amick Nichols

Rocks taken from fields along the old road into the homestead, looking west from the old Amick
homestead site, taken 2007

Barn west of old Amick Homestead, taken 2007

Middle of Second field in from road, picture taken from past the old Amick homestead
looking north, taken 2007

Road east near Henry Amick Grave, this is an old indian trail that leads
into Franklin over the rugged mountains, Taken 2007

Henry had land surveyed in 1796. Seven acres of land surveyed October 3, 1796 for Henry Emich, lying west side of his land on the Mountain between South fork and South Branch of the Potomac at the Sink Holes.[173]

Dahmer is located in Pendleton County, West Virginia, about 5 miles directly south of Franklin on Dry Creek. The Amick family homestead is located on Dahmer Road, east of Highway 220, and near County Road 23 and Dry Creek Road. This area is accessed from Harrisonburg, Virginia via Highway 33 on the north or Highway 257 from the south. Dahmer is not shown on the West Virginia State Highway map.

From 220 near Sugar Grove head north on road 23, this was taken coming down from Franklin on 23 and meeting 220. Taken 2007

From 1797: "From Whom Alienated-Nicholas Amick...To Whom Alienated-Henry Amick". Nicholas Emmick left Pendleton County for Rockbridge County Virginia and then moved to Kentucky.[174,175]

April 10, 1797, one hundred acres surveyed for Henry Emich, land described as "lying on the Mountain between the South Branch of the Potomac and the South fork and adjoining to Henry Swadely's and Henry Propst's land."[176]

Nicholas Emmick

Nicholas Emick married his second wife, Susanna Smith, the daughter of Henry Smith in 1795 in Pendleton County, VA.[177] Louise Reithel in her work on Nicholas Emmick described Susanna's lineage:[178]

> Peter Smith was an early resident of Augusta County, Virginia. While living there during the French and Indian Wars, he furnished provisions to The Virginia Militia, and was reimbursed by the Virginia Legislature in 1763. Henry, John, and Gaspar Smith were listed as soldiers from Augusta County who were in the Virginia Militia. In 1758, they were paid by the Virginia Legislature for their services. (1)

Peter Smith obtained a patent for 54 acres of land on the South Fork of the South Branch on 10 July 1767. Later records also show he obtained another patent for 65 acres of land on the northwest side of South Fork on 1 March 1779. At that time, both these tracts of land were a part of Augusta Co. VA. In 1787, Pendleton County was formed from parts of Augusta and Hardy Counties, VA, and then Peter Smith's land became a part of Pendleton Co. VA. (See References 2, 3, and 4.)

Land deeds show that Peter and Mary Smith signed over two tracts of land to Frederick Smith on 3 Oct. 1791. The first tract was for 17 acres at South Fork of the South Branch, and the second tract on the northwest side of South Fork was for 65 acres. (2) On 6 Feb. 1792, Peter Smith signed a deed giving 27 acres of land at South Fork on the South Branch to Henry Smith. (3) Henry Smith obtained a patent for 80 acres of land adjoining his other land on 30 Mar. 1796. (4)

Many early settlers in Pendleton County were of German birth or ancestry, and a German dialect continued in use in the county into the twentieth century. Many signatures and witnesses to the early land deeds were frequently signed in German script. (5)

Nicholas Emick (Emmick) purchased 90 acres of land at South Fork on the South Branch on 16 July 1793 in Pendleton Co. (West) Virginia. Henry Emick (Ame/Amick) was already living in the same area, and both belonged to the Pendleton County Militia. (See Part II, Chapt. 1.) Several members of the Smith family also belonged to the same Militia group. They were Frederick, John, and William Smith. Members from the Simmons family were Leonard, John, Sr., John, Jr., and Michael Simmons. (6)

Henry Smith (Sr.) died in 1797 in Pendleton County, (West) Virginia, and an inventory of his estate was listed. (7) John Smith, the son of Henry Smith of South Fork, purchased 140 acres of land from Michael and Mary Hoover on 8 Dec. 1805. Some of this land had once been a part of the 1767 land patent of Peter Smith of South Fork. (8)

The land heirs of Henry Smith, deceased, were listed in a deed of sale between the heirs and John Smith on 2 July 1811 in Pendleton County, (West) VA. The heirs listed were:
Henry (signed Henrich) Smith and wife, Christina Smith. Leonard Simmon and wife, Catharine Simmon. Christian Stone and wife, Mary Stone. (9)

Susanna Smith was listed by O. F. Morton as the daughter of
Henry Smith and Christina (?) Smith. She married Nicholas
Emick (Emmick) in 1795 in Pendleton Co. (West) Va. (10)
Nicholas and Susanna (Smith) Emmick later moved to
Rockbridge Co. Va., and again moved before 1810 to
Breckinridge Co. Kentucky.

References Chapter 1
(1) Gleanings of Virginia History, pp. 32, 36, 37, 38, 106,
compiled by William P. Boogher.
(2) Pendleton County (West) Virginia Deed Book Records,
1788-1813, pg. 15 by Rick Toothman.
(3) Ibid. pg. 17.
(4) Ibid. pg. 194.
(5) Ibid. pg. VII. Editorial Notes.
(6) A History of Pendleton County, West Va., pg. 397, by
Oren F. Morton.
(7) Virginia Wills and Administrations (1632-1800),
Pendleton Co., Va. (1787-1800) pg. 481 by Torrance.
(8) Pendleton Co. (West) Virginia Deed book Records, 1788-
1813, pg. 136 by Rick Toothman.
(9) Ibid. pg. 194.
(10) A History of Pendleton County, (West) Va., pg. 299 by
Oren F. Morton.

Nicholas Amick, of Pendleton County, Virginia, conveyed a tract of land to
his cousin Henry Amick on July 3, 1797, for consideration of two pounds
lawful money of Virginia paid him by Henry Amick "a certain tract of land
containing forty acres veering survey date twenty-seventh day of November
1793, and lying in Pendleton county on the forks of Mill Run Gap between the
land of Sophia Propst and Henry and Nicholas Amick's. At a court held for
Pendleton County on Monday August 7, 1797, this indenture of Bargain &
Sale from Nicholas Amick to Henry Amick was acknowledged by Nicholas
and ordered to be recorded."[179]

350

Know all men by these presents that I Nicholas Amick of the County of Pendleton State of Virginia in Consideration of the Sum of two pounds lawful money of Virginia paid me by Henry Amick of the County of Pendleton & State Aforesaid the receipt whereof I do hereby Acknowledge do hereby Give Grant Bargain Sell & Convey unto the said Henry Amick his heirs & assigns forever A Certain Tract or Parcell of land Containing forty acres by Survey, bearing Date the 27th day of november one thousand Seven Hundred & ninety three Lying & being in the County of Pendleton on the forks of Mill Run Gapp between the land of Sophiah propst & Henry Amicks and Nicholas amicks, and is Bounded as follows to wit begining at two Sugar trees by a Branch, & running thence South 51 Degrees East 32 poles to a Sugar tree & 2 Lyms at the head of a Spring, and thence North 20 Degrees East 64 poles to two Lyms by A Branch & thence North 73 Degrees East 76 poles to a white & Spanish oak and thence North 55 Degrees East 40 poles to a Chesnut oak & hiccory in the forks of the Run & thence North 54 Degrees West 90 poles to a white oak & Black oak & hiccory on a hill side & thence South 29 Degrees West 160 poles to the Begining To have & to hold the said Granted & Bargained Premises with the privilages and appurtenances thereof to him the said Henry amick his heirs & assigns forever to his & their well behoof forever & I the said Nicholas Amick for my Self my heirs Executors & Administrators do Covenant with the said Henry Amick his heirs & assigns that I am lawfuly Seized in fee of the Premises that they are free from all Incumbrances that I have G Good right to Sell & Con

Pendleton County, West Virginia Deeds, Book 2, pp. 350

351.

The Same to the s.d Henry amick to hold as aforesaid and
That I will Warrant and Defend the same to the s.d Henry
Amick his heirs & Assigns forever Against the lawful
Claims & Demands of all Persons In witness whereof I
have hereunto Set my hand & Siol this third Day of July in
the Year of our Lord one Thousand Seven Hundred &
ninety Seven ⁓   Nicholas Amick

Signed Sealed and Delivered
in the presence of ⁘

At a Court held for Pendleton County on monday
the 7.th day of August 1797
& Sale from Nicholas Amick & his wife to Henry Amick
This Indenture of Bargain
was acknowledged by the s.d Nicholas & ordered to be recorded
                                   Teste A. Smith C.P.C.

Pendleton County, West Virginia Deeds, Book 2 pp. 351

Nicholas and Susanna Emmick sold their land on February 8, 1799 to Abraham Pitsenbarger. The deed of sale was signed Niclaus Emig, and Susanna (X, her mark) Emick. The Indenture of February 8, 1799 between Nicholas Emick and Susanna of Pendleton, VA, and Abraham Pitsenbarger deeded the property to Abraham.[180]

78   This Indenture made the 8th day of February in the Year of our Lord One Thousand Seven Hundred and Ninety nine Between Nicholas Emick & Susanna his wife of the County of Pendleton and State of Virginia of the One part & Abraham Pittsbarger of said County and Commonwealth of the Other part Witnesseth that for and in Consideration of the sum of Nineteen Pounds Virginia Currency to me in hand paid the receipt whereof is hereby acknowledged and thereof doth Acquit and Discharge the said Abraham Pittsbarger his and Assigns and the said Nicholas Emick & Susanna his wife their heirs and assigns doth grant Bargain and Sell unto the said Abraham Pittsbarger two certain Tracts or Parcels of Land One Tract Containing thirty acres by Patent Bearing date the twenty first day of September One Thousand Seven Hundred and Ninety two Bounded as follows, To wit, Beginning at two White Oaks on a ridge & running thence North Eighty nine degrees East ninety two poles to a Walnut on the top of a ridge North forty degrees East one Hundred poles along the top of said ridge to a Walnut and ash North five degrees west forty poles to a Walnut & Lynn in the head of a hollow of Swadleys Mill run North fifty seven degrees West forty Poles to a black Oak and White Oak on Sideling Ground North thirty Eight degrees East thirty — poles to two Chesnuts on a Cliff of Rocks North Sixteen degrees East thirty six poles to a hickory and Walnut on a hill side towards the South fork North Sixty Eight degrees west Eighteen poles to two Chesnut trees on the Sum of the south Branch & South fork Waters South thirty four degrees west two Hundred and Seventy three poles to the Beginning One Other Tract Containing twenty seven acres By Patent bearing date the twenty seventh day of November 1793 & Bounded as follows Viz Beginning at a walnut and ash on a ridge Corner of his former land and running thence North five degrees west forty Poles to a Walnut and Lynn in a hollow and thence North fifty seven degrees west forty poles to a black and White Oak on Sideling ground and North thirty Eight degrees East thirty poles to two Chesnut Oaks on a Ridge of Rocks and thence south fifty One degrees East Eighty poles Leaving his former land and Crossing a hollow to a Sugar on a hill side & South forty six degrees west Eighty two poles to the Beginning Both his Tracts of Land Lying and Being in the County of Pendleton first mentioned Tract Between the south Branch and South fork Last mentioned lands on the head of Mile run Gap a west Branch of the south fork and adjoining on the East Side of his former Land To have and to hold the said Tracts or Parcels of Land with their Appurtenances unto the said Abraham Pittsbarger and his heirs and assigns forever without Let or Molestation from him the said Nicholas Emick and

Pendleton County, West Virginia Deeds, Book 3, p. 78

Pendleton County, West Virginia Deeds, Book 3, p. 78

Nicholas and Susanna took his children: Nicholas, Betsey, Sally and Anny; from his previous marriage to Rockbridge with them. Louise Reithel in her work on Nicholas Emmick states:[181]

> These children were very young when their mother died, and were probably taken to live with relatives. Later research records indicate the children had close relationships with the Jacob Michael family who lived in Augusta Co. VA. at this time. And, also with the William Willson family who lived in Rockingham County, VA. About 1800, or shortly afterwards, Nicholas Emick, the Jacob Michael family, and the William Willson family moved to Rockbridge County, Virginia.

On November 27, 1801, Nicholas Emick purchased from John and Judy Gabbert 97 acres of land adjoining land of George Gabbert lying along Buffalo Creek off the North Fork of the James River in Rockbridge County, Virginia.[182]

Nicholas and Susanna Emick sold 185 acres of land in Rockbridge county Virginia, on April 6, 1807 to William Willson. This land was located on the

North Fork of the James River, and cornered by the land of Jacob Michael, Philip Coutz, David Lytle, and William Paxton, owner of a mill.[183]

Louise Reithel in her work on Nicholas Emmick states:[184]

> Soon after selling their land in Rockbridge County, Virginia, Nicholas and Susanna Emmick moved to Breckinridge County, Kentucky. He was listed as Nicholas 'Emmie' on the 1810 Federal Census of Kentucky living in Breckinridge County. In 1829, Hancock County was formed from a part of Western Breckinridge Co., Ohio and Daviess counties, KY. This placed the Emmick farm in the new Hancock Co. KY. Nicholas and Susanna Emmick remained there the rest of their lives.

An Indenture June 21, 1818 between Nicholas Amick and Susanna (late Susanna Smith) of Breckenridge County, Kentucky and John Smith of the County of Pendleton, Virginia gives tracts of land to John and establishes that Susanna is the sister of John Smith and daughter of Henry Smith.[185] The acknowledgement dated June 21, 1819 confirmed that Susanna Smith was voluntarily selling property to John Smith.

225 Singular the appurtenances thereunto belonging or in any wise appertaining
To have and to hold the said Tract of Land with its appurtenances unto
the said David McMullen his heirs and assigns forever To the only proper use
and behoof of him the said David McMullen his heirs and assigns forever
and the said Henry Hedrick and Mary his wife for themselves their heirs
Executors and administrators do Covenant with the said David McMullen
his heirs and assigns that they the said Henry Hedrick & Mary his wife &
their heirs Executors and administrators the said Tract of Land with its
appurtenances unto the said David McMullen his heirs and assigns
against the Claim or Claims of them the said Henry & Mary Hedrick
and their heirs and of all and every person or persons, whatsoever
shall and will warrant and forever defend by these presents. In Witness
whereof the said Henry Hedrick and Mary his Wife have hereunto set
their hands and seals On the day and year first above written —
Signed Sealed and delivered
in the presence of

Henry Hedrick (seal)
Mary X Hedrick (seal)
   mark

At a Court held for Pendleton County the 3rd day of August 1819
This deed from Henry Hedrick and Mary his wife To David McMullen
was acknowledged by the said Henry and Mary (she the said Mary being
first privily examined as the law directs) and ordered to be recorded —
Examd   Teste L Dyer CPC

This Indenture made the 21st day of June in the year of our
Lord One thousand eight Hundred and eighteen between Nicholas Amick
and Susannah his wife late Susannah Smith Both of the County
of Breckenridge and State of Kentucky of the one part and John
Smith of the County of Pendleton and State of Virginia of the other part
Witnesseth That the said Nicholas Amick and Susannah his wife
lately Susannah Smith one of the legal heirs and representatives
of Henry Smith decd for and in Consideration of the sum of Twenty
five pounds Current money of the united States to them in hand paid
do bargain and sell unto the said John Smith his heirs and assigns
each their Respective parts in Two Certain Tracts or parcels of Land for
-merly by the said Henry Smith Deceased, Namely a Tract of Twenty

241

326 Seven Acres lying in the said County of Pendleton and on the South
fork being part of a Tract of fifty four Acres first granted to Peter
Smith by patent bearing date July 10th 1767 which said 27 Acres
is bounded as follows to wit Beginning at a hickey Sapling in a
field former Corner and with the former lines N.55.W.45 poles
Crossing the fork to a pine and hickey bushes on a bank thence N.45
E.116 poles to a white oak at a fence division Corner thence with the
fence S.40.E.38 poles Crossing the fork to a pine on a high bank
former Corner Thence S.44.W.106 poles to the Beginning
and a Tract of Eighty four acres Joining the above which was
patented to the said Henry Smith dec. March 30th 1796 which
is Bounded as follows Viz Beginning at a white oak his to
Corner and thence South west 36 poles with his line to a white oak
S.N.80.W.84 poles to two Spanish Oaks on the side of a ridge
N.30.E.204 poles to a Chesnut and Chesnut Oak S.N.27.W.36 poles
to a Black oak and white oak Corner to another tract of his land
and with a line of the same S.85.East 136 poles to a white oak
on his old line and with it South west 80 poles to the Beginning
Together with all its appurtenances to have and to hold said two
tracts of Land with all its appurtenances to the sole use and behoof
of him The said John Smith his heirs and assigns forever and the
said Nicholas Amick and Susannah Amick his wife formerly
Susannah Smith one of the legal heirs and representatives of
Henry Smith dec. do covenant with the said John Smith his
heirs and assigns that they said Nicholas Amick and Susan
=nah his wife aforesaid and their heirs the said Land with its
Appurtenances unto the said John Smith his heirs and
assigns against all persons whatsoever will warrant and
forever defend. In Witness Whereof the said Nicholas Amick
& his wife Susannah aforesaid have hereunto set their hands
& seals the day and year above Written

         Nicholas   his   Amick   (Seal)
                mark

         Susanna   her   Amick   (Seal)
                Mark

Pendleton County, West Virginia Deeds, Book 7, pp. 425-227

227 Kentucky Breckenridge County Set

I Jo Allen Clerk of Breckenridge County Court do Certify that this day before me in my Office the within Indenture was duly Acknowledged by the within named Nicholas Amick and Susannah his wife to be their act and deed for the purposes therein Expressed — And she the said Susannah Amick being examined by separate and apart from her said husband declared that she freely and Voluntarily, signed sealed and acknowledged the same without the threats or persuasions of her said husband and that she was willing the same should be recorded all of which I do certify to the County Court of Pendleton County in the State of Virginia where the land lies there to be Recorded.

In Testimony whereof I have hereunto set my hand and affixed the seal of the said County of Breckenridge aforesaid this twenty first day of June One Thousand eight hundred and Nineteen and in the 28 year of the Commonwealth —

Jo Allen

Kentucky Set

I James Moorman presiding Justice of the County Court of Breckenridge County and State aforesaid do Certify and make Known that Jo Allen whose attestation is to the above Certificate was at the date thereof and still is Clerk of said Court and that the attestation is in due form agreeably to the Laws of this Commonwealth.

Given under my hand and seal the 21 June 1819

James Moorman

At a Court held for Pendleton County the 7th day of September 1819

This deed from Nicholas Amick and Susanna his wife to John Smith was Certified to have been duly Acknowledged before the Clerk of Breckenridge County State of Kentucky as appears by his attestation thereunto annexed And Ordered to be Recorded.

Examd   Teste
                                                  Z. Dyer C.P.C.

Henry and Nicholas Militia Records

Henry and Nicholas Emich are listed on the muster roles of Pendleton County Militia districts for September 1794 in Captain Jacob Hoover's Company.[186] Hoover's Company is listed in Militia Districts of 1794, as being on the South Fork from Swadley's up to Michael Hoover's and John Harold's, and including John Conrad and Jacob Moats on Black Thorn and Nicholas Emick on the South Fork Mountain.[187]

Pendleton County Militia Districts, Companies, and Officers
Districts of 1794

Patton's-South Fork up to Henry Swadley's.

Hoover's-South Fork from Swadley's up to Michael Hoover's and John Harold's, and including John Conrad and Jacob Moats on Blackthorn and **Nicholas Emick** on South Fork Mountain.

McCoy's-From above Michael Hoover's to Alexander McQuain's and thence to the Bath line.

Jones'-From Balsor Hammer's on South Branch across to the mouth of west fork of Dry Run, including the head of North Fork.

Hopkins'-From Jacob Conrad's on South Branch to Hardyline, including Graham.

Gragg's-From mouth of West Dry Run to Hardy line.
  Militia Companies As Ordered by the First County Court 1788 and Officers Assigned to Them
Patterson's-From Charles Hedrick's up South Branch to the. line of Janes' company.

Upper South Fork Company-Captain, Jacob Hoover; Lieutenant, - Gillespie; Ensign, Thomas Hoover.

Lower South Fork Company-Captain. Roger Dyer; Lieutenant, William Patton; Ensign, William Dyer.

Crabbottom Company - Captain, Adam Hull; Lieutenant, William Janes; Ensign, Jacob Gum.

Capt. Jacob Hoover's Company
Muster Roll of Pendleton Militia, Sept. 6, 1794

Conrad, John	**Propst, George.**
Cowger, John	**Propst, Jacob**
Crummett, Conrad	**Propst, Leonard**
Crummett, Frederick	Puffenbarper, George
Eckard, Philip	Ruleman, Christian
Eckard, William	Ruleman, Joseph
Elsey, Thomas	Sibert, Philip
Emick, Henry	**Simmons, John, Sr.**
Emick, Nicholas	**Simmons, John, Jr.**
Garner, John	**Simmons, Leonard**
Harold. Christian	**Simmons, Leonard**
Harold, John	**Simmons, Michael**
Harold, Michael	**Smith, Frederick**
Hoover, George	**Smith, John, S**
Hoover, Lawrence	**Smith, William. S**
Hoover, Michael	Snidler, Jacob
Huffman, Henry	Stone, Christian
Huffman, Michael	Stone, Peter
Howe, Henry	Swadley, Henry
Howe, Jacob	Vance, Abraham
Kelly, George	Varner, George
Kow, Christian	Varner, -
Mick, Mathias. M	Warner, Conrad
Moats, George	Whiteman, Henry
Moats, John	Wilfong, Henry
Pitsenbarger, Jacob	Wilfong, Jacob

A History of Pendleton County West Virginia
By Oren F. Morton, Franklin, West Virginia, 1910

John Arvin Dahmer in an interview recorded by Barbara Nichols stated: "they trained once a month, at a meeting that often deteriorated into a drunken brawl."[188]

Henry Amick and Family

Henry Amick is mentioned in Pendleton County Wills in 1799:

> Pendleton County W.Va. Will Book 1 Pages 266-269 October 18, 1799 Sale Bill of Zachariah Rexrode - Purchasers Henry Amick - John Cowgar -Philip Eckert -Elizabeth Heviner - John Hicks - George Hover - Christian How - George How - Sebostian Huver - Henry Jones - Aran Kee - John Miller - Henry Props - Leonard Props - Michael Props - Henry Rexrode - John Rexrode - Leonard Rexrode - Christian Roleman - William Smith; No Total[189]

Cody Hicks' (related to John Hicks above) wife is Edith Walker. This may be the link to the Walkers. The Walker name shows up frequently in relation to the Amicks on Sewell Mountain.

The sixth of April 1802 "William Smith and Phebe his wife of Pendleton County sold to Abraham Pittsenberier and Henry Amick of said county, in consideration of thirty pounds, current money of Virginia, seventy-five acres in Pendleton County, called land lying on a branch of Black Thorn, a branch of the South Branch of Potomac."[190]

This Indenture made the sixth day of April one Thousand Eight Hundred and a two Between Wm. Smith and phebe of the County of Pendleton of the one part and abraham Pittsbarier and henry Amich of said County of the other part witnesseth that for and in Consideration of the sum of Thirty pounds Current money of virginia on of before the delivering of these presents the recipt and payment whereof is hereby acknowleag Hhath grantea Bargaind & sola by these presents do Grant bargain and sell unto the said Abm Pittsbarier & Henry Amich one certain tract or Parcel of Land Containing Seventy five acres by Survey bearing Date The second day of february one Thousand seven hundred and Eighty Seven lying and being in the County of Pendleton on a branch of Black Thorn on branch of the South Branch of Potomack and Boundea is followeth to with Beginning at three Chesnuts and a white oak and running South Seventy four degrees west Thirty poles to three white oaks North forty seven degrees West seventy six poles to a white oak and Chesnut North thirty two Degrees East Eighty Eight poles to a Chesnutt & Chesnut oak north sixteen degrees west Eighty poles to two Chesnutt oaks in a ridge North fifty five Degrees East Seventy four poles Croping a branch to three pines on a Laurel bank south two hundred and Thirty Seven poles to the Beginning with its Apurtamances to have & to hola the said Tract or Parcel of Land with its apurtamances to the said abrm Pittsbare & henry amich and their heirs & asigns for ever to the only use and behoof of them the said ab m Pittsbarier

Pendleton County, West Virginia Deeds, Book 3, p 355

First October 1805, "William McCoy and Elizabeth his wife of Pendleton County sold to Henry Amick of that county, for consideration of thirty-three pounds current money, seventy-five acres of land on the head of a branch of the Black Thorn of the South Branch of the Potomac between the lands of Henry Hawks". This was the Amick homestead farm.[191]

199

current money of the State aforesaid to them in hand paid have granted bargained &
sold and by these Presents do grant bargain and sell unto the said John Bean his heirs
and Assigns one certain Tract or Parcel of land containing Seventy tens by bearing
date the nineteenth day of February one thousand seven hundred and ninety four lying
and being in the County of Pendleton on the west side of the South fork and adjoining the lands of Samuel Morral on the west side of Wyggances and Dies lands and
bounded as followeth towit: Beginning at two white oaks on the north side of same run
near the Mouth of the Gap corner of John & Samuel Morrals land and running thence
South 64 degrees East 58 Poles to two white oaks former corner of John & Samuel
Morrals land North 34 degrees East 110 Poles leaving said line to two white oaks and
walnut on a ridge North 40 degrees West 100 Poles to a branch of chesnut thence &
thence South 48 degrees West 50 Poles to two pines and thence North 7 degrees West
110 poles to the Beginning. To have and to hold said Tract of Land with its appurtenances unto the said John Bean his heirs Executors administrators or assigns
forever. To the sole use and behoof of him the said John Bean his heirs forever.
And they the said John Evick and Mary his wife for themselves and their heirs
Executors and Administrators the said Tract or Parcell of land unto the said John Bean
his heirs or assigns shall and will warrant and forever defend

Signed Sealed & acknowledged   his
in Presence of   John X Evick
                                                                   mark

                                                                    her
                                                              Mary X Evick
                                                                   mark

At a court held for Pendleton County on Tuesday the first day of October one
Thousand eight hundred and five This Deed from John Evick and Mary his wife to
John Bean was acknowledged in court by the said John and Mary she being first
privily examined as the law directs and ordered to be recorded

                                        Teste   Z. Dyer

This Indenture made the first day of October in the year of our Lord one
Thousand eight hundred and five between William McCoy and Elizabeth his wife of
the one Part and Henry Amick of the other Part all of the County of Pendleton and
State of Virginia. Witnesseth that the said William McCoy and Elizabeth his wife
for and in consideration of the sum of Thirty three pounds current money, to them
in hand paid by the said Henry, have granted bargained and sold and by these
Presents do grant bargain and sell unto the said Henry Amick and his heirs and
Assigns one certain Tract or Parcel of Land containing Sixtyfive acres lying and
being in the County aforesaid on the head of a branch of the black House, of the south
branch between the lands of Henry Vaucks and Nicholas Amick and bounded as
followeth. To wit Beginning at several pines on the North East side of Vaucks land
and thence South Twenty degrees East one hundred and twelve Poles to two
chesnut oaks and black oak on some rocks S 58 E 32 Poles crossing a

200.

path to a white oak N. 84° E 94 Poles to a large white Oak on a hill side N 9°
East 86 Poles to a white Oak and 6 thence East thence South eighty degrees
West one hundred and thirty five Poles to the beginning. Together with all &
singular the Appurtenances thereunto belonging or in any wise appertaining to
the same To have and to hold the said Tract of Land with its appurtenances
to the said Henry Arrick his heirs and assigns forever. And the said William
McCoy and Elizabeth his wife for themselves and their heirs do covenant with
the said Henry and his heirs and assigns that they the said William and
Elizabeth and their heirs the said Tract of land with its appurtenances unto
the said Henry Arrick his heirs and assigns against the claim or claims of the
William McCoy and Elizabeth his wife and their heirs and of all and every person
or persons whatever shall and will warrant and forever defend by these Presents
In witness whereof the said William McCoy and Elizabeth his wife have hereunto
set their hands and affixed their seals the day and year first above written —
In Presence of

William McCoy {seal}
Elizabeth McCoy {seal}

At a Court held for Pendleton County on Tuesday the first day of October one
thousand eight hundred and five this deed from William McCoy and Elizabeth
his wife to Henry Arrick was acknowledged in Court by the said William and
Elizabeth she being first privately examined as the law directs and declared to be recorded

Teste

This Indenture made the Twenty first day of September in the year of our
Lord one thousand eight hundred and five between Michael Fisher and his wife
of the County of Harrison and State of Virginia of the one Part and Jacob
Fisher and Charles Hedrick of the County of Pendleton and State aforesaid of
the other Part Witnesseth that the said Michael and his wife Fisher for and in
consideration of the sum of one hundred dollars in hand paid do bargain &c
unto the said Jacob Fisher and Charles Hedrick their heirs and assigns a certain
part or Parcel of Land lying in Pendleton County on the east side of the south
Branch of Potomack adjoining and between Gailer and running water land on
the head of North Mill Creek, namely one full ninth part of the land held
by George Fisher Sen. of which said lands being purchased with money the said
George Fisher obtained for lands in the County of Rockingham on a Branch
of Cooks Creek which said lands was devised by Jacob Conrad deceased to his
daughter Elizabeth and her Children with Proviso that her husband George Fisher
should have a life Estate in the same, which said Fisher sold to Frederick
Swartz by consent of his wife Elizabeth and her Children and the said land
being in lieu of the aforesaid devised and entailed land said Michael Fisher is
because one of the heirs of the same being one the sons of the said Elizabeth Fisher

Deeds of Pendleton County, [now] West Virginia, Book 4, p. 200

Philip Wolf, original homestead was sold to William McCoy, who sold it to Henry Amick in October 1805 [same page as previous].[192]

John Arvin Dahmer in the interview recorded by Barbara Nichols continued:

> Henry Amick had a two story house built of logs with a narrow stairway, it has not survived to the present, only sunken ground of the foundation remains and it is only slightly visible today.
>
> The old Indian trail went through the upper pasture, and whites followed and used it. It just went over the ridge to the left and was the shortest way into Franklin.
>
> Henry's barn was up on the top of the rock back of the house. The nob east of his farm was known as Amick Nob, and they ranged hogs in the woods for acorns from oak trees there.[193]

Elias Amick was born in Virginia around 1808. The 1850 census for Indiana listed him as Elias Amick age 42 and born in Virginia.[194]

Elias Emmick
SPENCER CO, INDIANA 1850[195]
1021 75B EMMICK ELIAS 42 M FARMER $1,600 VA HAMMOND TP
1021 75B EMMICK SARAH 29 F $500 IN HAMMOND TP
1021 75B EMMICK JN'O W. 10 M   IN HAMMOND TP
1021 75B EMMICK MARY A. 8 F   IN HAMMOND TP

In the *Biographies of the 49th*, Mary Emmick, the daughter of Elias and Sallie Emmick, is listed as married to William Peckinpaugh and his father, referring to Henry Amick, is noted as fighting with Washington in the Revolutionary War.[196]

> CAPTAIN WILLIAM HENRY PECKINPAUGH was born Feb 22, 1838 in Crawford County, Indiana. Was married to Emeline McCown, on August 19, 1857, She died on April 20, 1859, with one child that died in Infancy.
>
> He then married after the war to Mary Ann Emmick, daughter of Elias and Sallie Emmick. (Elias father came from Holland and fought in the Rev. War with Washington) William Henry Peckinpaugh was Captain in Co. F 49th. Ind. Volunteers. He enlisted in Nov. 1861 and spent 3 years in the Army frequently serving on the Brigadier General's Staff as Acting Ass't. Adjutant General and sometimes as Provost Marshal. He was injured in action. After leaving the Army he

engaged in the practice of law until the time of his death. His Photo is listed in the Photo's of the men of the 49th's page.

Listed in the 1810 census: Henry Eamicke, Pendleton County, over 45 years of age, wife also over 45 years of age. Living with them were four males and five female children.[197, 198]

The Third Generation

The third generation family…

Family Tree Third Generation

Henry AMICK (1762 – 1830)
+Elisabeth Barbara NIEMAND (1764 – 1810)
  Henry AMICK (1788 –) *moves to Ohio*
  +Elizabeth SHROYER
  Jacob AMICK (1789 – 1869)
  +Rachael SHROYER (1793 – 1895)
    John AMICK (1815 – 1890)
    Samuel H. AMICK (1816 – 1900)
    Elizabeth AMICK (1819 -
    Catherine AMICK (1824 – 1917)
    Henry EMMICK (1814 – 1912)
    Jacob AMICK Jr. (1826 – 1909)
    Rachael AMICK (1830 – 1905)
    Mary AMICK (1833 – 1926)
  John the Miller AMICK (1790 – 1846)
  +Catherine BOWERS (1790 –)
    Lucy AMICK (1814 – 1854)
    Johannes AMICK (1815 –)
    Gideon AMICK (1819 – 1873)
    Eli AMICK (1820 – 1863)
    Mary Ann AMICK (1821 – 1896)
    Jesse AMICK (1822 –)
    Arnold AMICK (1823 – 1897)
    Barbara AMICK
    Asa AMICK (1827 – 1865)
    Ann AMICK (1827 – 1890)
    John AMICK (1830 –)
    Catherine AMICK (1832 – 1911)
    Joseph AMICK (1835 –)
    James Parker AMICK (1836 – 1881)
    Peregrine Houston AMICK (1839 – 1932)
  And continues…

Family Tree Third Generation Continued

      Mary AMICK (1797 –   )
      +Christian PROPST
      Barbara AMICK (1799 –   )
      +Henry EYE
      Elizabeth AMICK (1800 – 1856)
      Reuben AMICK (1805 –   )
      Elias AMICK (1808 – 1881)
    Christina AMICK moves to Spencer Indiana
      +Elias PARKER
+Catherine
      Catherine AMICK

Family Tree Third Generation Continued

Nicholas EMMICK (1766 – 1836)
+Catherine Hertzel (1769 – 1793)
      John Nicholas AMICK (1785 - 1850) *born 1772 per census*
      +Mary "Polly" LEAMON (1780 - 1869)
            Jacob AMICK (1806 - 1850)
            William Henry AMICK (1807 – 1883)
            Eva AMICK (1810 –   )
            John AMICK Jr. (1808 –
            Nicholas AMICK (1821 – 1880)
            David AMICK (1824 –   )
      Sally AMICK
      Anny AMICK
      Elizabeth "Betsy" AMICK
      +John MOHLER
            Samuel MOHLER
            Jno MOHLER
            Henry MOHLER
            Mary MOHLER
            Hezekiah MOHLER
            M.Jane MOHLER
+Susanna SMITH (1777 – 1833) second wife
      Mary EMMICK (1797 -)
      +James HENDERSON
            William HENDERSON
            John HENDERSON
      Jacob EMMICK (1799 – 1850)
      +Sarah Jane ASKINS
            Sarah Jane EMMICK (1833 -)
            George EMMICK (1838 - 1861)
            Mary Ann EMMICK (1840 - 1861)
      +Elizabeth CROOKS
            Felix EMMICK (1846 -)
      +Elizabeth BLANTON
      Elizabeth EMMICK (1803 – 1830)
      +David TURNER
      Katherine EMMICK (1805 - 1834)

Family Tree Forth Generation Continued

Nicholas EMMICK (1766 – 1836)
+Susanna SMITH (1777 – 1833) second wife continued
     George EMMICK (1811 – 1886)
     +Leticia ERSKINE
          Clarence EMMICK (1847 - 1924)
          Steven Powers EMMICK (1852 – 1914)
          George EMMICK Jr. (1854 – 1938)
          John C. EMMICK (1859 – 1906)
          Michael Hogg EMMICK (1863 - 1941)
     Allettia EMMICK
     +William RUST
          Felix Emmick RUST
          Francis M. RUST
          Nancy RUST
     Eliza Jane EMMICK
     +Vincent RUST
          John N. RUST
          James E.RUST
          Benjamin RUST
          Mary E. RUST
     Nancy EMMICK (1819 - 1859)
     +Waters ERSKINE
          Susanne ERSKINE
          Eliza Jane ERSKINE
          Norman ERSKINE
          Edna ERSKINE
          Nancy ERSKINE
          Aurilla ERSKINE
          Roberta ERSKINE
          Rosetta ERSKINE

The War of 1812

Henry Amick's [Henry, Georg] son Jacob was in the War of 1812; Henry may also have served. Jacob is listed in *War of 1812: Virginia Bounty & Pension Applicants* by Patrick G. Wardell:[199]

> Amick, Jacob (BLW), died 6 Sep 1859, Nicholas Co., VA; md 5 Jun 1814 Rachael Stroyer (P), Pendleton Co. VA. She died c1894, LNR Pool, Nicholas Co. WV, 1885.

Also listed is another Jacob Amick which may confuse the records. This may be the Winchester line of Amicks documented by Daisy Amick.

> Amick, Jacob (P, BLW), died 22 Sep 1892, LNR Back Creek, Frederick Co. VA 1871; md 19 Dec 1850 Jane McKee, Capon Springs, VA.

No other Amicks are listed in this work.

In the 1870s with the death of Jacob Amick, his wife Rachel had to apply for widows benefits. The confusion with the other Jacob Amick in Pendleton County in the War of 1812 caused confusion and many documents where created and referenced at that time. Our Jacob was married to Rachel Stroyer while the other Jacob was married to Jane McKee. It is likely the other Jacob was in Mastin's company and our Jacob's company was not known by Rachel (she cites Botkin's Company which is not found and this lead to confusion). The list of documents:

The National Archives, War of 1812 Pension and Bounty Land Warrant Application Files, National Archives Catalog ID: 564415, Record Group 15,

Our Jacob:

> W O Pension Number: 11769,
> W C Pension: 6928,
> Soldier Given Name: Jacob,
> Soldier Surname: Amick
> Widow Given Name: Rachael
> Window Maiden Name: Stroyer
> Bounty Land Warrant Number: 100943
> Bounty Land Acres Granted Number: 40
> Bounty Land Act Year: 1850

Service: Pvt., Capt. Francis T. Mastin's Co., Va. Mil.
Marriage Date: 05-Jun-1814
Soldier Death Date: 06-Sep-1859
Window Death Date: 1894

The "other" Jacob:
S O Pension Number 453,
S C Pension Number: 115,
Soldier Given Name: Jacob,
Soldier Surname: Amick,
Window Given Name: Jane,
Window Maiden Name: McKee,
Bounty Land Warrant Number: 38676,
Bounty Land Acres: 40,
Bounty Land Act Year: 1850,
Service Pvt., Capt. Francis T. Mastin's Co., Va. Mil.,
Marriage Date: 19-Dec-1850,
Soldier Death Date: 22-Sep-1892

Another citation for Jacob Amick and wife Rachel is the pension records:[200]

War of 1812 Pensioners lists Jacob AMICK, wife Rachel
(STROYER). Widow's certificate 6928, md. 5 Jun 1814 in
Pendleton County, Va. Soldier died 6 Sep 1859 in Nicholas
County, W. Va., widow died about 1894. Jacob served with
Francis T. MASTIN's Co., Va Militia. Widow also lived in
Greenbrier County, W. Va and Nicholas County, W. Va.

A search for Mastin's company only finds a reference for the Revolutionary
War.
There is a muster roll for a company of infantry "under the command of
Captain Jesse Hinkle, from the Forty-Sixth Regiment commanded by
Lieutenant Colonel John Hopkins, then by Lieutenant Colonel W. Street, and
later by Lieutenant Colonel Isaac Boothe. The company was enlisted for six
months, beginning July 21, 1814. But for some reason not known, it was
continued in service until after Feb. 1, 1815. In the War Department at
Washington, DC are muster rolls dated August 30, 1814; October 30, 1814;
December 30, 1814; and February 16, 1815. From these records the following
record was compiled for H. M. Calhoun by Virgil A. Lewis, June 19, 1912."
The four muster roll dates are indicated in the roster by (A), (B), (C), (D) in the
order of their occurrence.

Private:
Amick, Henry--discharged, Nov 12

Additional references for the Amick name are found at:
http://.sierrahome.com/familytree/records/

War of 1812 Search results showing all 6 records:

Danny Amick	57th Regiment Virginia Militia
Henry Amick	5th Regiment Virginia Militia
Henry Amick	6th Reg't (Coleman's, January-May, 1814), Virginia Militia
Henry Amick	6th Reg't (Sharp's) Virginia Militia
Jacob Amick	1st Reg't (Taylor's) Virginia Militia
Jacob Amick	39th Reg't (Fowler's) Maryland Militia

Companies had different names as their commanders changed. One of the above may be our Jacob and one might be our Henry but more research is needed.

The reference below to Jacob Amick in the war is not correct. Note he is born only in 1810...

Jacob Amick, who served in the war of 1812 and Rachel were natives of Va, but moved to Kane County, Illinois after receiving payment of 85 acres for serving in the war. They had five children, Mary Elizabeth, Matthew, Pleasant. Hiram (my grandfather) and Myron J.----Joan (Livingstone?), Amick Genforum message 356, Oct 15, 2000.

In reference to JACOB AMICK, b. Abt. 1810, VA; d. Abt. 1850, IL; m. RACHEL REBECCA CORRON, January 26, 1827, Greenbrier Co., VA; b. January 05, 1806, Greenbrier Co., VA; d. April 28, 1878, Chicago, Cook Co., IL.

After the War

Old Henry Amick's son, Henry Amick Jr. fought in the War of 1812. Henry Jr. married Eliza Shroyer[201] and later moved to the state of Ohio. Old Henry Amick's son Jacob Sr. also fought in the War of 1812. He married Eliza Shroyer's sister Rachel Shroyer in 1814. Old Henry Amick's son John the miller Amick married Catherine Bowers in Dahmer, Pendleton County on February 20, 1814. Old Henry's daughter Mary married Christian Propst. His daughter Barbara married Henry Eye. Elizabeth married Peter Pitsenbarger. Elias Amick and Christina Amick Parker and her husband James Parker moved out to Spencer County Indiana across the Ohio River from the Emmick Plantation. Rueben Amick and his wife Anna Brennerman moved out to Ohio.

Barbara Amick died about 1812. John Arvin Dahmer in an interview with Barbara Nichols states: "She [Barbara Amick] was buried with Henry and a daughter Elizabeth."[202]

Marriage Certificate of John and Catharine (Bowers) Amick
Married February 20, 1814 at Pendleton County, Virginia

John Amick married Catherine Bowers in Dahmer, Pendleton County on February 20, 1814 by the Rev. Ferdinand Lair, an early Methodist circuit rider minister.[203,204]

John Arvin Dahmer, in an interview recorded by Barbara Nichols states: "The William McCoy's raised Catherine Bowers but treated her badly. The McCoy's were neighbors of Henry Amick, so after Henry and his family took her in, John Amick fell in love with her, and later married Catherine."[205]

John's older brother Jacob Amick married Rachael Shroyer June 5, 1814.[206] Oldest brother Henry Amick married Rachael's sister, Elizabeth Shroyer on April 10, 1817.

Jacob Summers & Elizabeth Woods	Fardinand Lair	June 24th 1813
John Dean & Catharine Hearn	ditto	March 25th 1814
John Amic & Catharine Berver	ditto	February 20th 1814
George Summers & Elizabeth Wilson	Gerard McorgAn	July 27th 1813
James Campbell & Jane Dyer	Fardinand Lair	March 4th 1814
Peter Harper and Susanna huma	Moses Henkle	October 3rd 1811
Andrew Dilly & Susanna Smith	ditto	December 5th 1812
D' amiel Hartman & Polly ritter	ditto	December 24th 1811
Abraham Ketterman & Sarah Phil	ditto	October 30th 1811
Richard heskendall & Mary Siler	ditto	May 24th 1814
John Bergerhoff & Sarah Cose	ditto	August 3nd 1813
John Casner jr & Eve wise	ditto	September 23th 1813
Joseph Sauly & Phebe Henkle	ditto	November 12th 1811
Silas Blain & Elizabeth Sines	ditto	June 24 1814
Aaron Vansco & Hannah Bennet	ditto	September 6th 1814
Daniel Shoemaker & Barbara Borra	ditto	October 16th 1811
Jacob Specimen & Phebe Castle	ditto	October 10th 1811
Jacob Amick & Rachael Moyer	Robert Bolton	June 5th 1814
Thomas Summers & Catharine Harkott	ditto	July 17th 1814
Thomas Killingsworth & Hannah Lusk	ditto	September

Pendleton County, West Virginia, Register of Marriages, 1800-1852, p. 7
John and Catherine third from top, Jacob and Rachael third from bottom.

June 4, 1816 "Henry Amick County of Pendleton, Va. To William Syfers of said county in consideration of [left blank in deed] conveys two certain tracts of land in said county on a branch of the Black torn". First tract originally granted to Henry Hawk and conveyed to Henry Amick containing 75 acres. The second tract containing 12 acres and part of two tracts of land, ten acres being part of a 45 acres and two acres part of a tract originally granted to Philip Wolf.[207]

287 At a court held for Pendleton County the 4th day of June 1816
This deed from John Bodkin and Elizabeth his wife to Jarred
Armstrong was certified to have been acknowledged in the manner
prescribed by law and admitted
                              A copy Teste J. Dyer C. P. C.

This Indenture made the fourth day of June in the year
of our lord one thousand eight hundred and sixteen between
Henry Amick of the County of Pendleton and state of Virginia
of the one part and William Syfers of said county and state of
the other part Witnesseth that the said Henry Amick for and
in consideration of the sum of
current money of Virginia unto him in hand paid by the
said William Syfers at or before the sealing and delivery
hereof the receipt whereof he doth hereby acknowledge and
thereof do release acquit and discharge the said William Syfers his
heirs Executors and administrators by these presents the said Henry
Amick hath granted bargained sold alien enfeoffed released and
confirmed and by these presents do grant bargain sell alien enfeoff and
confirm unto the said William Syfers his heirs and assigns two certain
tracts or parcels of land lying and being in the said County of
Pendleton on a branch of Black thorn the first tract was originally
granted To Henry Hoult and by him conveyed to the said
Henry Amick. Containing seventy five acres and bounded as
follows To wit Beginning at three chesnuts and a white oak
S. 74. W. 30 poles to three white oaks. S. 47. W. 76. poles to a white oak
and chesnut. N. 32. E. 80 poles to a chesnut and chesnut oaks N. 16 W. 80
poles to two chesnut oaks on a ridge. N. 55. E. 74. poles crossing
a branch to three pines on a laurel bank south 237 poles to the
Beginning the other tract contains twelve acres and is part
of two tracts of land 10 acres part of a tract of 45 acres and two
acres part of a tract of land originally granted to Philip Wolf & is

287

At a Court held for Pendleton County the 4th day of June 1816
This deed from John Bodkin and Elizabeth his wife to Jarred
Armstrong was certified to have been acknowledged in the manner
prescribed by law and admitted
                    A Copy Teste J.H.Dyer. C.P.C.

This Indenture made the fourth day of June in the year
of our lord one thousand eight hundred and sixteen between
Henry Amick of the county of Pendleton and state of Virginia
of the one part and William Syfers of said county and state of
the other part Witnesseth that the said Henry Amick for and
in consideration of the sum of
current money of Virginia unto him in hand paid by the
said William Syfers at or before the sealing and delivery
hereof the receipt whereof he doth hereby acknowledge and
thereof do release acquit and discharge the said William Syfers his
heirs Executors and administrators by these presents the said Henry
Amick hath granted bargained sold alien enfeoffed released and
confirmed and by these presents do grant bargain sell alien enfeoff and
confirm unto the said William Syfers his heirs and assigns two certain
tracts or parcels of land lying and being in the said County of
Pendleton on a branch of black thorn the first tract was originally
granted To Henry Houck and by him conveyed to the said
Henry Amick containing seventy five acres and bounded as
follows To wit Beginning at three chesnuts and a white oak
S.74. W.30. poles to three white oaks S.47. W.76. poles to a white oak
and chesnut N.32. E.80 poles to a chesnut and chesnut oak N.16 W.80
poles to two chesnut oaks on a ridge N.55. E.94. poles crossing)
a branch to three pines on a laurel bank South 237. poles to the
Beginning the other tract contains twelve acres and is part
of two tracts of land 10 acres part of a tract of 45 acres and two
acres part of a tract of land originally granted to Philip Wolf & is

Deeds of Pendleton County [now] West Virginia, Book 6, pp. 287-288
Also note the Indenture for Henry Amick that follows this

On April 4, 1820 Henry Amick [Jr.] and his wife Elizabeth sold the land he had received from his father on the east side of the mountain in the Brandywine Gap.[208]

396. This Indenture made the fourth day of April in the year of our Lord one thousand Eight hundred & twenty Between Henry Emick Jr and his wife Elizabeth Emick of the County of Pendleton and State of Virginia of the one part and John Keister of the County and State aforesaid of the part hath sell that in Consideration of fifty Dollars to them in hand paid by the said John Keister do Bargain and sell unto the said John Keister his heirs or assigns a certain tract or parcel of land Containing Seventy four acres By Survey which was granted to the said Henry Emick by patent bearing date the 30th Day of November 1818 Situated in the County of Pendleton on the East side of the Mountains in the Brandiwine gap adjoining John Profit and Keister's Land and bounded as follow ...to wit Beginning at a large Spanish oak on the north point of a ridge thence N 46 E 26 poles to two Elms N 4 E 36 poles Crossing a hollow to two white oaks on a hill side N 55 W 6 poles to a black oak thence S...E 30 poles to a white oak on a stony Ridge N 11 E 48 poles to a hickory N 50 W 60 poles to two Red oaks on proper line and with the same S 30 W 36 poles to a Red oak on a hill side poops Corner S 33 W 36 poles to a Walnut and Corner and with said line N 17 W 30 poles to a walnut Corner with the same N 65 E 50 poles to a hickory and ash above the head of a spring thence S 74 E 50 poles to a sugar and Iron wood on a hill side South 20 poles Crossing a hollow to a sugar and Iron wood on the point of a ridge S 79 W 45 poles to three red oak on a ridge former Corner S 24 E 10 poles Crossing Keister's line to a sugar and Locust Props Corner and thence S 60 E 125 poles to the Beginning — To have and to hold the said tract or parcel of land with its appurtenances to the only use and behoof of him the said John Keister his heirs and assigns forever and the said Henry Emick and his wife Elizabeth for themselves and their heirs do Covenant with the said John Keister his heirs and assigns that they the said Henry Emick and his said wife the said land with its appurtenances unto the said John Keister his heirs and assigns against all persons whatsoever will warrant and forever defend In witness whereof the said Henry Emick and Elizabeth his said wife have hereunto subscribed their names and affixed their seals the day and year first above written Signed sealed and Delivered in presence of

Henry Emick (Seal)
Elizabeth Emick (Seal)

Pendleton County Deed Book 7, p.396, dated 4 April 1820

Henry Amick Jr. is still listed in Pendleton County in 1820. Jacob is listed in Nicholas County. Henry Amick Sr. is living with his wife and small children. John Amick is listed as manufacturing in the Pendleton County, US Census of 1820.[209]

The census Index lists:

```
32a  5   Amick          Henry, Jr.       pg0032.txt
40a 23   Amick          Henry, Sen'r     pg0039.txt
40a 24   Amick          John             pg0039.txt
```

		WHITE MALES					WHITE FEMALES						OCCUPATIONS		
			10 to 16	16 to 18	16 to 26	26 to 45	45 up	10 to 10	16 to 16	16 to 26	26 to 45	45 up	# of For-eign	AGR	COM	MFG
PG# LN#	LAST NAME	FIRST NAME														
32a 1	Armstrong	John, Jr	2	.	.	.	1	.	3	1	.	1	.	.	1	.	.
32a 2	Armstrong	William	.	1	.	3	.	1	.	1	.	.	3	.	4	.	.
32a 3	Arbogast	Henry	1	2	.	1	.	1	2	1	2	1	.	.	3	.	.
32a 4	Arbogast	George	.	.	1	1	.	1	.	1	1	1	1	.	2	.	.
32a 5	Amick	Henry, Jr	1	.	.	1	.	.	1	.	1	.	.	.	1	.	.

CENSUS YEAR: 1820   STATE: (W)VA   COUNTY: Pendleton   MICROFILM#: M33-140

		WHITE MALES						WHITE FEMALES						OCCUPATIONS		
			10 to 10	16 to 16	16 to 18	26 to 26	45 up	10 to 10	16 to 16	16 to 26	26 to 45	45 up	# of For-eign	AGR	COM	MFG
PG# LN#	LAST NAME	FIRST NAME														
40a 23	Amick	Henry, Sen'r	1	1	.	.	.	1	.	2	.	1	.	.	2	.	.
40a 24	Amick	John	3	.	.	.	1	.	.	.	1	.	.	.	.	.	1

From *Bucks County, Pennsylvania Administration Records* #5035, Bk. 28 (August 1822)[210]

> 28 Aug 1822
> To Benjamin Field, Registrar for the probate of Wills and granting letters of Administration in and for the County of Bucks. I Henry Amey do renounce all my rights of Administering to the Estate of my dec'd Mother in Law Barbara Stoneback in favor of James Jones Esq.
>   Signed
>   Henry Amey
>   Witnesses Thomas Jones, T. C. Field.

From Barbara Nichols this document is the only absolute proof of the marriage of Henry Emig/Amey to Barbara Niemand, daughter of Barbara (Keller) (Niemand) Steinbach (Stonebeck). Henry traveled back to

Pennsylvania and signed as "late of Hilltown, Bucks County, Pennsylvania" to decline interest in his mother-in-law's estate.[211]

From the Pendleton County book of Deeds an Indenture in 1823 states:[212]

> Henry Emick and Catherina his wife of Pendleton County granted Jacob Eye of that county, for consideration of seventy-seven dollars, money of the United States, land in Pendleton County between the South fork of the Potomac and Black Thorn containing seventy-five acres, also ten acres lying on the east side of the above and granted to Henry Emich by patent bearing date, 27 Dec 1799.

This is followed by an Indenture on December 3, 1823 on page 418 and 419 for Henry's and his wife Catherine selling the land to Jacob Eye.[213]

nue appertaining to have and to hold the said tract of land with its appurte=
nances unto the said Jacob Eye his heirs and assigns forever to the only proper
use and behoof of him the said Jacob Eye his heirs and assigns forever and the said
Henry Emick and Catharine his wife for themselves their heirs executors and Adminis=
trators doth covenant with the said Jacob Eye his heirs and assigns that they
the said Henry Emick and Catharine his wife their heirs executors and administrators
the said tract of land with its appurtenances unto the said Jacob Eye his heirs and
assigns against the claim or claims of them the said Henry Emick and Catha=
rine his wife their heirs and of all and every person or persons whatsoever shall
and will warrant and forever defend by these presents In Witness whereof
the said Henry Emick and Catharine his wife hath hereunto set their hands
and seals on the day and year first above written —

                         his
                     Henry X Emick (Seal)
                         mark

                             her
                  Catharine X Emick (Seal)
                          mark

Pendleton County to wit:

     We James Johnson and George W Amiss Justices of the peace in
the County aforesaid in the State of Virginia do hereby certify that Catha=
rine Amick the wife of Henry Amick parties to a certain deed bearing
date on the 3rd day of December and hereto annexed personally appeared
before us, in our County aforesaid and being examined jointly and apart from her
husband, and having the Deed aforesaid fully explained to her, she the
said Catharine Amick acknowledged the same to be her act and
deed, and declared that she had willingly signed sealed and delivered
the same and that she wished not to retract it. Given under our
hands and seals this 3rd day of December 1823 —
                         James Johnson (Seal)
                         George W Amiss (Seal)

Pendleton County, West Virginia Deeds, Book 8, pp. 417-419

419, In the Clerks Office of the County Court of Pendleton December
3rd 1823- This Deed from Henry Amick and Catharine his wife
to Jacob Eye Snr. was presented to me ___ Dyer Clerk of said
County. and acknowledged by the said Henry as the Law directs ___
                                        Teste Z Dyer CC.

At a Court held for Pendleton County the 7th day of January 182_
    This Deed being ___ acknowledged before Magistrate by the
said Catharine in a manner prescribed by Law and admitted to
Record ___
Examd   Teste Z Dyer CC.

This Indenture made the seventh day of November in the year of our
Lord one thousand eight hundred and twenty three Between Samuel Moral
and Elizabeth his wife Both of the County of Pendleton and State of Virginia
of the One part and John Davis of said County and State aforesaid of the other
part Witnesseth that the said Samuel Moral and Elizabeth his wife for and
in Consideration of the sum of seven hundred Dollars lawful money of the United
States to them in hand paid by the said John McDavis the receipt whereof is
hereby acknowledged hath granted bargained and sold and by these presents doth grant
Bargain and sell unto the said John Davis his heirs and assigns forever
three certain tracts or pieces of land lying and in Pendleton County lying
on the East side of the South fork of the South Branch of Potomack as
so forth the first tract Containing Ninety eight acres being part of a larger
tract of land Granted to Robert Green by patent bearing date the
Twenty first day of June One thousand seven hundred and forty seven and
conveyed by Deed from Green to Mathew Patton May the 29th day
1761 and Conveyed by deed from Patton to Robert Davis May the 21st
day 1764 and Bounded as follows Beginning at two red oaks Dickenson
corner of the old Original Tract Thence with Dickensons division line
N 20° East 68 poles to a white pine corner of the same N. 57. W
34 poles to a white oak N 20° E 24 poles to a white oak on the ___

The 1823 LAND BOOK FOR PENDLETON COUNTY, West Virginia lists Henry, Henry Jr. and Jacob as well as several Eyes:[214]

ENTRY #	DIST	LAST NAME	FIRST NAME	ACRES	LOCATION	DIR	NOTES
962	U	AMICK	HENRY	103	HOMEPLACE	7 S	
963	U	AMICK	HENRY	40	ADJ HOMEPLACE	7 S	
964	U	AMICK	HENRY	53	ADJ HOMEPLACE	7 S	
965	U	AMICK	HENRY	60	ADJ HOMEPLACE	7 S	
966	U	AMICK	HENRY	40	ADJ HOMEPLACE	7 S	
967	U	AMICK	HENRY	10	ADJ HOMEPLACE	7 S	
968	U	AMICK	HENRY	45	ADJ HOMEPLACE	7 S	
969	U	AMICK	HENRY	28	ADJ HOMEPLACE	7 S	
970	U	AMICK	HENRY	32	ADJ HOMEPLACE	7 S	
971	U	AMICK	HENRY	7	ADJ HOMEPLACE	7 S	
972	U	AMICK	HENRY	100	ADJ HOMEPLACE	7 S	
973	U	AMICK	HENRY	70	ADJ HOMEPLACE	7 S	
974	U	AMICK	HENRY	60	ADJ HOMEPLACE	7 S	
975	U	AMICK	HENRY	16	ADJ HOMEPLACE	7 S	
997	U	AMICK	HENRY JR	25	SWADLEYS MILL RUN	7 E	
994	U	AMICK	JACOB	40	NEAR JOHN AMICKS	4 S	
995	U	AMICK	JACOB	80	SWADLEYS MILL RUN	7 E	
1185	U	EYE	CHRISTIAN	20	CALF PASTURE	12 S	
1186	U	EYE	CHRISTIAN	110	HEAD HOOVER MT RUN	14 S	
1187	U	EYE	CHRISTIAN	50	ADJ MITCHELL	12 S	NEW GRANT
1183	U	EYE	GEO EST.	50	THORN MT	18 S	
1167	U	EYE	HENRY EST	200	S FORK MT	10 S	
1195	U	EYE	JACOB JR	200	BET FORK AND THORN	12 S	NEW GRANT
1159	U	EYE	STOPHEL EST	110	THORN	10 S	

Henry had amassed 664 acres of land by 1823 with his son Henry owning 25 acres and son Jacob 120 acres.

In the census for 1830, Henry Jr. and John the miller have left the county. Jacob has returned and Henry Amick Sr. is living with second wife and four young daughters.[215]

Propst Church

Author, David Emmick, at the marker on original foundation of
Propst Lutheran Church in the cemetery, taken 2007

John Amick is listed in the Propst Church records written as the original
German spelling of Johannes Emig. This is the same as his great-grandfather;
Georg Emig in early Bucks County, Pennsylvania records: "Member enrolled
or present in the church 1814."[216]

Robert Amick in front of the new Propst Church building overlooking the cemetery, taken 1984

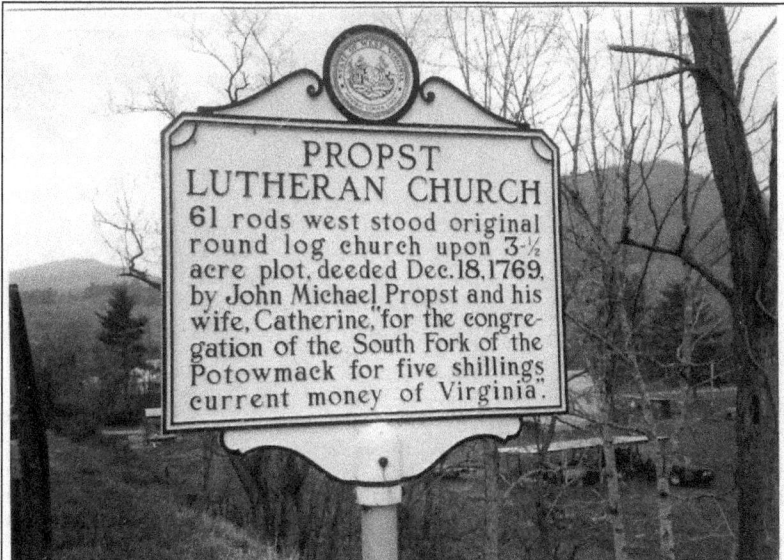

PROPST
LUTHERAN CHURCH
61 rods west stood original
round log church upon 3-½
acre plot, deeded Dec.18,1769,
by John Michael Propst and his
wife, Catherine,"for the congregation of the South Fork of the
Potowmack for five shillings
current money of Virginia".

Road marker for Propst Lutheran Church
About 1981 in Pendleton County, Virginia, now West Virginia
Photo by Barbara Nichols 1984

Marker on original foundation of Propst Lutheran Church in the cemetery, taken 2007

Marker on original foundation of Propst Lutheran Church in the cemetery, taken 2007

"Johannes Emig & his wife, Their daughter Lewesy born the 6 Feb, 1814, Baptized the 15 May, 1814. Godparents, Johannes Bauers & his wife (Lucy Mick)."[217]

"Johannes Emig born 13, April, 1815 Baptized 8 May, 1815. Sponsors, Johannes Emig & wife, namely, father & mother."[218]

"Johannes Emig, His son Gideon is born the 31 March 1819. Baptized the 20 May, 1819. Godparents are the parents."[219]

Henry Amick's Death

Henry Amick's grave stone, picture taken on the lawn in front of the Pendleton County Historical Society where it is kept to avoid further deterioration. The grave site is marked with a new stone. Taken 2007

Sketch of Henry Amick's grave stone, his grave faces east and is marked with a field stone 16"x12"x2". Inscribed H A; the SR 19 is likely for September 19 and 183c for 1830. The flying A in this sketch is overdone when compared with the photo. The V-Bar letter A is common in Bucks County German graves and may be used to avoid chipping the stone.
Sketch by Barbara Nichols

Henry Amick died around 1830. The Thorn area cemetery lists:[220]

> #2 Thorn Area Cemeteries – Barbara listed as Amick ? -- Amick - ?, W-Henry Amick ?, also listed: Amick - ? D- Henry Amick ?

From Barbara Nichols: This is Henry, wife Barbara and daughter Elizabeth. A new stone marker provided by John the miller Amick descendants states: Henry Amick, 1762-1830, Rev Soldier PA.[221]

Old Henry Amick died in 1830. A funny story is told about Old Henry's funeral. John Arvin Dahmer in an interview recorded by Barbara Nichols states:

> When Henry Amick died, the family Pitzenbarger relatives were standing around wondering how to get his body down the narrow circular stairs. He was a very large man and actually died with his boots on. One burly man spoke up with his usual colorful vocabulary and said he would go up and bring him downstairs. He went up, grabbed Henry by the heels of his work boots, and dragged him down feet first. His head went bumperty, bumperty, bump as it hit the steps on the way down.[222]

May 15, 1832, Henry Amick's personal estate was appraised at $25.53. Appraisal was signed by William Syford, Henry Huffman and George Mitcher. A bill of sale for Henry's personal estate is dated and lists sale for $22.63 with $824 due from notes given by Jacob and Elias Amick to their father. Each was to pay $100 per year to Henry's estate from 1831 through 1838.[223]

Reuben, Henry's youngest son, was declared an orphan March 19, 1832 by the Rockingham County, Virginia Court.   His guardian was Peter Brenneman of Rockingham County appointed by the court.[224] On March 22, 1832, Ruben married Annie Brenneman in Rockingham County, VA.[225]

Pointing to Henry Amick's grave with small rail fence near the tree line. This is the third field in from road 23. Taken 2007

View west from Henry Amick's grave site;
you can see the roofs of the Pitsenbarger farm below. Taken 2007

View from the Pitzenbarger farm up the slope [east] to the Henry Amick Gravesite,
taken 2007

Author at Henry Amick grave, looking west toward Pitsenbarger farm buildings, taken 2007

Henry Amick grave

Henry Amick, 1762-1830, Rev Soldier PA, Precious Memory
New marker, the original stone is in the Franklin Historical Society

From Pendleton County, West Virginia Deeds, Book 11:[226]

> Henry's wife Catherine Amick of Pendleton County signed by mark an indenture on 20 Mar 1834 for a consideration of fifty dollars "current money of the United States received from John Propst, son of George and Frederick, assigning Catherine's right of dower as the widow of Henry Amick, dec'd, for several tracts of land lying in Pendleton County between South Fork and South Branch, known as Wolf land. The first tract included forty-five acres, the second, forty-five acres, also, and plus a tract of sixteen acres.

107. In the Clerks office of the County Court of Pendleton March 13th 1834

This Deed from Martin Judy to Adam Judy was presented in the clerks office and acknowledged by the said Martin as the Law directs and admitted to record

Teste
Z Dyer C C

Examined

This Indenture made the 21st day of March 1834, Between Catharine Amick of the County of Pendleton and state of Virginia of the one part, and John Propst son of George of Frederick of the other part. Witnesseth, that the said Catharine Amick for and in consideration of the sum of Fifty dollars current money of the United States unto her in hand paid by the said Jno Propst at or before the sealing and delivery hereof, the receipt whereof is hereby acknowledged, hath granted, sold, aliened, enfeoffed, released and confirmed, and by these presents doth grant, bargain, sell, alien, enfeoff, and confirm unto the said John Propst his heirs and assigns all her right of Dower as the Widow of Henry Amick dec'd in and to several tracts of land lying and being in the County of Pendleton between the South Fork and South Branch and known by the Wolf Tune first a Tract of 65 acres, second a Tract of 45 acres and a tract of 9 acres. These three tracts it is believed are all the lands known by the Wolf lands, but as the parties to this Indenture are not certain that that is the case, it is hereby expressly agreed that if there should be any other tracts of land adjoining the above that belonged to Henry Amick dec'd and in which the said Catharine is entitled to dower, she hereby conveys the same to the said John Propst together with all and singular the rights, improvements hereditaments and appurtenances whatsoever to her right of dower in the said lands belonging and the reversions and remainders, rents, issues and profits thereof. To have and to hold all and singular the premises with the appurtenances hereby granted unto the said John Propst his heirs and assigns, to the only proper use and behoof of him the said John Propst his heirs and assigns forever. And the said Catharine Amick Widow as aforesaid hereby covenants for herself and her heirs that she seized of good and indefeasible estate of Dower in the premises, and that she hath good right to convey the same to the said John Propst in manner aforesaid. And lastly that the said Catharine Amick and her heirs, all and singular her dower in the premises hereby granted with their appurtenances, unto the said John Propst his heirs and assigns, against the said Catharine Amick and her heirs and all and every other person, shall warrant and forever defend by these presents. In Witness whereof the said Catharine Amick hath hereunto set her hand and seal the day and year first above written sealed and delivered

in presence of

                                              her
                                    Catharine X Amick (seal)
                                              mark

In the Clerks office of the County Court of Pendleton March 21st 1834

This Deed from Catharine Amick to John Propst son of George of Frederick was presented in the clerks office and acknowledged by the said Catharine as the Law directs and admitted to record

Teste
Z Dyer C. C.

Examined

From *Nicholas County, West Virginia Book of Deeds* July, 11, 1835 the indenture of ...[227]

> Jacob Amick and Rachael his wife: John Amick and Catherine his wife: Peter Pitsenbarger and Elizabeth his wife: Henry Eye and Barbara his wife; Christian Propst and Mary his wife, the heirs of Henry Amick dec'd of Nicholas County, Virginia, of the first part and John Propst of Pendleton County, same state, of the second sold land in Pendleton County containing sixty-five acres lying at the head of Black Thorn of the South Branch between the lands of Henry Houck and Nicholas Amick's old land.

This document was signed by the heirs showing they had all moved to Nicholas County by 1835.

And from *Pendleton County, West Virginia Deeds, Book 11* (1835):[228]

> John Amick and his wife Catherine; Christian Propst and his wife Mary; Peter Petsenbarger and his wife Elisabeth and Henry Eye and his wife Barbara, heirs of Henry Amick, dec'd, of Nicholas County sold to Jacob Amick of the same county, three tracts of land in Pendleton County. The first contained one hundred three acres, near a line of Henry Stone. The second, contained sixty acres, and the last contained sixty acres on the mountain between the South Fork and Black Thorn Branch, adjoining Henry's former land at the Sink Holes.

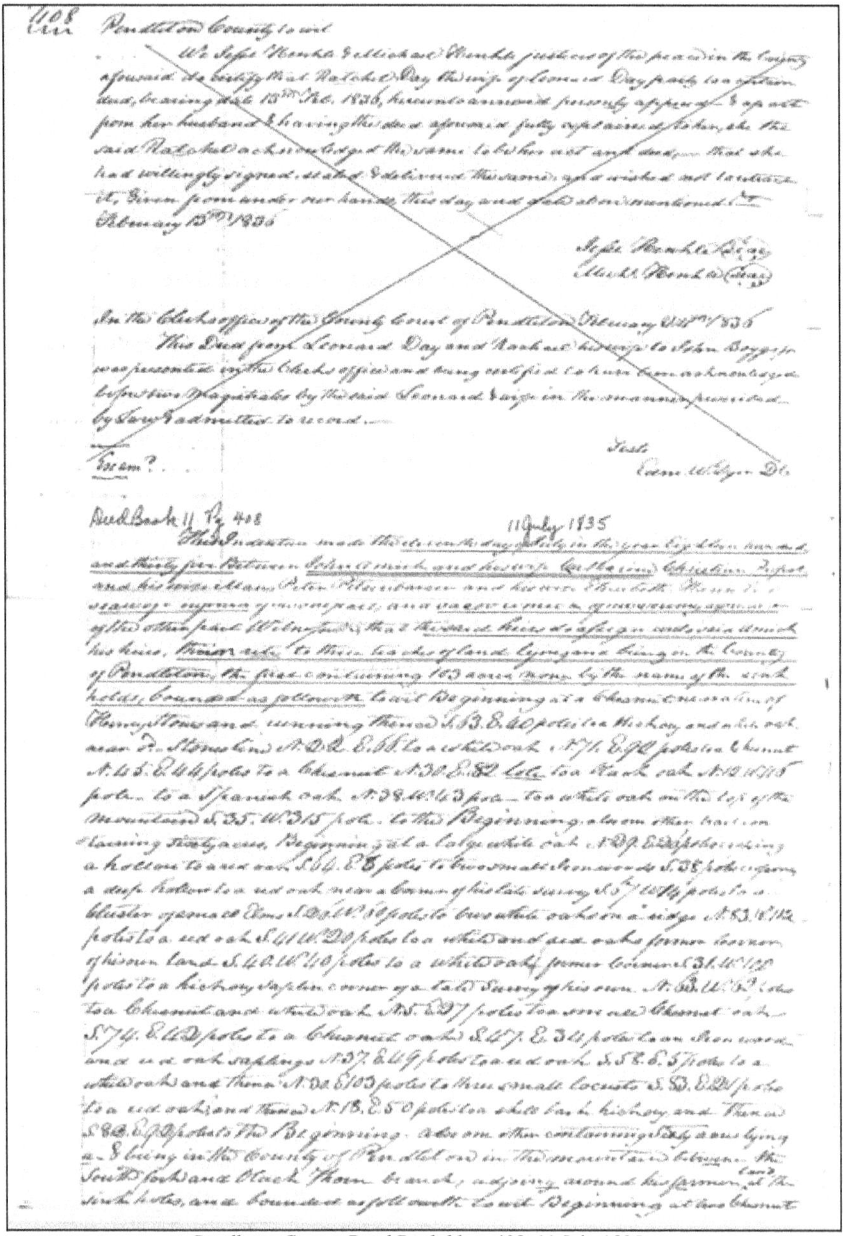

408

Pendleton County to wit

We Jesse Monks & Elliott Monks justices of the peace in the county aforesaid do certify that Rachel Day the wife of Leonard Day party to a certain deed, bearing date 13th Feb. 1836, hereunto annexed personally appeared & apart from her husband & having this deed aforesaid fully explained to her, she the said Rachel acknowledged the same to be her act and deed & that she had willingly signed sealed & delivered the same and wished not to retract it, Given from under our hands this day and date above mentioned the February 13th 1836

Jesse Monks (Seal)
Elliott Monk (Seal)

In the Clerks office of the County Court of Pendleton February 24th 1836

This Deed from Leonard Day and Rachel his wife to John Boggs was presented in the Clerks office and being certified to have been acknowledged before two Magistrates by the said Leonard & wife in the manner prescribed by law & admitted to record.

[illegible]?

Teste
Esau Wilson Dc

Deed Book 11 Pg 408   11 July 1835

This Indenture made the eleventh day of July in the year eighteen hundred and thirty five Between John Amick and his wife Catharine Christian Pepot and his wife Mary Peter Pitsenbarger and his wife Elizabeth Monk [illegible] of the one part and [illegible] of the other part Witnesseth that the said three heirs deeds [illegible] unto said Amick his heirs [illegible] to three tracts of land lying and being in the County of Pendleton, the first containing 163 acres more by the name of the [illegible] holds, bounded as follows to wit Beginning at a chesnut on a tin of [illegible]

[remaining text largely illegible handwriting]

Pendleton County Deed Book 11, p. 408, 11 July 1835

In a copy, undated, in possession of John Arvin Dahmer

Jacob Amick, by his Attorney, John Kenney stated:

> Henry Amick, in the year 1830-31, died interstate, leaving a wife and ten children, and before he had made any conveyance of the lands to his children.
> Shortly after the death of said Henry Amick, his wife who was the step mother of all the children except the youngest, declined the provision which was intended for her and her children and claimed her dower right from the lands of Henry Amick. Jacob Amick purchased her interest in the whole land for about $300 and got a conveyance from her for the same which is of record in the Clerk's Office of the County court of Pendleton County, Virginia...Jacob Amick purchased the interest of his Brother, John Amick, the interest of Christian Propst & Mary, his wife, who was a daughter of Henry Amick, the interest of Peter Pitsenbarger and Elizabeth his wife, another daughter of said Henry Amick, the interest of Henry Eye and Barbara his wife, likewise a daughter of Henry Amick, in and to all of the estate both real and personal of his father Henry Amick for which he has deeds in the Clerks Office in Pendleton Co....He has likewise purchased the interest of his brother Eli Amick in the same, for which he has receipt of the purchase money and has title bond. He has purchased the interest of his Brother Reuben Amick and paid for it. He has agreed to take his fathers debts...The other interest in said estate belonging to his brother Henry, in the state of Ohio, his sister Teney (_?__ wife of Jacob (_?_) of Kentucky, and his Sister Catherine [half-sister] under the age of 21, who moved with her Mother to the state of Ohio.[229]

From Barbara Nichols: "All children identified except for oldest Henry. He received his share in the land earlier and sold it on the 4th of April 1820."[230]

Esther, born 1804 is not mentioned but a "sister Teney," is mentioned but not listed in any other documents. Esther may be the "sister Teney" mentioned.

The Door

Teresa Munn with the door found in the attic,
taken by Jeff Munn 2013

None of the current buildings date to the Henry Amick period. The buildings
left are from the Pitzenberger period – sometime after 1830. In the attic of one
of the old buildings a door was found that dates to the Amick period. Jeff
Munn describes finding the door: [231]

> The door was actually found by a preservation historian who
> was our guest one weekend. I was giving her the tour of the
> old house and she wanted to see the rafters in the attic. While
> up there she noticed the door in a pile of wood back in a far

corner. She immediately recognized it as a door and asked if she could see it. I had no idea what she was talking about. We literally had to crawl on hands and knees to get to it under the eaves and drag it out. She was the one who said it pre-dated the 1840's house by a long shot. So that's how it all got started.

Jeff describes the door as 35" wide and 63" and made from two tongue and grooved planks that are 17.5" wide over 3/4" thick. The strap hinges are hand forged and are approx. 21" long. All the nails in the door are hand forged and very large. They were driven thru the door and bent over back into the wood on the backside. Three cross braces are on the back of the door.

Faint EYE carving with flour for highlights, taken by Jeff Munn 2013

The door has a number of carvings on it. They are numerous and in various orientations. Not all of the carvings are oriented vertically on the door almost as though at some time the "door" was used as a table. There is an H and an A carved as well as an "eye". The "eye" is faint, but is vertically above the latch system. In fact, both the HA and the "eye" are oriented on the latch side and about head height so as to be prominent. The numerous other carvings, likely carved after the door was used as a table, appear to be double "V"s or a strange "W". One is an "H" with a triangle added on top of the crossbar.

H and A carving on the door, taken by Jeff Munn 2013

The "A" in the HA appears to be made to replicate the Masonic compass and square and is similar to the H and A on Henry's grave.

The Propst Family in Pendleton County

Propst Family
Michael PROPST (1679 – 1785) arrived on ship Samuel in 1733
+Barbara
      Johann Michael PROPST Sr. (1712 - 1786) settled Propstburg
      +Anna Maria KELLER (widow of Peter KELLER)
          Philip PROPST (1735 – 1780)
          Daniel PROPST (1736 – 1782)
          Leonard PROPST (1737 – 1801)
          + Mary Catherine MILLER
               Christian PROPST (1795 – 1867)
               +Mary AMICK (1797 – 1874) daughter of Henry
          Johann Michael, Jr. PROPST (1738 – 1738)
+Maria Margaretha CORELL
          John George PROPST (1739 – 1750)
          Frederick George PROPST (1740 – 1741)
          Johann Michael Jr. (II) PROPST 1743 – 1829)
          Margaretha Barbara PROPST (- 1745)

Propst Family Tree
Michael PROPST (1679 – 1785) continued
+Catherine E. (- 1804)
        Frederick George PROPST (1744 – 1801)
        +Barbara SWADLEY
                Jacob PROPST (1769 – 1849) powder maker
                +Rachel CRUMMETT (1770 -   )
                        Jacob PROPST (-)
                        John J. PROPST (1806   -) powder
                        +Elizabeth PROPST (1809   -   )
                Daniel PROPST (- 1850)
                +Elizabeth EYE
        Catherina Barbara PROPST (1745 -   )
        Maria Elizabeth PROPST (1746 -   )
        Maria Eva PROPST (1751 – 1785)
        George Peter PROPST (1751 – 1792)
        +Anna Maria Appolonia EYE
        Heinrich PROPST (1759 – 1820)
        +Mary "Molly" CRUMMETT
        +Barbara EYE
                John PROPST (1805-1876)
                +Elizabeth HOOVER (1811 -)
                        Noah PROPST (1830 – 1879) CW
                        +Susanna BRIGHT
                        William PROPST (1837 –
                        + Sarah EYE
                        Valentine PROPST (1838 -) CW
                        Abel PROPST (1839 – 1867) CW
                        Morgan PROPST (1845 – 1936) CW

CW - indicates Civil War veteran

The family tree is taken from:
        http://www.rootsweb.com/~wvcalhou/mpropst.htm and
        http://www.rootsweb.com/~wvcalhou/fpropst.htm
        http://groups.msn.com/CindyChristinasGenealogyGroup/uncomfirme
        dpropsts.msnw

The lineage of Michael Propst and his children is hard to trace because of the
large families, the marriages between cousins, and the sons of each family

using the same Christian names. The Pendleton County West Virginia History by Oren F. Morton was used in part compiling the web sites above.

The Propst family is an important family to Amick genealogy and research. The family comes from the same area in Germany and settles into Pendleton County before the Amicks. Of significant note is the reference to the Propst family making gun powder in the Civil War. This establishes a line of gun powder making between the Amick and Propst families from 1820 to 1864. The Amick and Propst families do not inter-marry although a few marriages exist. This may be due to a (to us unknown) genetic family relationships. The family relationships would pre-date the journey to America since the families are tracked there. Since the Amicks moved into Pendleton County following the Propsts and since religion and skills seem to overlap in the families, the Propst family is detailed here to help with further research.

(John) Michael Propst (Probst) was a soldier in the French and Indian War and was exempted from the Revolutionary War in 1775.[232] This may place Michael Propst with George Washington at Fort Necessity and possibly in the Freemason's. George Washington held meetings at a cave near Charleston that has retained the name Washington's Masonic Cave. The military lodges at the time were Scottish Right. The Freemasons may be an additional family link between the Amick's, Propst's and Keller's.

These notes are taken from a Web site: Propsts in America found at: http://members.tripod.com/~CampD/propsts_in_america.htm.[233]

THE WEST VIRGINIA PROPSTS
The first known immigrant Propst family was Hans Michael Propst (1679) (age 54) and his wife Barbara (1670) (age 53), with their two children Johann Michael (21) and Anna Barbara (8). They arrived in America on Aug 17 1733 in Philadelphia on the ship "Samuel", Hugh Percy, Master, coming out of Rotterdam. On the ship's papers, the names were shown as Michael Propts, Barbli Bropts, Johan Michal Propts, and Barbara Bropts. On one set of immigration clearance (arrival) papers, the names were shown as "Michael Probst" and "Johs. Michall Probst."

And continues...

Shortly thereafter, they went to Bethlehem, Pennsylvania, but apparently spent little time in that part of Pennsylvania (and none in the Allemaengle), but instead migrated quickly southwestward, into what is now Lancaster and York, then, in the early 1750s, across the Susquehanna River, and through

Maryland down into the Shenandoah River Valley of northern Virginia into what was originally Rockingham and Augusta County, Virginia, and which later became Pendleton County, West Virginia. They lived in the Lancaster area until 1745 before moving on into Augusta County. Whether Hans Michael stayed in Lancaster or moved into Virginia with Johan Michael is not known.

Hans Michael Propst's origins are uncertain. What does seem certain is that he was not related to the Swiss/German Probsts, although he may have been living in the Palatinate. Hans Michael's birth year was determined to be 1679 from the ship's manifest which listed him as being 54 years old in 1733. (And how accurate were the ship's records?) They were just a few of the tens of thousands of Germans who emigrated to America in the 1700s to settle in "Penn's Sylvania", a land opened up to immigrants looking for a new life free of political and religious persecution. Records in Frederick Co, MD, state that Johann Michael Propst and his father Hans Michael Propst came from Wurttemberg, Germany (Bavaria), but a search of the records of Wurttemberg immigrants failed to list them. So it is not known for sure from whence in Germany they came, but it appears most likely that they came from Bonnigheim, a small village near Wurttemberg. Hans Michael was the son of Hans Michael, and the grandson of Johannes Propst.

Johann Michael Propst
In Lancaster, in Dec 1733, in the Muddy Branch Lutheran Church in Cocalico Township, Johann Michael Propst (b. 1712) married Anna Maria Keller, widow of Peter Keller; ceremony by Rev. Johann Caspar Stoever. They had four children - Philip, Daniel, and Leonard, and Johann Michael, Jr. (I). What happened to Anna Maria is not known for sure, but she probably died as a result of childbirth in July 1738 with Johann Michael, Jr., who also died as an infant.
(Note: the family history of the Kellers has not been revealed. There were Kellers living in Lancaster at the time, although no Kellers were found among the names of immigrants from 1720-1735.)

and continues...

> It didn't take Johann Michael, Sr., long to recover from her death, for while still in Lancaster, Johann Michael married Maria Margaretha Corell in Lancaster County on Dec. 3, 1738, again by Rev. Stoever. They had four children while living in New Holland, Lancaster County - John George, Frederick George, Johann Michael Jr (II), and Margaretha Barbara.
>
> From "Index and Abstract of Deeds in Lancaster County, Pennsylvania": In 1735, John Smoze of Leacock Township, Lancaster Co, sold 153 acres of land there to Michael Probtz, a tailor, for 78 pounds. In 1741, Michael had also bought some land on King Street in Lancaster. On July 1 1743, the Smoze land was resold by Michael and wife Margaretha to John Fierre for 82 pounds.
>
> Maria Margaretha apparently died around 1745, for shortly after the birth of their fourth child, he married Catherine Elizabeth (last name unknown). They had six children -- Catharina Barbara, Maria Elizabeth, Frederick George, George Peter, Maria Eva, and Heinrich. It is possible that some or all of those six children could have been the offspring of Maria Margaretha Corell, and the marriage to Catherine Elizabeth took place later.

and continues...

> Sometime after the birth of Margaretha Barbara in 1745 (recorded in Lancaster County), after selling his land in Lancaster County, and before 1749, he and his family left the Lancaster area and migrated southwestward. They probably followed one of the two most common routes: (1) the Old Philadelphia Wagon Road, which ran westward from Philadelphia to Gettysburg, and then headed south into Maryland (through what are now Hagerstown and Frederick) and on into Virginia and North Carolina, or (2) The Moravian Trail, a more easterly parallel route. While enroute to Virginia, they passed through Frederick County, Maryland, for there are records there showing their presence. Those records show Johann Michael and his father Hans Michael; no mention is made in the one Frederick County record found to date of any of the children other than Philip. (Two Brobsts are shown in Frederick County as well, but they were of the immigrant sons

of Christophel Probst from Kandel [John Brobst, b 1768 in Berks Co, and Daniel, b 1796 in Berks Co]).

After leaving Maryland, they continued down into the Shenandoah River Valley of Northern Virginia into "Germany Valley", an area that was originally in Rockingham County, Virginia, which later became Augusta County, Virginia. That area is located just south of Brandywine, in what is now Pendleton County, West Virginia. His parents probably (but not proven) moved with him, as well as the six surviving children of his first two marriages, and perhaps his sister Barbara, also.

Schuyler Brossman states: "He was in Pendleton County, Virginia, now West Virginia, in the 1740s. Some of his visitors there were Moravian Missionaries who knew him when he lived in Lehigh County, Pa, before they went on to Va." Brossman evidently was referring to Hively's history of the Old Propst Church. While it seems clear that they may have passed through Lehigh County on their way from Bethlehem to Lancaster, it is doubtful that they actually lived in Lehigh County; this may have been just some confusion with the Probsts who did live in Lehigh County.

Exactly when he left Lancaster and arrived in Pendleton (then Augusta) County is not certain. One record states he was there in 1749. However, it is questionable whether he was actually there that early. Another record states he settled in Pendleton County in 1753, and is listed as one of the early Pioneers there. Whatever his actual arrival date, and whether with or without his father, he established the village of Propstburg, Pendleton County, West Virginia. Certainly, he arrived in that area between 1746 and 1753, and not much before 1749.

Propsts in America continues…

By the late 1750s, they were well settled in "Germany Valley", along a small creek leading into the South Fork. For many decades, this area was called "Probstburg". In 1756, he and William Dyer were appointed road overseers, replacing William Hevener. He was appointed a "Processioner" on the South Fork of the Potomac in 1767. For many decades, this area was called "Germany Valley" and the village was "Probstburg". In 1769, he and his wife Catherine sold, for 5 shillings, 3½ acres of his 415 acre tract in Propstburg for the building of the first Lutheran Church in West Virginia. (He also owned 240 additional acres elsewhere in Germany Valley.) Today, the third "Old Propst Church" stands on that site, along with the cemetery where Michael and his wife, Catherine, are buried. The fate of Michael's parents is not known. Johann Michael died in 1786. His will, dated Dec 19, 1785, gives some details of his family. The historic marker in Propstburg, WV, shows his wife's name as Catherine in 1769. Family records show that Catherine was clearly the mother of Heinrich, born between 1759 and 1764.

Morton's History of Pendleton County states: "The Pioneer Propst willed 100 acres to his son Henry and 20 pounds ($66.67) to each of his three daughters. His son Philip was the first person to be buried in the yard of the oldest church in Pendleton. The inventory of the property of Frederick who died in 1801, amounted to 2,321.80. The sons mostly remained around the original homestead, the locality being known as "Propstburg". The dispersion of the family has been chiefly southward and westward, the connection being especially numerous between the upper courses of the South Branch and South Fork. The family furnished more soldiers to the Confederate Army than any other in the county. Jacob and his son John J. were noted powder-makers in their day and the product was considered of superior quality. The remains of one of the old mills is on the farm of Laban H. Propst."

and continues…

History of "Propst Country", WV

Prior to 1700, the Shenandoah Valley of Virginia was inhabited primarily by Indians, French soldiers, and wild animals. The Indians were of the Algonquin family; primarily the Senedos Tribe which was exterminated around 1732 in a battle between the Delawares and the Catawbas.

The first non-French whites to see this territory were in a party of about fifty explorers, led by the Alexander Spotswood, Governor of Virginia, in 1716. The area became colonized with European settlers in about 1732, and became known as the Augusta Territory in 1738. So the Propsts, who arrived in 1733 or 1734, were among the very first settlers in this area.

In Virginia, Augusta County was established in 1745; Rockingham County was formed in 1778 from Augusta

County. In 1787, an Act of the Virginia Assembly was passed
creating Pendleton County. This Act transferred the northwest
boundary of western Rockingham County some 25 miles
southeastward, that is, from the Allegheny Mountain to its
present position on the Shenandoah Mountain. When West
Virginia was created from western Virginia in the mid 1800s,
Pendleton County became part of West Virginia.

Of note is another family of Propts that came in on the ship *John and William*
with the other line of Amicks [York/Lancaster line].

They came from Rotterdam to Philadelphia in 1732 on the
Pink (a kind of ship) John and William. Fourteen families
from Northern Bas-Rhine went to Pennsylvania together in
1732 aboard the ship Pink John & William. Johannes Emich
knew many of these families as they came from neighboring
villages. A few are associated with him in Pennsylvania
records.

Johannes was the only one from Uttenhoffen, Niederbronn-
less-Baines. Seven families resided at Lemback, Soultz, north
and east of Uttenhoffen: Balser Gerlach and wife Maria;
Ludwig Hugel; Christian Low, Conrad Low and wife; Anna
Gluf Lowein, Philip Lowein, Christian Lowein, Barbara
Lowein and Margaret Lowein; Johannes Nagel; Hans Georg
Sprecher and wife Catharina Spreakering, Jacob Weber and
wife Dorothy.

Johannes was the only one from Uttenhoffen, Niederbronn-
less-Baines. (Bever). Two from Langensoultzbach, Woerth:
Hans Michael Hoffman & wife Eva Hausman (name listed in
error). One family from Windstein, Niederbronn-les-Bains
and Langensoultzbach: Lorentz Roser (Laurence Rosier, sick,
and Dorothy Rosar). Lastly one from Oberseebach,
Wissembourg: **Jacob Philip Probst and wife Cathrina
Proops, Michael Proops, and Felder Proops.** these families
are all listed in Annette Kunsellman Burgert's *Eighteenth
Century Emigrants from the Northern Alsace to America.*

And from the Pennsylvania Gazette of 1732 a mutiny on this voyage is
reported:[234]

Sunday last arrived here Capt. Tymberton, in 17 weeks from
Rotterdam, with 220 Palatines, 44 died in the Passage. About
three weeks ago, the Passengers, dissatisfied with the length of

the voyage, were so imprudent as to make a Mutiny, and being the stronger Party have ever since had the Government of the Vessel, giving Orders from among themselves to the Captain and Sailors, who were threatened with Death in case of Disobedience. Thus having Sight of Land, they carried the Vessel twice backwards and forwards between our Capes and Virginia, looking for a place to go ashore they knew not where. At length they compelled the Sailors to cast Anchor near Cape May, and five of them took the Boat by force and went ashore from whence they have been five Days coming up by Land to this place, where they found the Ship arrived. Those concerned in taking the Boat are committed to Prison.

1732 John & William

This is listed here because of the similarity of names and the increased possibility of relations to this other Amick and Propst line. The pink (a type of ship) *John & William* brought the Corolina branch of the Amick family. There were Propsts listed on this ship as well. This does re-enforce that the two lines of family are related.

> [List 28 A, B, C] *John & William (pink)*
> Captain: Constable Tymperton
> From: Rotterdam
> By Way of: Dover
> Arrival: Philadelphia, 17 Oct 1732
> 71 men, 98 women & children. Sixty one Palatines, who with their families, making in all one hundred and sixty nine persons

Black Powder

Thorn Springs, Looking toward McCoy Mill on Dry Run Creek and Thorn Creek from route 220. The road past the mill goes up to Dahmer and the Amick homestead, several miles up stream from here on the Thorn is the Saltpeter and Powder Works. Taken 2007.

In early years of the colonies England restricted the manufacture of black powder. However, during the Revolutionary War the colonists manufactured low grade black powder in the forests. The State of Pennsylvania was actively searching for sources of black powder and the need for powder during the war was great. In the early years, gun powder manufacture was a family affair. The DuPont's had a small family mill, as did the Hazards; there was no large commercial production as there is today. The Amicks were millers and had grain mills. The Bucks County Safety Committee was encouraging the making of black powder. One of Old Henry Amick's neighbors, Kechlien, was on the safety committee in search of sources for powder. Kechlien was also an auditor of Henry's father's estate.

John the miller Amick had a black powder mill after the Revolutionary War and may have learned the craft from his father Henry, and grandfather Henry. It is uncertain how they learned the trade. If they learned it from necessity and from the application of milling and engineering principles or whether it had been passed down from their family in Europe.

The original market for black powder was blasting. Blasting for the railroads, particularly the Baltimore and Ohio may have contributed to Henry's move to Pendleton County. The Amicks were one of only 208 or more powder mills.

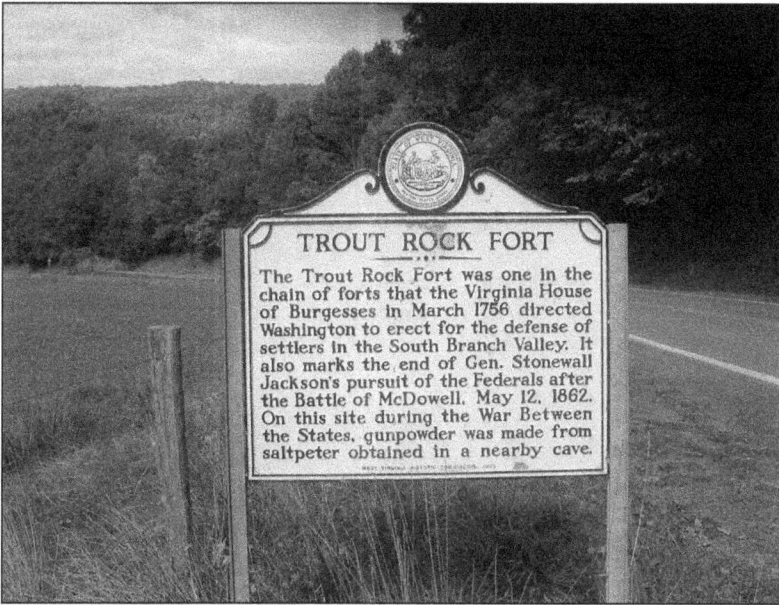

Road Marker for Trout Rock, route 220, taken 2007.

Trout Rock Fort was one of the forts the Virginia House of Burgesses directed then Colonel Washington to erect in defense of the settlers in the South Branch Valley. There is, however, no evidence that the fort was actually constructed. The reference to "Trout Rock Fort" may be to a strategic supply of the ingredients of black powder: sulphur and saltpeter from the caves. It would be important to keep this strategic area secret and yet be able to reference it by a name. This would put the production of black powder at the site sometime around 1756. Clearly the site was making powder around 1820 and continued through the War Between the States in 1864. Trout Rock is now the John Guilday Caves Nature Preserve. There are many caves throughout the valley including a large complex at Sinnet Cave and Thorn Mountain Cave but the Little Cave, Trout Cave and Hamilton Cave at Trout Rock are better known and documented. Many of the caves in the area show signs of saltpeter production.[235] John Penninger was the first to have the land surveyed for deed on July 19, 1787. The caves were worked for saltpeter from then until the end of the Civil War. Four thousand pounds of saltpeter were extracted per year in 1810 but by 1820 the caves were nearing exhaustion.[236]

Powder Mill run road is right at the Trout Fort location on Route 220
Note the cliff above the sign in the photo,
this is the location of the caves and source of the saltpeter. Taken 2007

Looking upstream (south) on Thorn Creek from side of Route 220, the bend is the location of the
Trout Rock saltpeter works. You can still see some remnants of structure at the creek side in the
center of the picture. Taken 2007

Another view looking upstream (south) on Thorn Creek, the bend is the location of the Trout Rock saltpeter works, they were completely destroyed during floods in the 1930s. Taken 2007

Gun powder involves sulphur, saltpeter (nitre) and charcoal. Sulphur occurs naturally and can be mined. Saltpeter is leached from excrement or guano. It can come from outhouses or can be mined from caves. Bats leave guano on cave floors. Charcoal is made from burning wood without air. The ingredients are ground separately to a fine powder and then mixed in a slurry of water and sometimes alcohol. The slurry is pumped through sieves for size and dried. This is called "kernalization" and was invented by the French. Prior to that the powders were dry mixed and the gunpowder was like flour. Kernalized black powder manufacturing remained a trade secret in the Guilds for centuries.

Powder was in great demand after the War of 1812 for the construction of the B&O Railroad across the Allegheny Mountains. John the miller would make the powder and possibly Jacob would transport it up to the mountains. Jacob became a blaster using powder to move rock and clear a path. John was called "John the miller" to distinguish him from the other Johns in the family. He moved to Thorn Creek in Pendleton County and built a powder mill. John pulverized charcoal to make powder.

Powder mills are exceptional. Very few powder mills existed and it was a unique but necessary skill. It was a skill passed down from father to son. Powder mills require distinct engineering skills similar to flour mills. Flour is also highly combustible, and mills need to be sensitive to spark danger. Powder mills were earth bermed at times to keep a blast contained if it happened.

John the miller Amick built his house on Thorn Creek about 5 miles south of Franklin near a small spring. This is near the Trout Rock saltpeter works. The powder mill was about an eighth of a mile down stream from the house on the bank of Thorn Creek. You can still see sulfur in the clay banks of the creek. The powder mill was built on a big S bend in the creek. The mill was made entirely of wood with no nails or metal that might spark and cause a fire. One morning John and Catherine returned home for breakfast. A tremendous explosion was heard. A powder mill was very volatile. It had exploded hurling a large log across the creek into a tree. The neighbors, hearing the explosion from miles away, came running. Determining John and Catherine must be dead, they discussed which family would take which orphan. The neighbors found the family safe and sound. John and Catherine had been at breakfast at the house and not down at the mill.[237, 238]

John Arvin Dahmer in an interview with Barbara Nichols continues:

John and Catherine Amick moved shortly after their marriage to the banks of the Black Thorn, a branch of the Thorn Creek, where John built a powder mill. He also built a house near a good spring on the banks of the creek; with the mill about one-eighth mile down stream. While visiting in the area in 1981, John A. Dahmer took this compiler, with an Amick cousin, Robert Amick, his wife Connie and their youngest son Henry, to this site on the Thorn. Only the creek and spring now remain.

The powder mill was built where the stream makes a big S bend under a present-day dirt cliff visible from the road up Thorn Creek about five miles from Thorn Spring south of Franklin. The mill race was broken out of the rock in the first bend by first building fires on the large flat rock of the stream bed, then pouring water on the hot rocks to fracture them and thus finally making the water race across the bend. Water then could be let in or shut off at will.

One morning after returning home from the mill for breakfast, John and his family heard a tremendous explosion. The powder mill had blown up! A log was thrown up by the explosion and lodged in the fork of a tree across the creek. John A. Dahmer stated, "It remained there for years as a reminder of the incident."

John Amick pulverized charcoal when making powder, and his entire mill was made of wood, using wood pegs instead of metal nails, so it is unknown what could have caused the explosion. John used local materials in his manufacturing of the gun powder. After the powder mill explosion, the neighbors came hurrying over expecting to find only young orphans. However, the whole family was alive to everyone's amazement. It was shortly after the accident that John moved his family to Nicholas County, making the trip over the mountains by horseback. They were settled on Anglins Creek by 1821.[239]

Geneva Amick Dyer in Fourteen Children states:

The first authentic history I have is of our grandfather, John Amick, born Sept. 6th, 1790, presumably in Pendleton county, W. Va. He married Catherine Bowers, Feb. 1813. This marriage was in Pendleton county and grandmother was at that time a little past twenty years of age, having been born Dec. 9th, 1792. It is to her I owe much of this information. They owned, and operated a gunpowder mill. One morning after having started the mill in operation, and had gone home for breakfast, there was an explosion, which destroyed the mill. Neighbors who lived many miles away heard the explosion, and hurried to grandfather's home confident the parents had been killed, each one deciding as they came, which one of the six or seven children, they would take to rear. Soon afterward they moved to Nicholas county, W. Va., carrying their possessions on horseback. [240]

The family black powder business continued with the Propst family relatives until the Civil War. It is not clear that any of John's children continued the trade.

In the Civil War

Black Powder making in Franklin and the valley were key in the Civil War and the Union attacked the valley several times. The Amick in-laws, the Propsts were running a powder mill just south of Franklin up to the Civil War. The Propst's continued production of black powder into the time of the War Between the States:[241]

> The family furnished more soldiers to the Confederate Army than any other in the county. Jacob and his son John J. were noted powder-makers in their day and the product was considered of superior quality. The remains of one of the old mills is on the farm of Laban H. Propst.

On August 9, 1863, Averell left Moorefield and marched 11 miles to Petersburg, leaving Gibson's battalion on the South Fork. His command was badly in want of horse-shoes and nails, clothing, and ammunition, requisitions for which had been made by his quartermaster, at Cumberland, on the seventh.

The order of Brigadier-General Kelley to move was received on the fifteenth, at Petersburg, but it was not until noon of the seventeenth that horse-shoe nails arrived. Some ammunition for Ewing's battery was also received, but Averell was unable to increase his supply for small-arms, which amounted to about thirty-five cartridges to each man. This was sufficient for any ordinary engagement, but they had a long march before them, entirely in the country occupied by the Confederates, and he felt apprehensive that the supply would be exhausted before the expedition should be ended.

It was his opinion that the delay which would ensue by awaiting the arrival of ammunition would be more dangerous to them than undertaking the expedition with the supply they had. Therefore, on the eighteenth, Colonel Oley, 8th West Virginia, was sent with his regiment up the North Fork of the South Fork. On the morning of the nineteenth, Averell moved with the 3rd West Virginia, 14th Pennsylvania Cavalry, and Ewing's battery nearly to Franklin sending forward two squadrons to destroy the saltpeter works 5 miles above.

Four miles south of Franklin in Pendleton County, West Virginia, in March of 1864, the Union destroyed the salt-peter works. This is near the site of the

Amick homestead and the powder mill of John the Miller that exploded in the 1820s. This would be near or is the site of Laban Propst's farm.

March 8 the Salt Peter works were destroyed again:[242]

> HDQRS. FIFTEENTH Regiment NEW YORK VOL. CAV.,
> Camp near Burlington, W. Va.,   March 8, 1864
> SIR: I have the honor to report to you, for the information of the colonel commanding, that in obedience to an order received from division headquarters on the 28th day of February, 1864, I moved with my command, 400 strong, at 8 p. m., on the 29th ultimo, toward Petersburg, W. Va., and arrived there at daylight on the 1st instant, meeting with no opposition and finding no enemy there. I strongly picketed all approaches to the place, and camped my command in a ravine about 1 mile from town.
> During the day I directed the detached portions of the command that had reported to me to take three days' ration in haversacks and two days' forage for animals on the horses, and be prepared to move at 8 p.m. One of the wagons of my command containing supplies not coming up I could only take two days' rations for men and animals for the Fifteenth New York Cavalry. The command that I had been informed would report to me at Petersburg on the 1st instant to take charge of my wagons did not arrive until 8 p. m. Before I could have formed the command, drawn in my pickets, and crossed the river, it would have been 2 o'clock, and from the bad condition of the roads it would have been impossible for me to have reached Franklin at daylight on the 2nd instant, and owing to the snow-storm of the previous twenty-four hours my men and animals had been unable to obtain any rest, and upon the suggestion of Captain Pease, of your staff, I decided not to move until the evening of the 2nd instant.
> At 7 p m., on the 2nd, I moved forward and arrived at Franklin a little after daylight on the 3rd. Finding no enemy there I moved forward, with one squadron, to the saltpeter-works, 4 miles south of the town, and completely destroyed the buildings and all the materials for carrying on the works. Being satisfied from the information that had been obtained that there was no force of the enemy in the Crab Bottom country, and learning that the enemy's forces had been ordered to concentrate on the South Fork, I decided to move directly to Circleville, distant 15 miles. I left Franklin at 3 p.

m., crossed the North Mountain, and reached Circleville at 7 p.m., and camped. Moved forward at daylight down the North Fork. Near evening I received information from a citizen (Mr. Carr) that a part of the force left in charge of my train at Petersburg had been captured and the balance of it had fallen back. I pushed forward and took up a position at the junction of the Greenland and North Fork roads, arriving there at 3 a. m. of the 5th, having marched 37 miles.

In the mean time I had sent Lieutenant Gibson, of the Ringgold Calvary, with 10 men to ascertain what force (if any) of the enemy were in my front. I received a report from him at daylight, that he had been into Petersburg and there was no force there. I immediately moved forward, arriving there at 12 m. Finding no rations or forage there for my command I decided to move at once to Burlington, where I arrived at 11 p m.

My command has marched, since leaving camp, 172 miles over a very rough road, and for two days with but little subsistence, the country being entirely destitute of anything but hay. My loss in material, from examination, has been 12 horses. The 6-mule wagon that accompanied the command was precipitated down a precipice and destroyed. From 2 prisoners that were captured I received information that on the day of my arrival in Franklin the enrolling officer for the Confederate Government, with a provost guard, was to have arrived there, and the men that had been conscripted were ordered to report there on that day. My arrival was very opportune, and the destruction of the saltpeter-works must have been a loss to the Confederate Government of $8,000 or $10,000.

I desire to express my sincere thanks to Lieutenant McKenzie and Nugent, of the staff of the colonel commanding, and Lieutenant Gibson, of the Ringgold Cavalry, for the prompt and efficient manner in which they preformed all the duties assigned to them, but I would particularly request that Lieutenant Crago, of the Ringgold Battalion, will not be again assigned to any command under me. To Captain Pease I am under special obligations for his assistance in the general movements of the command.

> I have the honor to be,
> very respectfully,
> your obedient servant,

A. I. ROOT,
Lieutenant Colonel,
Commanding Fifteenth New York
Vol. Cavalry.
Lieutenant M. J. RUSSELL,
Acting Assistant Adjutant-
General

The Propst Cemetery

Propst Cemetery, taken 2007

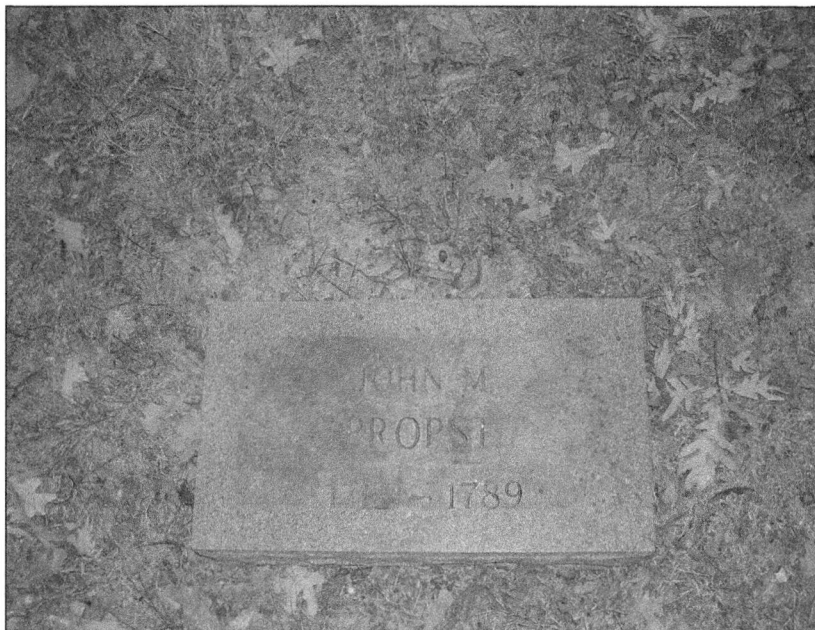

John M. Propst, 1712 – 1789
Propst Cemetery, taken 2007

John and Elizabeth Eye
Propst Cemetery, taken 2007

The Pitsenbarger Family

Pitsenbarger Family Tree

Abraham PITSENBARGER (-1781)
    from Hesse-Darmstadt, Germany
    Served as a private in Michael Reader's Co. VA Rev War
+Elizabeth TISSINGER
    Jacob PITSENBARGER (1767 - 1840) *died Ohio*
    +Margaret BUTCHER (1768 – 1848)
    Abraham Jr. PITSENBARGER (1770 - 1840)
        died Nicholas County
    +Mary COWGER
        John PITSENBARGER (1797 – 1877)
        +Rachel PROPST (1801 – 1863)
        Peter PITSENBARGER (1798 – 1864)
        Elizabeth AMICK (1800 -   )
        Jacob PITSENBARGER (1800 – after 1850) *Iowa*
        +Catherine SIMMONS (1807 – 1850)
        William PITSENBARGER (1803 – 1887)
        Eve AMICK (1810 -   )
        Elizabeth PITSENBARGER (1810 -)
        Abraham PITSENBARGER (1812 – 1887)
        +Nancy McCLUNG (1813 -)
            daughter of Samuel and Sarah
    Elizabeth Ann PITSENBARGER (1774 - 1820) *died Ohio*
    +John MOATS (1767 – 1851)
    Peter PITSENBARGER (1774 – 1837) *died Ohio*
    +Mary FRY (1789 – 1853)
    John PITSENBARGER (1776 – bef 1794)
    Philip PITSENBARGER (1780 – 1840)

Robert Amick near Amick homestead in Pendleton County.
These buildings date to Pitsenbarger who bought the farm from Henry.
Taken by Barbara Nichols 1984 looking at Amick knob.

Abraham Pitsenbarger was from Hesse-Darnstadt and settled in Lancaster County Pennsylvania before moving to Shenandoah County Virginia before 1780. He served as a private in Michael Reader's Co. VA during the Revolutionary War. Abraham married Elizabeth in Lancaster Co. and most of the children were born there. His son Abraham Jr. bought Nicholas Emmick's farm when Nicholas moved to Rockbridge and then to Kentucky. His son Peter married Henry Amick's daughter Elizabeth. His son William married Nicholas' son John's daughter Eve Amick. John was from Nicholas' first marriage.

The Pitsenbarger Genealogy is available at:
http://www.calweb.com/~wally/darke/w-pits3.htm

Pitsenbarger homestead. Taken 2007

Robert Amick near Amick homestead in Pendleton County,
these buildings date to Pitsenbarger who bought the farm from Henry.
Taken by Barbara Nichols 1984.

Pitsenbarger homestead. Taken 2007

Pitsenbarger homestead. Taken 2007

Pitsenbarger homestead. Taken 2007

Looking west toward Pitsenbarger homestead. Taken 2007

Root cellar on north side of farm buildings, taken 2007

Of note is the move to Ohio. These three Pitsenbargers move at about the same time as Henry Amick Jr.:

Jacob PITSENBARGER (1767 - 1840) *died Ohio*
Died - 25 Mar 1848 Wayne Twp, Darke Co., OH

Elizabeth Ann PITSENBARGER (1774 - 1820) *died Ohio*
Died - 1 May 1820 Jackson Co., OH

Peter PITSENBARGER (1774 – 1837) *died Ohio*
Died - 3 Dec 1837 Wayne Twp, Darke Co., OH

The Pitsenbarger graveyard looking north toward Amick Knob,
this is the second field in from road 23. Taken 2007

Graves of J. Alben (18879 – 1967) and Sarah (1875 – 1959) Pitsenbarger
Pitsenbarger Graveyard near Amick home stead on road 23, taken 2007

Graves of Gilbert Pitsenbarger (1884 – 1973)
Pitsenbarger Graveyard near Amick home stead on road 23, taken 2007

The Nicholas Family

Nicholas Family Tree

Unknown relationship to Bucks County Nicholas family

Zepheniah NICHOLS (1705 -   )
+ unknown
    George NICHOLS (1727 - 1813)
    + Barbara
        Elizabeth NICHOLS
        George NICHOLS (1767 -)
        William Cary NICHOLS (1769 -)
        Catherine NICHOLS (1773 -)
        Barbara NICHOLS (1774 - 1850)
        Francis NICHOLS (1775 -1864)
        Henry NICHOLS (1783 - 1877)
        James NICHOLS
        Nathan NICHOLS
    Levan NICHOLAS (1730 - 1821)
    +Lucretia
        Levan NICHOLS Jr. (1756 -)
        Zepeniah NICHOLS (1763 -)
        + Rebecca DAVIS (1790 -1850)
            William NICHOLS (1794 -1869)
            Zepeniah NICHOLS Jr. (1800-)
            Hugh NICHOLS (1801 -)
            James NICHOLS (1802 -)
            Robert NICHOLS (1805 -)
            Miles NICHOLS (1807 -)
            Johnathan NICHOLS (1808 - 1843)
            Andrew NICHOLS (1815 - 1884)
        William NICHOLS
        Lucretia NICHOLS
        James William NICHOLS

Road Builders

Cousins James and Zepeniah Nicholls settled in Pendleton County about the same time as the Amicks. The family name has various spellings: Nichols, Nicholls and Nicholas.

Old Henry's mother was Catherina Nickla daughter of Valentine and Anna Elisabeth Nicola. Fighting with Old Henry in the same company in the Revolutionary war were his cousins Daniel, Henry and Jacob Nicholas. James and Zepeniah Nicholls were both road builders and probably worked the B&O Railroad line. It is not known how the two lines of Nicholas are related. The Amicks and Propsts made blasting powder which would have been sold primarily to this road.

With the completion of the B&O Railroad James Nicholls moved from Pendleton County to settle near Cross Lanes before Nicholas County was organized in 1818. The James River and Lewisburg Turnpike and the Wilderness Road were begun in 1817. His cousin Zepeniah Nichols came to Nicholas County about 1820. James was overseer of the road from the mouth of the Gauley to Little Elk Creek in 1824. [243] The Nichols families were road builders from Pendleton County. Many of the Nichols family moved on into Clay County building roads but a few stayed in Nicholas. Zepeniah's son John Nicholas was the Road Superintendent for the West Fork.

Jacob Amick worked with them on the Wilderness Road before 1820. He is in the census as living there. Jacob Amick worked building the Wilderness Road for many years and then returned home to Pendleton County before moving back with the whole family.

Descendants of Johan Georg EMIG

First Generation

1. **Johan Georg EMIG** was born 7 Jul 1714 in Germany. He died 5 Mar 1773 in Haycock, Township, Bucks County, Pennsylvania and was buried 1773 in Trinity Church, Springfield Township, Bucks, Pennsylvania.

Johan married **Maria Elisabeth** on 1736/1738 in Germany. Maria was born in Germany. She died 12 Oct 1799 in Haycock twp, Bucks, Pennsylvania.

They had the following children:

+   2   M   i   **Johan Heinrich EMIG** was born 1737/1739 and died Dec 1777.

+   3   M   ii   **Johan Philip EMIG** was born 1745.

+   4   M   iii   **Johan Georg EMIG** was christened 21 Apr 1751 and died 13 Apr 1829.

Second Generation

2. Johan Heinrich EMIG (Johan Georg) was born 1737/1739 in Germany. He died 11 Jun 1777 and was buried 1777 in Haycock twp, Bucks, Pennsylvania. Johan married **Anna Catharina NICHOLAS**, daughter of Johann Valentine NICHOLAS and Anna Elisabeth SCHENCK, on 4 Dec 1759 in Keller's Church, Bedminster Twp, Bucks, Pennsylvania. Anna was born about 1739/1740 in Pennsylvania. She died 1832 in Richland Twp, Bucks, Pennsylvania.

They had the following children:

+   5   F   i   **Maria Elizabeth EMICH** was born 5 Sep 1760 and died 12 Aug 1761.

    6   ii   **Child EMIG** was born 1761 in Haycock Twp, Bucks, PA. Child died 12 Aug 1761 in Haycock Twp, Bucks, PA and was buried 13 Aug 1761 in Bucks, PA.

+   7   M   iii   **Henry AMICK** was born 7 Jun 1762 and died 1830.

+   8   F   iv   **Julianna EMICH** was born 29 Apr 1765 and died 31 Aug 1841.

    9   F   v   **Catherine Margaret EMICH** was born 9 Jan 1768 in Bedminster Twp, Bucks, Pennsylvania and was christened[1] 3 Apr 1768 in Keller's Church, Bedminster Twp, Bucks, Pennsylvania. She died 12 Oct 1842 in Bedminster Twp, Bucks, Pennsylvania and was buried 1842 in Keller's Church, Bedminster Twp, Bucks, Pennsylvania.

+   10   M   vi   **John Philip EMICH** was born 11 Dec 1769 and died 27 Oct 1850.

+   11   F   vii   **Mary Magdalene EMICH** was born 30 Jan 1772 and died before 15 Oct 1841.

    12   M   viii   **John George EMICH** was born 6 Apr 1774 in Bedminster Twp, Bucks, Pennsylvania and was christened 20 Aug 1774 in Keller's Church, Bedminster Twp, Bucks, Pennsylvania. He died after 1827.

          John married **Barbara HESS**, daughter of Conrad HESS and Anna Dorothea FRANKENFIELD, on 14 May 1797 in Springfield Twp, Bucks, PA. Barbara was born 14 Feb 1772 in Springfield Twp, Bucks, PA.

3. Johan Philip EMIG (Johan Georg) was born 1745 in Germany.

Johan married **Barbara HAHN** before 1766.

They had the following children:

+   13   M   i   **Johannes Nicholas EMMICK** was born 15 Sep 1766 and died 1

Aug 1836 in Hancock county, Kentucky.

14 F ii **Maria Magdalena EMIG** was born 20 Oct 1768 in Haycock Township, Bucks County, Pennsylvania and was christened 13 Nov 1768 in Tohickon Church, Bedminster, Pennsylvania.

15 M iii **Henry EMIG** was christened 11 Nov 1770 in Tohickon Church, Bedminster, Pennsylvania.

16 F iv **Catharine EMIG** was born 25 Nov 1772 and was christened 4 Dec 1772 in Tohickon Church, Bedminster, Pennsylvania.

4. **Johan Georg EMIG** (Johan Georg) was christened 21 Apr 1751 in Bedminster, Bucks County, Pennsylvania. He died 13 Apr 1829 in Haycock, Bucks County, Pennsylvania.
Johan married **Anna Margaretha LERCH**, daughter of Anthony LERCH and Anna Margaretha LAUER, on 1771 in Bedminster, Pennsylvania. Anna was born 31 Dec 1754 in Lower Saucon Township, Northampton, Pennsylvania. She died 13 Apr 1829 in Haycock, Bucks County, Pennsylvania.
They had the following children:

+ 18 M i **George EMIG** was born 23 Apr 1774.

19 F ii **Anna Maria EMIG** was christened 2 May 1778. She died Apr 1805 in Bucks County, Pennsylvania.

Anna married **Johann Jacob WEIRBACH** on 1795 in Bucks County, Pennsylvania.

20 M iii **Johannes EMIG** was born 7 Apr 1779. He died 29 Jun 1849.

Johannes married **Margaret HESS**, daughter of Conrad HESS and Anna Dorothea FRANKENFIELD. Margaret was born 21 Oct 1783 in Springfield, Bucks County, Pennsylvania.

21 M iv **Samuel EMIG** was born 8 Apr 1782 and was christened 24 May 1782 in Springfield, Bucks County, Pennsylvania.

22 v **Petrus EMIG** was born 22 Aug 1784 and was christened 3 Oct 1784 in Springfield, Bucks County, Pennsylvania.

23 M vi **Anthony EMIG** was born 17 Jan 1789 and was christened 22 Mar 1789 in Springfield, Bucks County, Pennsylvania. He died 1842 in Richland, Bucks County, Pennsylvania.

24 M vii **Joseph EMIG** was born 27 Aug 1793. He died 8 Apr 1842 in Springfield, Bucks County, Pennsylvania.

25 F viii **Catharine EMIG** was born 8 Nov 1795 and was christened 28 Mar 1796 in Springfield, Bucks County, Pennsylvania.

26 M ix **David EMIG** was born 28 Jun 1798.

27 F x **Magdalena EMIG** was christened 30 Sep 1800 in Springfield, Bucks County, Pennsylvania.

Third Generation

5. **Maria Elizabeth EMICH** (Johan Heinrich, Johan Georg) was born 5 Sep 1760 in Bedminster Twp, Bucks, Pennsylvania and was christened 28 Sep in Keller's Church, Bedminster Twp, Bucks, Pennsylvania. She died 12 Aug 1761 in Bedminster Twp, Bucks, Pennsylvania and was buried 13 Aug 1761 in Bedminster Twp, Bucks, Pennsylvania.

Maria married **Daniel WIEGNER** on 1783 in Keller's Church, Bedminster.

They had the following children:

    28 M i   **Joseph WIEGNER** was born 12 Dec 1784 in Haycock, Bucks County, Pennsylvania and was christened 19 Dec 1784 in Keller's Church, Bedminster, Bucks County, Pennsylvania.

    29 F ii   **Elisabeth WIEGNER** was born 20 Oct 1786 and was christened 10 Jun 1787 in Keller's Church, Bedminster, Bucks County, Pennsylvania.

    30 F iii **Sarah WIEGNER** was born 23 Aug 1792 in Haycock, Bucks County, Pennsylvania and was christened 18 Nov 1792 in Keller's Church, Bedminster, Bucks County, Pennsylvania.

    31 M iv **George WIEGNER** was born 1 Jun 1794 in Haycock, Bucks County, Pennsylvania and was christened 5 Oct 1794 in Keller's Church, Bedminster, Bucks County, Pennsylvania.

    32 M v   **Henry WIEGNER** was born 30 Dec 1795 in Haycock, Bucks County, Pennsylvania and was christened 27 Jul 1796 in Keller's Church, Bedminster, Bucks County, Pennsylvania.

7. **Henry AMICK** (Johan Heinrich, Johan Georg) was born 7 Jun 1762 in Bedminster, Bucks, Pennsylvania and was christened 4 Jul 1762 in Keller's Church, Bedminster Twp, Bucks, Pennsylvania. He died 1830 in Dahmer, Pendleton, West Virginia and was buried 1830 in Dahmer, Pendleton, West Virginia.

Henry married **Elisabeth Barbara NIEMAND**, daughter of Johannes NIEMAND and Elisabeth Margaret Barbara KELLER, on 1783 in Keller's Church, Bedminster Twp, Bucks, Pennsylvania. Elisabeth was born 8 Aug 1764 in Haycock twp, Bucks, Pennsylvania. She died 1808/1810 in Dahmer, Pendleton, West Virginia.

They had the following children:

    33 F i   **Elisabeth AMICK** was born Nov 1784 in Haycock twp, Bucks, Pennsylvania and was christened- 9 Jan 1785 in Keller's Church, Bedminster Twp, Bucks, Pennsylvania. She died before 1800 in Dahmer, Pendleton, West Virginia.

    34 M ii   **Henry AMICK** was born 13 Jan 1788 in Haycock twp, Bucks,

Pennsylvania and was christened 9 Mar 1788 in Tohickon Church, Bedminster Twp, Bucks County, Pennsylvania.

Henry married **Elisabeth SHROYER** on 29 Apr 1817 in Dahmer, Pendleton, Va.

+ 35 M iii   **Jacob AMICK** was born 1788/1789 and died 1868.

+ 36 M iv   **John the Miller AMICK** was born 6 Sep 1790 and died 20 Nov 1846.

+ 37 F v   **Mary AMICK** was born about 1797.

+ 38 F vi   **Elizabeth AMICK** was born 1800 and died about 1855/1856.

+ 39 F vii   **Barbara AMICK** was born 1803.

+ 40 F viii   **Easter AMICK** was born 1804 and died 18 Sep 1894.

+ 41 M ix   **Elias AMICK** was born 1806 and died before 1881.

+ 42 F x   **Christina AMICK** was born 1808 and died 1876.

+ 43 M xi   **Reuben AMICK** was born 1812 and died 19 Apr 1899.

Henry also married Catherine.
They had a child:

  44 F xii   **Catherine AMICK**.

8. Julianna EMICH (Johan Heinrich, Johan Georg) was born 29 Apr 1765 in Bedminster Twp, Bucks, Pennsylvania and was christened 11 Jun 1765 in Kellers Church, Bedminster Twp, Bucks County, Pennsylvania. She died 31 Aug 1841 in Juniata, Pennsylvania and was buried 1841 in Juniata, Pennsylvania.

Julianna married **John NIEMAND**, son of Johannes NIEMAND and Elisabeth Margaret Barbara KELLER, on 1783/1784 in Bedminster, Pennsylvania. John was born 15 Apr 1761 in Haycock Township, Bucks County, Pennsylvania and was christened 14 Jun 1761 in Tohickon Reformed Church, Bedminster, Pennsylvania.

They had the following children:

  45 F i   **Sarah NIEMAND** was born 7 Sep 1784 in Haycock Township, bucks County, Penn. and was christened 28 Oct 1784.

      Sarah married **Samuel MYERS** in Tohickon Reformed Church, Bedminster.

  46 M ii   **Johannes NIEMAND** was born 22 May 1787 in Haycock Township, Bucks County, Penn. and was christened 1 Jul 1787 in Tohickon Reformed Church, Bedminster, Penn. He died 1801.

  47 M iii   **Samuel NIEMAND** was born 24 May 1789 in Haycock Township, Bucks County, Pennsylvania and was christened 5 Jul 1789 in Tohickon Reformed Church, Bedminster, Pennsylvania. He died 29 May 1837 in Greenwood Township, Juniata County,

Pennsylvania and was buried 1837 in Niemand Cemetery, Monroe Township, Juniata County, Pennsylvania.

Samuel married **Frances SELLERS**.

48 F iv   **Elizabeth NIEMAND** was born 20 Mar 1791 in Haycock Township, Bucks County, Pennsylvania and was christened 7 Oct 1792 in York, York County, Pennsylvania. She died 1873 in Newberry Township, Miami, Ohio.

Elizabeth married **Michael MYERS** on 9 Mar 1813 in Mifflin County, Pennsylvania.

49 F v   **Julianna NIEMAND** was born 26 Apr 1793 in Haycock Township, Bucks County, Pennsylvania and was christened 9 Feb 1794 in Keller's Church, Bedminster, Pennsylvania.

Julianna married **John SHALLENBERGER**.

50 F vi   **Catharina NIEMAND** was born 20 Aug 1794 in Haycock Township, Bucks County, Pennsylvania and was christened 4 Aug 1796 in Keller's Church, Bedminster, Pennsylvania.

Catharina married **Benjamin PANNEBAKER**.

51 M vii   **Gideon NIEMAND** was born 25 Mar 1797 in Haycock Township, Bucks county, Pennsylvania and was christened 29 Oct 1797 in Keller's Church, Bedminster, Pennsylvania. He died 1813.

52 M viii   **Joseph NIEMAND** was born 25 Mar 1799 in Montgomery Co. Pennsylvania. He died 28 Apr 1874 in Pennsylvania.

53 M ix   **John NIEMAND** was born 14 Jan 1801 in Haycock Township, bucks County, Pennsylvania.

John married **Mary PAGE**.

54 F x   **Maria Magdalena NIEMAND** was born 13 Feb 1809 in Cumberland County, Pennsylvania. She died 15 Dec 1885 in Cass County, Michigan.

Maria married **Abraham PAGE**.

10. **John Philip EMICH** (Johan Heinrich, Johan Georg) was born 11 Dec 1769 in Bedminster Twp, Bucks, Pennsylvania and was christened 1 Jan 1770 in Keller's Church, Bedminster Twp, Bucks County, Pennsylvania. He died 27 Oct 1850 in Monroe, Juniata, Pennsylvania and was buried 1850 in Niemond's Church, Monroe, Juniata, Pennsylvania.

John married **Christina BAUER**.

They had the following children:

55 M i   **Gideon EMIG** was born 16 Nov 1794 in Bedminster, Bucks County, Pennsylvania. He died 9 Oct 1833.

+ 56 M ii   **Henry EMIG** was born 28 Mar 1796 and died 13 Aug 1863.

57 F   iii **Elisabeth EMIG** was born 2 Mar 1798 in Bedminster, Bucks County, Pennsylvania. She died 4 Jun 1891.

Elisabeth married **Daniel STRUCK**. Daniel was born 22 Aug 1795. He died 11 Nov 1893.

58 M   iv **Samuel EMIG** was born 8 Dec 1799 in Bedminster, Bucks County, Pennsylvania and was christened 25 May 1800. He died 12 Jul 1854.

Samuel married **Salome EMICH**. Salome was born 12 Apr 1809. She died 15 May 1850.

59 M   v   **George EMIG** was born 8 Mar 1802 in Bedminster, Bucks County, Pennsylvania. He died 7 Feb 1809.

+ 60 M   vi **Philip EMIG** was born 15 Apr 1805 and died 8 Feb 1846.

61 F   vii **Sarah EMIG** was born 17 Sep 1807. She died 22 Mar 1851.

Sarah married **David STRUCK**. David was born 13 May 1807. He died 15 Apr 1847.

62 M   viii **Jonathon EMIG** was born 1 Apr 1809.

63 F   ix **Julianna EMIG** was born 5 Mar 1813. She died 19 Aug 1904.

Julianna married **Thomas WATTS**. Thomas was born 3 Jan 1801. He died 28 Nov 1885.

64 F   x   **Mary EMIG** was born 9 Jul 1823.

Mary married **Henry DREESE**.

65 F   xi **Lucinda EMIG** was born 13 Apr 1824. She died 11 Sep 1893 in Denver, Miami, Indiana.

Lucinda married **George A. BOOKS**.

11. **Mary Magdalene EMICH** (Johan Heinrich, Johan Georg) was born 30 Jan 1772 in Bedminster Twp, Bucks, Pennsylvania and was christened 8 Jan 1772 in Keller's Church, Bedminster Twp, Bucks County, Pennsylvania. She died before 15 Oct 1841.
Mary married **Daniel DIEHL** on 1792 in Bedminster, Bucks County, Pennsylvania.
They had the following children:

66 M   i   **Samuel DIEHL** was born 1793. He died in Springfield.

Samuel married **Mary HEIST** on 18 Aug 1816 in Tohickon Church, Bedminster, Bucks County, Pennsylvania.

67 M   ii **John DIEHL**.

John married **Mary LOUX** on 4 Jun 1820 in Tohickon Church, Bedminster, Bucks County, Pennsylvania.

68 M   iii **Tobias DIEHL**.

69 M   iv **William DIEHL**.

70 F   v   **Elisabeth DIEHL**.

13. **Johannes Nicholas EMMICK** "Nicholas" (Johan Philip, Johan Georg) was born 15 Sep 1766 in Haycock twp, Bucks County, Pennsylvania and was christened 12 Oct 1766 in Tohickon Church, Bedminster Twp, Bucks County, Pennsylvania. He died 1 Aug 1836 in Lewisport, Hancock, Kentucky and was buried Aug 1836 in Emmick Cemetery, Hancock, Kentucky.
Nicholas married (1) **Catherine HERTZEL**, daughter of Johan Philip HERTZEL and Christina Barbara KREILING, on 14 Oct 1784 in Cumru Township, Berks County, Pennsylvania. Catherine was born 1769 in Northampton County, Pennsylvania. She died 1793 in Rockingham, Augusta, Virginia.
They had the following children:
+   71 M   i   **John Nicholas AMICK** was born about 1785 and died after 1850.
    72 F   ii   **Sally AMICK**.
                 Sally married **Chesley WOODARD** on 19 Sep 1822 in Rockbridge Co., VA.
    73 F   iii **Anny AMICK**.
+   74 F   iv   **Elizabeth AMICK**.
Nicholas also married (2) **Susanna SMITH**, daughter of Henry SMITH, on 1797/1798 in Pendleton, West Virginia. Susanna was born 1777. She died 5 Jul 1833 in Lewisport, Hancock, Kentucky.
They had the following children:
+   75 F   v   **Mary EMMICK** was born 1797.
+   76 M   vi   **Jacob EMMICK** was born 21 Mar 1799 and died 2 Nov 1850.
    77 F   vii **Elizabeth EMMICK** was born 1803. She died 1830.
                 Elizabeth married **David TURNHAM**.
    78 F   viii **Katherine EMMICK** was born 1805. She died 1834.
+   79 M   ix   **George EMMICK** was born 16 Sep 1811 and died 26 Sep 1886.
+   80 F   x   **Allettia EMMICK**.
+   81 F   xi   **Eliza Jane EMMICK**.
+   82 F   xii **Nancy EMMICK** was born 1819 and died 1859.
18. **George EMIG** (Johan Georg, Johan Georg) was born 23 Apr 1774 in Haycock, Bucks County, Pennsylvania.
George married **Maria Magdalena HESS** on 1797 in Springfield. Maria was born 13 Apr 1829 in Lower Saucon, Northampton, Pennsylvania.
They had the following children:
    84 F   i   **Margaret EMIG** was christened 27 Nov 1799 in Springfield.
    85 F   ii   **Anna Dorothea EMIG** was christened 17 Oct 1800 in Springfield.

Bibliography

Public Records

Pennsylvania

Pennsylvania Archives
This is a well-known collection of early government records printed by the Commonwealth in the 1800's. The first volune was printed by Joseph Severns & Co. in 1852. The Pennsylvania Archives are published in ten sets, called series and the Pennsylvania Colonial Records. There are 135 volumes in total, grouped by series number (1 through 9, plus the Colonial Record series), then by volume within each series.

Pennsylvania Colonial Records
A part of the Pennsylvania Archives. Colonial Records —Volumes I to X, "Minutes of the Provincial Council of Pennsylvania, from the Organization to the Termination of the Proprietary Government," contain material dating from the beginning of English rule in 1682 to its end in 1775. Volumes XI to XVI, "Minutes of the Supreme Executive Council of Pennsylvania, from its Organization to the Termination of the Revolution" include records from the early statehood period.

Pennsylvania State Archives; ARIAS; the Archives Records Information Access System located at: http://www.digitalarchives.state.pa.us/index.asp; Revolutionary War Military Abstract Card File and Militia Officers Index Cards, 1775-1800

Pennsylvania Land Records
Bucks County Pennsylvania, *Petitions for Roads,* 1721-1800

Warrants of Land, County of Bucks 1733-1889", Pennsylvania Archives, 3rd Series, vol. 24, Bucks Co., p.125 [also on FHL microfilm #984929]

Pennsylvania State Archives, Division of Land Records, Harrisburg PA. *Deed Book AA*, vol. 15
Bucks County, Pennsylvania Deeds, Book AA #10
Bucks County, Pennsylvania Deeds, Book 22 (12 June 1786)
Bucks County, Pennsylvania Deeds, Book 25 (1790)
Bucks County, Pennsylvania, Deeds, book 26

Bucks County, Pennsylvania Administration Records #5035, Bk. 28 (Aug. 1822); Dated 28 Aug 1822

Map of Lottery Land adjoining the Manor of Richland 1735
Copy of map at Bucks Co. Historical Society, [Spruance Library, 84 South Pine St., Doylestown, PA 18901

Map of Lower Haycock Township
Constructed from and compared with original drafts remaining on file in the Department of Interior Affairs of Pennsylvania, for the use and at the request of the Forestry Reserve Commission of Pennsylvania on 8 Dec 1924.
Copy of map at Bucks Co. Historical Society, [Spruance Library, 84 South Pine St., Doylestown, PA 18901

Pennsylvania Church Records
Bible Records, Bucks Co. Historical Society, 1676-1938, Copied by C. Arthur Smith, Vol. V, 1940

Kirchen Buch Der Evangelish Lutherischen on Der Toheka, p. 188 [FHL film #1312361] In German

Pennsylvania Court Records
Register of Wills; Clerk, Berks County Court House, Reading PA; Book I, p. 86.

Wills of Bucks County, Pennsylvania, Bk. B. 1773, pp. 315-316

Bucks County, Pennsylvania, Register of Wills, Doylestown, PA., Estate #1531
Bucks County, Pennsylvania, Register of Wills, 1782, Estate #1756

Bucks County, Pennsylvania, Orphans' Court Records, File #563, 13 Sep 1774, Bk. A-2
Bucks County, Pennsylvania, Orphans Court Record File #629. Bk. B. 1778

(West) Virginia Records

Virginia Land Records
Pendleton County, West Virginia, Inventory Book 4 (1832)

Pendleton County (West) Virginia Deed book Records, 1788-1813 compiled by Rick Toothman.

Pendleton County, West Virginia, Deeds Book 1 (1791)
Pendleton County, West Virginia Deeds, Book 2
Pendleton County, West Virginia Deeds, Book3
Pendleton County, West Virginia, Deed, Book 4
Pendleton County, West Virginia Deeds, Book 6
Pendleton County, West Virginia Deed, Book 7
Pendleton County, West Virginia Deeds, Book 8
Pendleton County, West Virginia Deeds, Book 11, (1834)

Virginia [now West Virginia] Surveys Record Book, Bk. A
West Virginia Surveyors' Record Book, A

1823 Land Book for Pendleton County, WV
Available online at: USGenWeb Archives

Pendleton County, West Virginia Land Tax Record, [FHL film #163912]
Surveyor's Book B

Rockbridge County, VA., Deed book 'D', 1798-1802
Rockbridge County, VA., Deed book 'F', 1806-1809,

Virginia Church Records
Pendleton County, West Virginia, Register of Marriages, 1800-1852

Marriages in Pendleton County, (West) Virginia, 1788-1853, compiled by
Mary Harter

Mary Harter, comp. *Pendleton County, Virginia Marriage bonds, 1791-1853,
and completed 1810 Census*, (Published by the author, undated)

Philips, Claude Summer; Ed. *Pendleton County Marriage Records, 1800-1851*,
(typed, 1926) p 1. [FHLibrary 975.491/v25p]

Marriage Certificate of John and Catharine (Bowers) Amick
Married 20 February 1814 at Dahmer, Pendleton County, Virginia
Copy by Barbara Nichols

George Smith, translator & transcriber, *The Church Book for the Propst
Congregation, Begun 27 April 1814 [by] Jacob Scherer, Evangel, Lutheran
Preacher,* [Hereinafter, *Propst Church Records.* (typed 1964) Original located
at the Va. State Library] with Emig listed, p 55 *"Propst Church Records"*

Pendleton County Marriage Records 1800-1851 – copied 1926
Copy of 975.491 V25p SLC

Grave Register of Pendleton County, West Virginia, (Pendleton Co. Historical
society, 1977)

Virginia Court Records

Pendleton County W.Va. Will Book 1 Pages 266-269
Not verified but found on Web.
http://members.aol.com/gadgone/page37.html

*Abstracts of Executor, Administrative, and Guardian Bonds of Rockingham
Co., VA. (1778-1864)* compiled by Marguerite B. Priode

Virginia Other Public Records
1810 Pendleton County, Virginia Census
Available online at:
ftp://ftp.rootsweb.com/pub/usgenweb/wv/pendleton/census/1810/1810pend.txt

Pendleton County Census: 1810, 1820

1830 Federal Census for Pendleton County, WV. - Lists Jacob and Henry, Sr.;
Available online at: USGenWeb Archives

Published Works

AMERICAN MILITARY HISTORY; Army Historical Series, Office of the Chief of Military History, United States Army; Chapter 4 The winning of Independence, 1777-1783; Available Online at:
http://www.army.mil/cmh-pg/books/AMH/AMH-04.htm
Chapter 7 THE THIRTY YEARS' PEACE *Extracted from AMERICAN MILITARY HISTORY;* ARMY HISTORICAL SERIES, *OFFICE OF THE CHIEF OF MILITARY HISTORY, UNITED STATES ARMY*
http://www.army.mil/cmh-pg/books/AMH/AMH-04.htm

Buch, Kirchen, Evangelich Lutheran Kirchen, at Toheka, 1759. [FHL Film #132361]

Davis, W. W. H.; A.M; *The History of Bucks County Pennsylvania*; originally published in Doylestown, PA 1876; reprinted by the Historical Society of Pennsylvania; The Lewis Publishing Co. in 1905. Vol. 1 and Vol. 2, [Spruance Library, 974.821, 109]
Available online at:
http://www.rootsweb.com/~usgenweb/pa/bucksp/davistoc.htm

Dyer, Geneva Amick, *Fourteen Children, The Family of John Amick of West Virginia.* (Typed and publ. by author, undated)

Dyer, Geneva Amick, *Fourteen Children, The Family of John Amick of West Virginia.* (Typed and publ. by author, undated) written in the 1940's

Emmick, Maude; *Family History*, self typed; about 1950

Fackenthal, B. F., Jr. *Trinity Union Church, Springfield Twp. Bucks Co. Cemetery Records,* Typed copy at Spruance Library, Doylestown, 84 Pine St., Doylestown, PA.

Fulbrook, Mary; *A Concise History of Germany*, Cambridge University Press, 1990

Hinkle, William John, *History of Tohickon Union Church, Bedminster, Bucks, Penn.*, 1925.

Hinkle, William J. *Keller's Lutheran Church Records*, Bedminster twp., Bucks County Penn., 1751-1870, [FHL microfilm #940443, items 7 and 9]

Hodges, Glenn; Daybreak On Old Fortification Creek

Giuseppe, M. S. *Naturalizations of Foreign Protestants in American and West Indian Colonies*, (Rev. Ed. Baltimore: Genealogical Publishing Co. 1964.

MacReynolds, George, *Place Names in Bucks County, Penn.,* 1942.

McNealy, Terry A. and Waite, Francis W., Bucks County Tax Records 1693-1778

McClung, Rev. William, *The McClung Genealogy*, 1904,
Available Online at:
http://freepages.genealogy.rootsweb.com/~rootsr/Greenb.htm

Morton, Oren F.; *History of Pendleton County, West Virginia*, (Baltimore: Regional Publ. Co. 1974,)

Munger, Donna Bingham, *Pennsylvania Land Records, History and Guide for Research*, (Wilmington, Del. Scholarly Resources).

Nichols, Barbara, *John Amick "The Miller" his Ancestors and some Descendants*; 2nd Edition, self published, 2004

Nichols, Lt. Col. Barbara J., Ret.; *My Family of Amick...Ame, Amey, Emich, Emig, Emigh, Emmerisch*; self published, Catalog number R929.2Am51N

Rhodes, J. F., *History of the United States*, Vol. III

Reithel, Louise E.; *Nicholas Emmick (1764-1836) His Forebears, Descendants and Related Families*; self-published, 1997

Ripp, Daniel; *A History of the Counties of Berks and Lebanon, Pennsylvania*

Stahl, Elmer, "Mills of Goshenhoppen, North Montgomery County, Penn." *Old Mill News*, vol. XVIII; 1, p. 11.

Strassburger Ralph B. & Hinkle, William J., ed.., *Pennsylvania-German Pioneers*, vol. 1, Baltimore, Md.: Genealogical Pub. Co., rev. ed., 1996.

Thrasher, Mattie L Emmick; *An Emmick Family History* (1973)

Tindall, George Brown and Shi, David E. *America, A Narrative History*, 4th Ed. Norton & Co., New York; 1996.

Yoder, Don, ed.; *Pennsylvania-German Church Records: Tohickon Reformed Church, Bucks County, Penn.*; Pennsylvania-German Society; Vol. 3

Yochim, Mrs. Eldred Martin; *DAR Patriot Index;* Centennial Edition, part 1; National Society of the Daughters of the American Revolution Centennial Administration; Washington: 1990; Lists: Amick, Henry: b 6-7-1762 PA d c 1830 VA m Barbara ----; Pvt PA
No other Amicks listed.

Wallace, Paul A., *Indian Paths of Pennsylvania*, Penn. Hist. & Museum Comm., 1965

Wardell, Patrick G.; *War of 1812: Virginia Bounty & Pension Applicants* Heritage Books, Inc.
A quick reference guide to ancestors having War of 1812 service who served, lived, died, or married in Virginia or West Virginia

Whisonant, Robert C., *Geology and History of Confederate Saltpeter Cave Operations in Western Virginia*, West Virginia Division of Mineral Resources, Vol. 47, November, 2001, No. 4, availableas adownload at: http://www.dmme.virginia.gov/DMR3/dmrpdfs/vamin/VAMIN_VOL47_NO0 4.pdf

Wright, F. Edward, *Bucks County, Penn. Church Records of the 17th and 18th Century*, vol. 1, "German Church Records: Keller's Lutheran Church." Westminster, Md.: Family Line Pub., 1994 [FHLibrary, 974.821/K2w]

Zanine, Louis J., Brigadier General John Lacey and the Pennsylvania Militia in 1778, *Pennsylvnaia History* (48, 1981), pp 129-142

Periodicals

Bucks County, PA Historical Society Papers, vol. VI, 1932, published through the B. F. Fuckenthal Fund

Lancaster PA., Gazette Abstracts, 1826-1891, pg. 273, Lancaster, PA

McClung Family Journals, Vol. 7, Donated by Arthur J. McClung and Mrs. John L. Rice; (McClung Family Journals, Vol. 6, p.29)
Available Online at:
http://freepages.genealogy.rootsweb.com/~rootsr/6-29b.htm

Pennsylvania Gazette of 13 Oct 1773, vol. 19 p. 131. Bucks County Historical Society [Spruance Library, 84 So. Pine St. Doylestown Penn. 18901]

Manuscripts

George Washington Papers at the Library of Congress, 1741-1799: Series 3b Varick Transcripts

Internet sites

Keller History at http://www.kellerkin.com/
This also includes a family tree. Contact Email: replyfrom-kellerkin@yahoo.com
And additional links: Keller Family Genealogy Forum; FamilySearch.org - Keller Group Record

Propsts in America found at:
 http://members.tripod.com/~CampD/propsts_in_america.htm

Propst 2 - The Family of Michael Propst
http://www.rootsweb.com/~wvcalhou/mpropst.htm

Wikipedia, http://en.wikipedia.org/wiki/Pennsylvania_Constitution_of_1776

Pennsylvania State Archives
http://www.docheritage.state.pa.us/documents/constitution.asp, this site has pictures of the documents

The Avolon Project of Yale Law School:
http://www.yale.edu/lawweb/avalon/states/pa08.htm

Thomas Jefferson, John Adams and the Declaration des Droit l'Homes et du Citoyen; available at http://www.nuff.ox.ac.uk/users/mclean/ddhc3.pdf

End Notes

[1] http://www.ghat.com/hatfintr.htm#tree
[2] Strassburger, Ralph B. & Hinkle, William J., ed., *Pennsylvania-German Pioneers*, vol. 1, pp 399-400
[3] Strassburger, Ralph B. & Hinkle, William J., ed., *Pennsylvania-German Pioneers*, vol. 1; pp 441
[4] Emmick, Maude; *Family History*
[5] Pennsilfaanisch Deitsch, Pennsylvania German or Pennsylvania Dutch in English, is a dialect of High German that is related to dialects spoken in the ancestral home of the Pennsylvania Germans in the Rhineland-Palatinate and also contains some elements of other southwestern German and Swiss dialects. From http://www.pgs.org/dialect.asp
[6] Emmick, Maude; *Family History*
[7] This may be a confusion with the York/Lancaster line of Amicks
[8] Dyer, Geneva Amick; *Fourteen Children, The Family of John Amick of West Virginia*, p. 1
[9] Brown, William G. *History of Nicholas County, West Virginia, Pioneer Families*; pp. 283, 284
[10] Fulbrook, Mary; *A Concise History of Germany*
[11] Shirer, William L., *The Rise and Fall of the Third Reich*, Simon and Schuster, New York, 1960; pp. 91-92
[12] Tindall, George Brown and Shi, David E.; *America, A Narrative History*. p. 143
[13] The Tun Tavern was a brew house built in 1685 near what is today known as Penn's Landing in Philadelphia. It is known as one of the first brew houses in the country, and its name is derived from the old English word "tun" meaning a barrel or keg of beer. The proprietor of the tavern in the early 1740s changed the name of the restaurant and served such distinguished guests as George Washington, Thomas Jefferson and Benjamin Franklin.
[14] Tindall, George Brown and Shi, David E. *America, A Narrative History*. p. 147
[15] Davis, W. W. H.; A.M; *The History of Bucks County Pennsylvania*
[16] Davis, W.W.H., A.M *The History of Bucks County Pennsylvania*, Doylestown, PA 1876 reprinted by the Historical Society of Pennsylvania; The Lewis Publishing Co. in 1905
[17] Davis, W. W. H.; A.M; *The History of Bucks County Pennsylvania*
[18] Davis, W. W. H.; A.M; *The History of Bucks County Pennsylvania*
[19] Davis, W. W. H.; A.M; *The History of Bucks County Pennsylvania*
[20] Hinke, William John, *History of Tohickon Union Church, Bedminster,*

Bucks, Penn, p. 69

[21] MacReynolds, George, *Place Names in Bucks County, Penn.*, p. 21

[22] Hinke, William John, *History of Tohickon Union Church, Bedminster, Bucks, Penn.*

[23] Giuseppe, M. S. *Naturalizations of Foreign Protestants in American and West Indian Colonies*

[24] http://freepages.genealogy.rootsweb.com/~buckscounty/bedminster.html

[25] *Kirchen Buch, Evangelich Lutheran Kirchen, at Toheka, 1759*; 974.821, chu 41; pp. 30-31

[26] Nichols, Lt. Col. Barbara J., Ret.; *My Family of Amick...Ame, Amey, Emich, Emig, Emigh, Emmerisch*

[27] Davis, W. W. H.; A.M; *The History of Bucks County Pennsylvania*

[28] *Bucks County, PA Historical Society Papers*, published for the Society by Frankenthal Publication Fund, 1932; Vol. VI, pp. 363-365,

[29] *Pennsylvania State Archives*; RG-17; Records of the Land Office, WARRANT REGISTERS, 1733-1957. [series #17.88]; Bucks County Warrant Register Pages, Page 171, line 74 (near bottom)

[30] Pennsylvania Archives, Series 3, Vol. XXIV, Chapter: Warrantees of Land in the County of Bucks. 1733-1889, p. 125

[31] *Warrants of Land, County of Bucks 1733-1889"*, Pennsylvania Archives, 3rd Series, vol. 24, Bucks Co., p.125

[32] *Application for Warrants, 1768*, A-E, 6 July 1768; Warrant Registers, Bureau of Land Records, Department of Internal Affairs, Commonwealth of Pennsylvania; Microfilming Job Number 2 – 1957;

[33] *Bucks County, Penn. Deeds*, Patent Book, Bk. AA #10, p. 433

[34] http://www.pennridge.org/works/nockhistory.html

[35] *Map of Lottery Land adjoining the Manor of Richland 1735;* Copy of map at Bucks Co. Historical Society

[36] Warrant Map; S.G.L No. 157, Haycock Township, Bucks County, Map No. 2; available at Spruance Library, Bucks Co. Historical Society

[37] Wright, F. Edward, *Bucks County, Penn. Church Records of the 17th and 18th Century*, vol. I, p. 164; "German Church Records"

[38] Klosak, Linda M., *Trinity Lutheran Church (Springfield) Cemetery*, Inscription copied and compiled by Linda M. Klosik, October 30, 1981; also Fackenthal, B. F., Jr. *Trinity Union Church, Springfield, Bucks, Penn., Springfield Cemetery.* p. 3; citation from Barbara Nichols

[39] For an excellent overview of Pennsylvania Dutch gravestones see: http://pagstones.com/pgs_stone_overview.page.html

[40] Senn, Rev Jacob *Tohickon rec Bucks Co in PA Germ Church Rec.*, Don Yoker Vol. III, p. 271

[41] *Wills of Bucks County, Pennsylvania*, Bk. B. 1773, pp. 315-316

[42] *Bucks County, Pennsylvania, Orphans' Court Records*, File #563, 13 Sep

1774, Bk. A-2, p. 363
[43] *Bible Records, Bucks Co. Historical Society, 1676-1938*, Copied by C. Arthur Smith, Vol. VIII, p. 136.
[44] *Bible Records, Bucks Co. Historical Society, 1676-1938*, Copied by C. Arthur Smith, Vol. VIII, p. 136.
[45] Hinkle, William J., Keller's *Lutheran Church Records, Bedminster twp., Bucks County Penn., 1751-1870*, citation from Barbara Nichols
[46] *Kirchen Buch, Evangelich Lutheran Kirchen, at Toheka, 1759*; citation from Barbara Nichols
[47] Wright, F. Edward, *Bucks County, Penn. Church Records of the 17th and 18th Century*, vol. 1, "German Church Records: Keller's Lutheran Church." p. 49
[48] Yoder, Don, ed. "Pennsylvania-German Church Records: Tohickon Reformed Church, Bucks County, Penn., *Pennsylvania-German Society*, Vol. III, p. 267
[49] Wright, F. Edward, *Keller's Lutheran Church*, p. 50
[50] Hinkle, William J., *Keller's Church Records*, p. 127
[51] Hinkle, William J., *Keller's Church Records*, p. 12
[52] Wright, Edward, *Bucks County, Penn. Church Records in the 17th & 18th Century*, Vol. 1, "German Church Records", p. 164
[53] Hinkle, *William J., Keller's Church Records*, p. 96
[54] Wright, Edward, *Bucks County, Penn. Church Records in the 17th & 18th Century*, Vol. 1, "German Church Records", p. 52
[55] Hinkle, William J., *Keller's Church Records*, pp. 96-99
[56] Wright, F. Edward, *Keller's Lutheran Church*, p. 54
[57] *Pennsylvania Gazette* of 13 Oct 1773, vol. 19 p. 131, Bucks County Historical Society
[58] Wright, F. Edward, *Keller's Lutheran Church*, p. 54
[59] Hinkle, William J., *Keller's Church Records*, pp. 100-101
[60] Davis, W. W. H.; A.M; *The History of Bucks County Pennsylvania*; 1905
[61] *Bucks County Pennsylvania, Petitions for Roads, 1721-1800*, p. 138
[62] *Petition for Roads*, pp. 545-546
[63] McNealy, Terry A. and Francis W. Waite, *Bucks County Tax Records 1693-1778*, p. 79
[64] *Bucks County, Penn. Orphans' Court Records*, File #629, Book B
[65] *Pennsylvania State Archives,* Division of Land Records, Harrisburg PA. *Deed Book AA*, vol. 15, pp. 635-636
[66] Munger, Donna Bingham, *Pennsylvania Land Records, History and Guide for Research*, p. xxix
[67] *Bucks County, Pennsylvania, Deeds*, book 26, p. 49
[68] *Bucks County, Pennsylvania, Register of Wills*, Doylestown, PA., No. 1531, Estate of Henry Emy, Register's Office 1777 (administration, not a will)
[69] *Bucks County, Pennsylvania, Orphans Court Record* File #629. Book B,

1778, p. 10
[70] *Orphans' Court Records*, File #629, Book B (1779) pp. 26-27
[71] Wright, F. Edward, *Bucks County, Penn. Church Records of the 17th and 18th Century*, Vol. I, p. 164; "German Church Records"
[72] Nichols, Barbara; *John Amick "The Miller" his Ancestors and some Descendants*, p.4
[73] The two lines are likely closely related and it is possible, but not likely, that Nicholas actually belongs to the York line and the reference to cousin Henry of Pendleton is a more abstract consideration of kinship. More research is needed. See the Book Supplement for more information on the York line of Amick.
[74] Wills- see Book Supplement
[75] Little documentation of early companies exist and only a few later war companies. Henry Emig is not listed in the few available documents of those not serving. It is likely that he served in the same company that his brother Georg Emig served in but few records exist of this company or regiment.
[76] *Pennsylvania Archives*, Series 5, Vol. V, Chapter: Associators and Militia Pennsylvania, pp. 3-4
[77] Zanine, Louis J., Brigadier General John Lacey and the Pennsylvania Militia in 1778, *Pennsylvania History* (48,1981), pp 129-142
[78] *Pennsylvania Archives*, Series 5, Vol. V, Chapter: Muster Rolls and Papers Relating to the Associators and Militia of the County of Bucks, p. 327
[79] *Pennsylvania Archives*, Series 5, Vol. II, Chapter: Fourth Pennsylvania Battalion. Col. Anthony Wayne. January 3, 1776-January 24, 1777, (a), p 148
[80] *Pennsylvania Archives*, Series 2, Vol. X, Chapter: Fourth Pennsylvania Battalion, Col. Anthony Wayne. January 3, 1776-January 24, 1777, p. 117-122
[81] *Pennsylvania Archives*, Series 1, Vol. V, Chapter: Pennsylvania Archives 1777, pp. 154-155
[82] *Pennsylvania Archives*, Series 5, Vol. V, Chapter: Muster Rolls and Papers Relating to the Associators and Militia of the County of Bucks, p. 363
[83] see Supplement on Brigadier General Lacey
[84] Keller History
[85] Keller History
[86] *Pennsylvania Archives*, Series 3, Vol. X, Chapter: Minutes of the Convention of 1776, pp. 756-758
[87] *George Washington Papers at the Library of Congress, 1741-1799*: Series 3b Varick Transcripts
[88] *George Washington Papers at the Library of Congress, 1741-1799*: Series 3b Varick Transcripts
[89] *George Washington Papers at the Library of Congress, 1741-1799*: Series 3b Varick Transcripts
[90] *George Washington Papers at the Library of Congress, 1741-1799*: Series

3b Varick Transcripts
[91] *George Washington Papers at the Library of Congress, 1741-1799*: Series
3b Varick Transcripts
[92] http://en.wikipedia.org/wiki/Order_of_battle_of_the_Battle_of_Long_Island
[93] Davis, W. W. H., A.M., *The History of Bucks County, Pennsylvania*,
Chapter XL, Bucks County in the Revolution, 1774 to 1783
[94] Keller History
[95] Pennsylvania State Archives; ARIAS; the Archives Records Information;
Revolutionary War Military Abstract Card File, Emich, George
[96] *Pennsylvania Archives*, Series 2,Vol. XIV, Chapter: Muster Rolls and Papers
Relating to the Associators and Militia of the County of Bucks, p. 192
[97] *Pennsylvania Archives,* Series: Colonial Records, Volume: XI; Chapter:
Minutes of the Supreme Executive Council, p. 302
[98] *The winning of Independence, 1777-1783* Extracted from *American Military
History; Army Historical Series*, Office of the Chief of Military History,
United States, pp. 73 and 74
[99] *The winning of Independence, 1777-1783* Extracted from *American Military
History; Army Historical Series*, Office of the Chief of Military History,
United States, From Chapter 4, pp. 74, 75 and 76
[100] Pennsylvania Archives, Colonial Records, Vol. XI, Chapter: Minutes of the
Supreme Executive Council, pp. 359-362
[101] *The winning of Independence, 1777-1783* Extracted from *American
Military History; Army Historical Series*, Office of the Chief of Military
History, United States, Chapter 4, p. 76
[102] *Pennsylvania Archives*, Series: Colonial Records, Vol. XI, Chapter:
Minutes of the Supreme Executive Council, p. 398
[103] *The winning of Independence, 1777-1783* Extracted from *American
Military History; Army Historical Series*, Office of the Chief of Military
History, United States, Chapter 4, pp. 80 and 81
[104] Library of Congress; In the 1790s, Washington biographer Mason Locke
Weems made up the story of Washington praying in an Oak Grove at Valley
Forge to demonstrate Divine sanction of the War for Independence. American
soldiers courage and endurance during the Valley Forge winter gained renewed
meaning during the American Civil War. John McRae's engraving of
Washington's "Prayer at Valley Forge" was based on an 1866 painting by
Henry Brueckner.
[105] Eyewitness testimony of Isaac Potts, a Valley Forge resident who shared the
following story with the Rev. Nathaniel Randolph Snowden (1770-1851), who
then recorded it in his "Diary and Remembrances." The report is controversial,
see citation above.
[106] Davis, W. W. H., A.M., *The History of Bucks County, Pennsylvania*,
Chapter XL, Bucks County in the Revolution, 1774 to 1783.

[107] Zanine, Louis J., Brigadier General John Lacey and the Pennsylvania Militia in 1778, *Pennsylvania History* (48,1981), pp 129-142

[108] Zanine, Louis J., Brigadier General John Lacey and the Pennsylvania Militia in 1778, *Pennsylvania History* (48,1981), pp 129-142

[109] http://johnsmilitaryhistory.com/barrenhill.html.

[110] See http://johnsmilitaryhistory.com/barrenhill.html for an excellant write up as well as the signage for the battle.

[111] *The winning of Independence, 1777-1783* Extracted from *American Military History; Army Historical Series*, Office of the Chief of Military History, United States, Chapter 4, pp. 82, 83, and 84

[112] Davis, W. W. H., A.M., *The History of Bucks County, Pennsylvania*, Chapter XL, Bucks County in the Revolution, 1774 to 1783

[113] *The winning of Independence, 1777-1783* Extracted from *American Military History; Army Historical Series*, Office of the Chief of Military History, United States, Chapter 4, pp. 82, 83, and 84

[114] *The winning of Independence, 1777-1783* Extracted from *American Military History; Army Historical Series*, Office of the Chief of Military History, United States, Chapter 4, pp. 82, 83, and 84

[115] *Pennsylvania Archives*, Series: Colonial Records, Vol. XI, Chapter: Minutes of the Supreme Executive Council, pp. 635-366

[116] *Pennsylvania Archives*, Series: Colonial Records, Vol. XI, Chapter: Minutes of the Supreme Executive Council, pp. 626-627

[117] *Pennsylvania Archives*, Series 5, Vol. V, Chapter: Muster Rolls and Papers Relating to the Associators and Militia of the County of Bucks, pp. 418-420

[118] *Pennsylvania Archives*, Series 5, Vol. V, Chapter: Muster Rolls and Papers Relating to the Associators and Militia of the County of Bucks, pp. 442-444

[119] *Pennsylvania State Archives*; ARIAS; the Archives Records Information; Revolutionary War Military Abstract Card File, Emig, George

[120] *Pennsylvania Archives, Series 5*, Vol. 5, pp. 426-428

[121] Yochim, Mrs. Eldred Martin; *DAR Patriot Index;* Centennial Edition, part 1; National Society of the Daughters of the American Revolution Centennial Administration; Washington: 1990

[122] *Pennsylvania Archives, Series 2*; 14:214

[123] *Pennsylvania State Archives*; ARIAS; the Archives Records Information; Revolutionary War Military Abstract Card File, Emig, Henry

[124] *Pennsylvania Archives*, Series 3, Volume: XIII, Chapter: Provincial Papers Proprietary and Other Tax Lists of the County of Bucks for the Years, 1779, 1781, 1782, 1783, 1784, 1785, 1786, p. 299

[125] *Pennsylvania State Archives*; ARIAS; the Archives Records Information; Revolutionary War Military Abstract Card File, Emig, Henry

[126] *Pennsylvania Archives*, Series 6, Vol. III, Chapter: Militia Rolls- 1783-1790, pp. 55-56

[127] Davis, W. W. H., A.M., *The History of Bucks County, Pennsylvania*, Chapter XL, Bucks County in the Revolution, 1774 to 1783

[128] *Pennsylvania Archives*, Series 2, Vol. XVII, Chapter: Names of Foreigners who took the Oath of Allegiance, 1727-1775, pp. 239-240

[129] Hinkle, Wm. J., *Keller's Lutheran Church Records*, p. 68

[130] *Kirchen Buch Der Evangelish Lutherischen on Der Toheka*, p. 188

[131] Nichols, Barbara, John Amick "The Miller" *his Ancestors and some Descendants*

[132] Hinkle, Wm. J., *Keller's Lutheran Church Records*, p. 22

[133] *Pennsylvania Archives*, Series 3, Volume: XIII, Chapter: Provincial Papers Proprietary and Other Tax Lists of the County of Bucks for the Years, 1779, 1781, 1782, 1783, 1784, 1785, 1786, p. 74

[134] *Pennsylvania Archives*, Series 3, Volume: XIII, Chapter: Provincial Papers Proprietary and Other Tax Lists of the County of Bucks for the Years, 1779, 1781, 1782, 1783, 1784, 1785, 1786, p. 176

[135] *Pennsylvania Archives*, Series 3, Volume: XIII, Chapter: Provincial Papers Proprietary and Other Tax Lists of the County of Bucks for the Years, 1779, 1781, 1782, 1783, 1784, 1785, 1786, pp. 299-302

[136] *Pennsylvania Archives*, Series 3, Volume: XIII, Chapter: Provincial Papers Proprietary and Other Tax Lists of the County of Bucks for the Years, 1779, 1781, 1782, 1783, 1784, 1785, 1786, p. 400

[137] *Pennsylvania Archives*, Series 3, Volume: XIII, Chapter: Provincial Papers Proprietary and Other Tax Lists of the County of Bucks for the Years, 1779, 1781, 1782, 1783, 1784, 1785, 1786, p. 436

[138] *Pennsylvania Archives*, Series 3, Volume: XIII, Chapter: Provincial Papers Proprietary and Other Tax Lists of the County of Bucks for the Years, 1779, 1781, 1782, 1783, 1784, 1785, 1786, pp. 554-555

[139] *Pennsylvania Archives*, Series 3, Volume: XIII, Chapter: Provincial Papers Proprietary and Other Tax Lists of the County of Bucks for the Years, 1779, 1781, 1782, 1783, 1784, 1785, 1786, p. 688

[140] *Pennsylvania Archives*, Series 3, Volume: XIII, Chapter: Provincial Papers Proprietary and Other Tax Lists of the County of Bucks for the Years, 1779, 1781, 1782, 1783, 1784, 1785, 1786, p. 794

[141] *Bucks County, Pennsylvania Deeds, Book 22* (12 June 1786) pp. 372-74

[142] *Bucks County, Pennsylvania Deeds, Book 22* (12 June 1786) pp. 372-374

[143] Wright, F. Edward, *Bucks County Pennsylvania Church Records of the 17th & 18th Centuries*, Vol. 1, "German Church Records of Tohickon." p. 225

[144] Nichols, Barbara; *John Amick "The Miller" his Ancestors and some Descendants*, p. 19

[145] The 1850 Census of the Western District, Nicholas Co. Va.

[146] *Bucks County, Pennsylvania Deeds, Book 25* (1790) pp. 457-459

[147] *Bucks County, Pennsylvania, Register of Wills, 1782,* Estate #1756

148 Keller History
149 Wikipedia,
http://en.wikipedia.org/wiki/Pennsylvania_Constitution_of_1776
150 Pennsylvania State Archives
http://www.docheritage.state.pa.us/documents/constitution.asp, this site has
pictures of the documents
151 The full text can be found at The Avolon Project of Yale Law School:
http://www.yale.edu/lawweb/avalon/states/pa08.htm
152 Thomas Jefferson, John Adams and the Declaration des Droit l'Homes et du
Citoyen http://www.nuff.ox.ac.uk/users/mclean/ddhc3.pdf
153 Strassburger, Ralph B., and Hinkle, William J. eds.; *Pennsylvania German
Pioneers*, Vol. I, 1727 – 1775, Baltimore, Genealogical Pub. Co., 1966, pp. 66-
70.
154 *Pennsylvania Archives*, Series 3, Vol. 24, p. 163
155 *Keller's Lutheran Church*, Bedminster Twp.., Bucks, Penn. [FHL film #
940443, item 91, pp. 68-70
156 *Pennsylvania Archives*, Series 3, Vol. 6, pp.31-32.
157 *First Census of US (1790) for Cumru RTwp. Berks Co. Pennsylvania*, p. 32
158 *First Census of US (1790) for Cumru RTwp. Berks Co. Pennsylvania*, p. 32
159 Barbara Nichols, *John Amick "The Miller" his Ancestors and some
Descendants*, p.19
160 Kershner, Rev. W.J. and Lerch, Adam G. *History of St. John's (Hain's)
Reformed Church in Lower Heidelberg Township Berks County, Penna.*
Reading, PA: I.M. Beaver, Publisher, 1916, pp. 59-69.
161 Tindall, George Brown and Shi, David E. *America, A Narrative History*, p.
343
162 Tindall, George Brown and Shi, David E. *America, A Narrative History*, p.
146
163 Wallace, Paul A., *Indian Paths of Pennsylvania*, Penn. Hist. & Museum
Comm., 1965, citation from Barbara Nichols
164 *The 1787 Census of Virginia*, Vol. 1, p. 639, cited by Reithel, Louse;
*Nicholas Emmick (1764-1836) His Forebears, Descendants and Related
Families*
165 *Deeds of Pendleton County, Virginia (now West Virginia), Book 1* (1791) p.
153
166 Morton, Oren F., *History of Pendleton County, West Virginia*, 1974, p. 167
167 Smith, George, translator & transcriber, *The Church Book for the Propst
Congregation*, Begun 27 April 1814 [by] Jacob Scherer, Evangel, Lutheran
Preacher, [Hereinafter, Propst Church Records (typed 1964). Original located
at the Va. State Library]
168 Nichols, Barbara, *John Amick "The Miller" his Ancestors and some
Ascendants*; John Arvin Dahmer, letter to Barbara Nichols, HC61 Box 28,

Franklin, WV 26807-9611, County Historian, confirmed by phone June 2007 by author to Johnnie Dahmer, son of John Arvin Dahmer,

[169] *Virginia [now West Virginia] Surveys Record Book, Book A*, p.214, citation from Barbara Nichols

[170] *Virginia [now West Virginia] Surveys Record Book, Book A*, p. 207

[171] *Virginia [now West Virginia] Surveys Record Book, Book A*, p. 208

[172] Reithel, Louise, *Nicholas Emmick (1764-1836) His Forebears, Descendants and Related Families*, pp.12-13

[173] *West Virginia Surveyors' Record Book, A*, p. 211, citation from Barbara Nichols

[174] *Pendleton County, West Virginia Land Tax Record*, p. 44, citation from Barbara Nichols

[175] Reithel, Louise, p. 13

[176] *Pendleton County (West) Virginia, Surveyor's Book B*, p. 82, citation from Barbara Nichols

[177] *Marriages in Pendleton County, (West) Virginia, 1788-1853*, p. 18 compiled by Mary Harter

[178] Reithel, Louise; *Nicholas Emmick (1764-1836) His Forebears, Descendants and Related Families*; page 43-45

[179] *Pendleton County, VA. Deed Book 2*, pp 350-351. Indenture of Bargain and Sale to sell land, dated 27 November 1793, between Nicholas Amick of Pendleton County, VA and Henry Amick of Pendleton County, VA

[180] *Pendleton County, Virginia Deed Book 3, 1788-1813*, p. 78, compiled by Rick Toothman

[181] Reithel, Louise; *Nicholas Emmick (1764-1836) His Forebears, Descendants and Related Families*, p. 13

[182] *Rockbridge County, VA., Deed Book 'D', 1798-1802*, p. 455; citation from Louise Reithel

[183] *Rockbridge County, VA., Deed Book 'F', 1806-1809*, p. 121, citation from Louise Reithel

[184] Reithel, Louise; *Nicholas Emmick (1764-1836) His Forebears, Descendants and Related Families*; p. 14

[185] *Pendleton County, West Virginia Deed Book 7*, Page 225

[186] Morton, Oren F., *History of Pendleton County, West Virginia*, 1974, pp. 395-397

[187] Morton, Oren F., *History of Pendleton County, West Virginia*, 1974, p 397

[188] Barbara Nichols, *John Amick "The Miller" his Ancestors and some Descendants*, p. 22

[189] *Pendleton County West Virginia Will Book 1*, pp. 266-269

[190] *Pendleton County, West Virginia Deeds, Book 3*, p 355

[191] *Deeds of Pendleton County, [now] West Virginia*, Book 4, p. 199

[192] *Pendleton County, West Virginia Deeds, Book 4*, p. 199

[193] Nichols, Barbara, *John Amick "The Miller" his Ancestors and some Descendants*, p. 22

[194] *1850 Census of Hammond Township, Spencer County, Indiana*, p. 123

[195] Source: http://www.rootsquest.com/~jmurphy/spencer/1850sp2h.htm

[196] 49th Indiana Biographies

[197] Harter, Mary, comp. *Pendleton County, Virginia Marriage bonds, 1791-1853*, p. 40, citation from Barbara Nichols

[198] 1810 Census Pendleton County, VA

[199] Wardell, Patrick; p. 6

[200] http://www.rootsweb.com/~vahighla/1812war.htm

[201] Note that the name as spelled "Shroyer" in the records is probably not correct; there is a Rev. Stoever in Lancaster County mentioned by the Propsts and a Boston Shawver who came from Greenbrier and settled on two 100 acres tracts of land on Anglins Creek. The Shroyer name is not on any other Pendleton County documents yet found and it may be one of these other spellings.

[202] Barbara Nichols, *John Amick "The Miller" his Ancestors and some Descendants*, p. 23

[203] *Pendleton County, West Virginia, Register of Marriages, 1800-1852*, p. 7

[204] Philips, Claude Summer, Ed. *Pendleton County Marriage Records, 1800-1851*, p 1, citation from Barbara Nichols

[205] Nichols, Barbara, *John Amick "The Miller" his Ancestors and some Descendants*, p.30

[206] *Pendleton County, West Virginia, Register of Marriages, 1800-1852*, p. 7

[207] *Deeds of Pendleton County [now] Vest Virginia, Bk. 6*, pp. 287-288

[208] *Pendleton County, West Virginia Deeds, Book 7*, p. 396

[209] US Census:http://ftp.us-census.org/pub/usgenweb/census/wv/pendleton/1820/

[210] *Bucks County, Pennsylvania Administration Records* #5035, Book 28 (Aug. 1822), citation from Barbara Nichols

[211] Barbara Nichols, *John Amick "The Miller" his Ancestors and some Descendants*

[212] *Pendleton County, West Virginia Deeds, Book 8*, pp. 417-418

[213] *Pendleton County, West Virginia Deeds, Book 8*, pp. 418-419

[214] *1823 Land book for Pendleton County*

[215] US Census: http://ftp.us-census.org/pub/usgenweb/census/wv/pendleton/1830/

[216] *Propst Church Records*, p. 4, citation from Barbara Nichols

[217] *Propst Church Records*, p. 4, citation from Barbara Nichols

[218] *Propst Church Records*, p. 4, citation from Barbara Nichols p. 55

[219] *Propst Church Records*, p. 4, citation from Barbara Nichols p. 62

[220] *Grave Register of Pendleton County, West Virginia*, (Pendleton Co.

Historical society, 1977) p. 100, Citation from Barbara Nichols

[221] Nichols, Barbara, *John Amick "The Miller" his Ancestors and some Descendants*, p.24

[222] Nichols, Barbara, *John Amick "The Miller" his Ancestors and some Descendants*, p.24

[223] *Pendleton County, West Virginia, Inventory Book 4* (1832) pp. 350-351

[224] *Abstracts of Executor, Administrative, and Guardian Bonds of Rockingham Co., VA. (1778-1864)* compiled by Marguerite B. Priode

[225] *Lancaster P.A., Gazette Abstracts, 1826-1891*, p. 273, Lancaster, PA

[226] *Pendleton County, West Virginia Deeds, Book 11*, (1834) p. 107

[227] *Nicholas County, West Virginia Deeds, Book 11* (1835) pp. 361-362

[228] *Pendleton County, West Virginia Deeds, Book 11* (1835) pp. 408-410

[229] Copy, undated, in possession of John Arvin Dahmer, Citation from Barbara Nichols

[230] Barbara Nichols, *John Amick "The Miller" his Ancestors and some Descendants*, p. 26

[231] Jeff Munn, email 10/3/2014.

[232] Propst -2 web

[233] Propst web

[234] *The PA Gazette*, Oct. 9-19, 1732 No. 203 Custom House, Philadelphia Entered Inwards Sloop John & William Constable Tymperton, From Dover. Philadelphia, Oct 19, 1732

[235] Whisonant, Robert C., *Geology and History of Confederate Saltpeter Cave Operations in Western Virginia*, West Virginia Division ofMineral Resources, Vol. 47, November, 2001, No. 4

[236] The John Guilday Caves Nature Preserve Management Plan, found online at: http://www.caves.org/preserves/jgcp/mp-jgcp.html

[237] Nichols, Barbara, *John Amick "The Miller" his Ancestors and some Descendants*, p. 31

[238] Dyer, Geneva Amick, *Fourteen Children, The Family of John Amick of West Virginia.* pp. 1-2

[239] Nichols, Barbara, *John Amick "The Miller" his Ancestors and some Descendants*, p.31

[240] Dyer, Geneva Amick, *Fourteen Children, The Family of John Amick of West Virginia,* pp. 1-2

[241] Propst web

[242] *The War of the Rebellion: A Compilation of the Official Records of the Union and Confederate Armies,* Series 1 - Volume 33, p. 228-229

[243] Brown, W. C.; *History of Nicholas County, West Virginia, Pioneer Families*; p. 363

www.ingramcontent.com/pod-product-compliance
Lightning Source LLC
Chambersburg PA
CBHW020603270326
41927CB00005B/147